GRAMMAR EXERCISES

Part One
Elementary/Intermediate ESL

Arthur A. Burrows
illustrations by Robert MacLean
Second, Revised Edition

Interplay ESL

PRO LINGUA ASSOCIATES

Published by Pro Lingua Associates
15 Elm Street
Brattleboro, Vermont 05301
802-257-7779 800-366-4775

SAN 216-0579

At Pro Lingua,
our objective is to foster
an approach to language learning and teaching which
we call **Interplay**, the **inter**action of language
learners and teachers with their materials,
with the language and the culture, and
with each other in active, creative,
and productive **play**.

ISBN 0-86647-050-6

This book was set David Chase of Brattleboro, Vermont, with display type in Century Oldstyle and the cover and title page in Tiffany set by Stevens Graphics of Brattleboro. This fourth printing was printed and bound by DB Hess Company in Woodstock, Illinois. The book was designed by the author.

Printed in the United States of America.

Fourth printing, 1997.
10,000 copies in print.

Acknowledgements

It is to Ray Clark that the lion's share of my appreciation is due. The original idea for our in-class text, *The Grammar Handbook*, and its companion text of grammar exercises was his, as were the choice and sequence of grammar points and the idea of focusing each lesson on both a cultural and a grammar topic. Furthermore, as I struggled through the lessons, he kept me going with suggestions and encouragement and, ultimately, helped me shape the book with his sharp editorial knife.

Grammar Exercises: Part One is based on Nancy Clair's *The Grammar Handbook* and follows her grammar explanations point for point. I rephrased and expanded upon her work, fitting it to the needs of a student working alone, but the simplicity and clarity with which she cut to the heart of complicated grammar points is wonderful. Her students, her readers, and I are all grateful. Her book is a pleasure to work with.

This is an unusual book so we felt that it should be extensively tested in the classroom. Ray Clark and Janie Duncan both used it with classes of elementary ESL students from a variety of countries and backgrounds. They both assured me that the lessons work and gave me valuable suggestions. Their students in the International Students of English Program at The Experiment's School for International Training were Dario Alvarez (Mexico), Felipe Barroilhet (Chile), Jaime Mehech (Chile), Setsuo Nakashima (Japan), Mauricio Palau (Colombia), Atef Salem (Egypt), Kimie Tsumita (Japan), Marcus Brassi (Brazil), Luigi Carena (Italy), Karin Carolla (Brazil), Luiz Duarte (Brazil), Manuel Fernandez (Costa Rica), Maximo Guzman (Mexico), Michele Landry (Canada), Jamel Latrous (Tunisia), Maria Lopez (Mexico), Guillermo Mendez (Mexico), Toru Takahashi (Japan), Mariko Tamaki (Japan).

The production of a complicated book like this one is painstaking and often frustrating. However, Patti Pound, who typed much of my manuscript, David Chase, who set the exercises on his word processor, Janice and Marshall Stevens, who set the explanations and display type, Marle Stevens, who did the cover, and Bob MacLean, who drew the illustrations, managed somehow to stay good humored and professional through it all. They are great people to work with.

And finally, to Janet and Stephen Greene and Bob Dothard, who taught me what I know about editing and producing a book, to my family, who put up with the process, and to all the host of friends, colleagues, and students at The Experiment, ALA, Northfield Mount Hermon School and elsewhere, who have helped me grow as a teacher, I wish I could thank you each personally. It's been fun.

A. A. Burrows
1985

To Brattleboro

"Exercises are only good if you take into account what they will do to your music making. Otherwise, they are useless."

Blanche Honegger Moyse

Contents

Preface on Interplay ESL

Grammar Exercises: Part One is the third in a collection of language textbooks we will be publishing over the next few years as the *Interplay for ESL* series. This ESL collection, once it is complete, will be a unique set of language materials that answers the needs of teachers who are looking for books that liberate, rather than restrict, the teacher, and encourage creativity in the classroom. The ESL collection will eventually form a comprehensive curriculum that will meet the needs of students ranging from the absolute beginner level to the advanced level.

Although the *Interplay for ESL* series as a total package will be based on a coordinated plan, it will also be distinguished by the fact that it is a modular program. Each and every book in the series can stand alone and is not rigidly linked to nor dependent on other books in the series. This book, for example, can be used by itself as an interesting and creative way to explore the grammar of basic English. It can also be used in close coordination with Pro Lingua Associates' *The Grammar Handbook: Part One* or to supplement or complement other ESL textbooks.

Interplay for ESL as a complete curriculum will be divided into two stages. Stage One, The Introductory Course, will be a short, integrated program designed for the beginning student with little or no English. Stage Two, the Basic Course, begins at the elementary level and will proceed to the advanced level. There will be two basic modules at each level of the Basic Course. One will be the grammar module; the other will be based on a communicative syllabus. In addition, there will be supplementary modules for strengthening the following skill areas: Conversation, Pronunciation, Listening Comprehension, Writing, Vocabulary, and Reading. A text for the last of these modules, Reading, is already available. *The Smalltown Daily* is a multilevel reader based on newspaper articles of general interest.

There are two books at the elementary level of the grammar module of the Basic Course. *Grammar Exercises: Part One* and *The Grammar Handbook: Part One* are designed to be used together or independently. The former is a self-study or homework text; the latter, for classroom use. These *Part One* texts are aimed specifically at "the false beginner," as explained in the introduction. Although they are well suited for this elementary level, either one can also be used as a review text for intermediate- and even advanced-level students.

For more information on how to use this unique text/workbook, we urge you to study the author's introduction and the first, explanatory lesson carefully.

Pro Lingua Associates
Arthur A. Burrows
Raymond C. Clark
Patrick R. Moran

Introduction

The first lesson of *Grammar Exercises: Part One* is an introduction for the student. It explains "how to use this book" while giving practice with the affirmative word order in English. In this way the lesson both describes and demonstrates the method of the book, which can also be summarized by these seven points:

1. **This book is designed for independent study or homework.**
   It can be used in the classroom, but the teacher will want to rely on its companion text, *The Grammar Handbook: Part One*, or other resources for a full classroom presentation and in-class practice.

2. **Each lesson has both a grammatical and a topical focus.**
   For example, Lesson 18 presents possessive pronouns, but it also works with information and vocabulary related to American sports. Why? It is our contention that by building grammar exercises using sentences which are all interrelated and focused on some entertaining and culturally stimulating topic, we can engage the student's imagination and put him into an acquisitive frame of mind.

3. **The book is appropriate for the "false beginner."**
   It is for the elementary to intermediate student who speaks and reads some English, but does so inaccurately, and needs work on basic English structures. The book is not intended for the beginning student.

4. **The exercises vary in difficulty.**
   The first exercises in each lesson provide the elementary student with practice on the basic grammar point of the lesson. More advanced students can go on to be challenged by the more difficult exercises at the end of the lesson.

5. **There are more than enough exercises.**
   The students do not have to complete each lesson. Although some students may become involved with the cultural topic and want to work their way through all the exercises and vocabulary, they should not be required to do so. The extra exercises given at the end of some of the lessons are motivation builders. They are often difficult, but they provide a mixture of extra idioms, cultural insights, and fun.

6. **Answers to most of the exercises are given in the appendix.**
   The student should be encouraged to check his answers, to puzzle out his errors using the grammar explanations, and then to make all the corrections. The teacher can then encourage him to bring any problems he cannot work out on his own for explanation and discussion in class. By correcting his own work, the student gets feedback immediately, when it is most effective. The student is thus encouraged to become self-reliant in his study and to treat his teacher, classmates, and English-speaking friends as resources.

7. **The sequencing of lessons is flexible.**
   The student or class can take up the grammar points as they are needed, coordinating this book with most curriculum designs. The lessons follow the order of the classroom presentations in *The Grammar Handbook: Part One* point for point, although the grammar is explained here in somewhat greater detail than would be appropriate in classroom paradigms. Used in conjunction with the classroom handbook, these lessons thus offer both a reinforcement and an enrichment of the class activities.

In keeping with the underlying concepts of **Interplay,*** this book is intended to be learner centered, to be flexible and fun, and to stimulate a free exchange of ideas between the student, his teacher, and his friends in and out of class.

*See "Interplay" in the appendix of *Language Teaching Techniques*, Raymond C. Clark; Pro Lingua Associates, Publishers; 1980; pp. 117-120.

Affirmative word order

1

How to use this book

In English, simple sentences (affirmative statements) usually have three parts.
They always have a subject and a verb, and the verb usually has a complement.
The usual word order is subject - verb - complement (**SVC**).

Subject	Verb	Complement
This book	*is*	*a grammar exercise book.*
It	*is*	*brown and orange.*
Part One	*explains*	*fifty-two grammar points.*
The first point	*starts*	*on page one.*

A. Read these sentences.

1. This is a book of grammar exercises.
2. The book teaches fifty-two grammar points.
3. Each point starts with an explanation.
4. Each explanation includes examples.
5. Several exercises follow each explanation.
6. The first exercises are easy.
7. The exercises become more difficult.
8. Each exercise starts with instructions.
9. Examples come after the instructions.
10. The examples include the answers.
11. The student studies the instructions and the examples,
12. and he writes the exercises following the same pattern.
13. The answers to each exercise are at the back of the book.
14. The student checks his answers carefully.
15. He studies his mistakes.
16. He corrects all the mistakes he understands.
17. These exercises are for self study homework,
18. but all students need help sometimes.
19. Good students ask for help.
20. The answers start on page 219.

B. Write the verbs from the sentences in Exercise A above.

1. _*is*_ 2. _*teaches*_ 3. _*starts*_ 4. _____ 5. _____
6. _____ 7. _____ 8. _____ 9. _____ 10. _____
11. _____ 12. _____ 13. _____ 14. _____ 15. _____
16. _____ 17. _____ 18. _____ 19. _____ 20. _____

C. Underline the subjects in exercise A above. Study the following examples, and then mark the sentences in A.

1. <u>This</u> is a book of grammar exercises.
2. <u>The book</u> teaches fifty-two grammar points.
3. <u>Each point</u> starts with an explanation.

D. Circle the complements in the sentences in exercise A above following these examples.

1. This is (a book of grammar exercises.)
2. The book teaches (fifty-two grammar points.)
3. Each point starts (with an explanation.)

E. These sentences are scrambled. (The parts are mixed up.) Rewrite them using the correct affirmative word order (SVC).

Notice: Sentences start with capital letters and end with periods.

is   a book for self study   this textbook

This textbook is a book for self study.

the title of the book   **Grammar Exercises**   is

The title of the book is Grammar Exercises.
Grammar Exercises is the title of the book.

has   the second example   two correct answers

The second example has two correct answers.

1. correct for this sentence   only one answer   will be

   _____

2. all the correct answers   gives   the appendix at the back of the book

   _____

3. should correct   you   your exercises carefully

   _____

4. all students   mistakes   make

   _____

5. you   from your mistakes   can learn

   _____

6. teaches   each lesson in this book   one grammar point

_____

7. some vocabulary   includes   each lesson also

_____

8. is listed   the vocabulary   in a box at the end of each lesson

_____

9. study   some students   the vocabulary before starting the lesson

_____

F.   Read the following paragraph. Underline any incorrect sentences. All the sentences should have the usual affirmative word order (SVC). Finally, rewrite all the incorrect sentences in the space below the paragraph.

> Learn we languages in many different ways. Learning is natural and fun for all humans. Many of us best by speaking and listening learn. Others need to read and write. Some of us quickly learn. Others need a lot of time to think and to practice. Little children learn naturally by speaking and listening. Adults the grammar of a language can study. Understanding the grammar helps us learn quickly, but grammar and grammar exercises are not enough. Need we vocabulary. Conversation practice also very important is. Several exercises are given for each lesson in this book. Some of us all of them need to write. Other students should use only one or two exercises, and then they should practice by talking to friends in English.

We learn languages in many different ways.

_____

_____

_____

_____

_____

_____

_____

_____

_____

Vocabulary summary

above	easy	mark	sentence
affirmative	example	mistake	start
answer	exercise	order	statement
back	explanation	paragraph	subject
below	follow	pattern	teach
carefully	help	point	title
circle	include	practice	underline
conversation	instruction	read	understand
correct	learn	scrambled	usual
difficult	make	self study	

Extra Exercise

Read the paragraph, underlining the verbs. Below the paragraph, list the vocabulary words which are new to you.

Many students <u>enjoy</u> an extra challenge. At the end of some of the lessons in this book, there is an extra exercise. The exercise gives you additional practice and extra vocabulary. The vocabulary is not listed in the vocabulary box. Many of the extra exercises are stories. They are more difficult than the first exercises, but they are fun and culturally interesting.

Negative word order 2

Exploring the Earth and the stars

> An English sentence may be made negative in two ways:
>
> 1. With the verb **to be, not** follows the verb.
>
>   *Columbus is a great hero.*
>   *Columbus is **not** a great hero.*
>
> 2. With all other verbs, **not** follows an auxiliary verb.
>
>   *Everyone loves Columbus.*
>   *Everyone **does not** love Columbus.*

A. Make these sentences negative by adding **not**.

The Atlantic Ocean is ^*not* east of China.

The Pacific is ^*not* west of Spain.

1. The Atlantic and Pacific are one big ocean.

2. The South Pole is in the Arctic Ocean.

3. Hong Kong is in Eastern Europe.

4. The Indian Ocean is between the Americas.

B. Make these sentences negative by adding the auxiliary **do** and **not**.

Mexicans ^*do not* like cold weather.

Japanese fishermen ^*do not* fish in the Red Sea.

1. Australians come from Africa.

2. Saudi Arabians own Samoa.

3. Brazilians speak Spanish.

4. The American Indians live in South Asia.

C. Make the first verb in these sentences negative. Add **not, do not,** or **did not.**

Notice: When the sentence is in the past, the verb changes (in the second example, own**ed** > own) when you use the negative. (See lesson 27, Simple past.)

Columbus was _∧ *not* a Spaniard.

He _∧ *did not own* ~~owned~~ a large sailing ship.

1. In 1491 Columbus was a famous sea captain.

2. He was a very rich man.

3. He wanted to go to America.

4. Columbus hoped to find San Francisco's Golden Gate.

5. His queen, Isabella, lived in Rome.

6. She gave Columbus twenty large ships.

7. He planned to sail west to find America.

8. Everyone believed the world was flat in 1491.

9. In 1492 the world changed.

10. Columbus proved the world was round.

11. He sailed around the world.

12. He discovered the United States!

13. He called the people "Americans."

14. Back in Spain, Columbus was a popular hero.

15. He returned with lots of gold and silver.

16. Queen Isabella wanted to call his new world "Columbia."

17. "Columbus was the first European here!" say the Scandinavians today.

18. The Irish believe the Vikings discovered the new world.

19. This argument is very important.

20. After Columbus and 1492, the Spanish civilized the Americas.

21. Everyone was rich and happy.

22. The Indians of the new world loved the great hero Columbus.

D. Look at this picture of the solar system. Read the paragraph. Some statements are not correct. By adding negatives and auxiliaries, correct the mistakes.

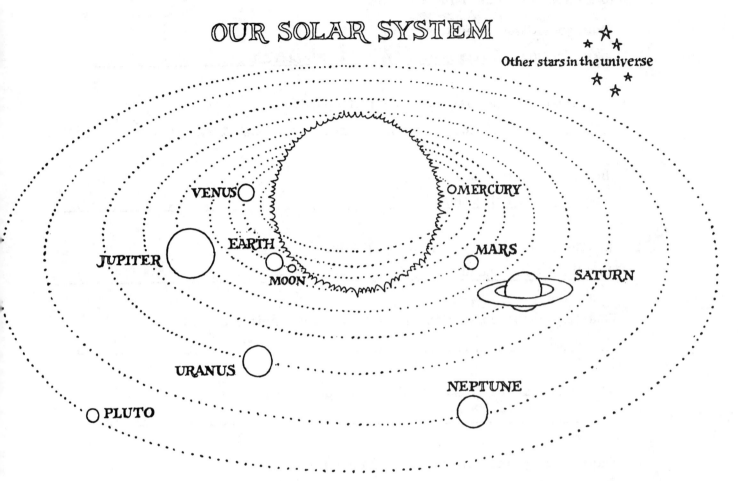

Today we know the world is not flat. It is round. It is a planet. We know the Earth is not the center of the Universe. The Sun and the stars go around the Earth. The Sun is the center of our solar system. It goes around the Earth. The Earth goes around it. The other planets also go around the Sun. The Moon is a planet. It goes around the earth. Other moons go around the other planets. There are five planets we can see with our eyes. We can see Uranus, Neptune, and Pluto without a telescope. All the planets go around the Sun. The Sun is a planet. It is a star. All the other stars go around the Sun. It is the center of our solar system. It is the center of the Universe. Before Copernicus (1543), people thought the Heavens went around Man. Now we know this is true. However, sometimes we forget. The Universe is made for us but we forget.

E. These statements are correct grammatically. They are not correct factually. Correct them by putting them in the negative and then writing the correct sentence below each sentence using the cue.

did not discover

Columbus ∧ ~~discovered~~ North America.

Leif Erikson *discovered North America.* _____

not

The first man in space was ∧ Alan Shepard.

_____ *The first man in space was* Yuri Gargarin

1. In 1778 Captain Cook colonized Hawaii.
   About 700 AD Polynesians _____

2. In 1909 Robert Peary reached the South Pole.
   In 1911 Roald Amundsen _____

3. Charles Lindbergh was the first to fly the Pacific alone.
   _____ Atlantic _____

4. The first man to climb Mt. Everest was Lord Everest.
   _____ Sir Edmund Hillary _____

5. Captain Magellan sailed alone around the world.
   Capt. Joshua Slocum _____

6. Laika, a Russian cat, was the first animal in space.
   _____ dog _____

7. John Glenn was the first man on the moon.
   Neil Armstrong _____

8. Sally Ride was the first woman in space.
   Valentina Tereshkova _____

9. The U.S.A. reached the Sun, Moon, Venus and Mars first.
   The U.S.S.R _____

10. Lunik 10 was the first space ship to leave our solar system.

Pioneer 10 _____

11. Apollo 11 returned to Earth with a little green Moon man.

moon rocks

_____

12. The first reusable space shuttle was Sputnik 1.

Columbia

_____

13. The first U.S.S.R.-U.S.A. joint space flight was in 1983.

1975

_____

14. The world's favorite spaceman is R2D2.

ET

_____

15. The space shuttle Columbia is named for a Viking sea captain.

_____

16. The best use for space is war.

_____

Vocabulary summary

animal	fly	peace	shuttle
alone	forget	people	silver
argument	gold	planet	solar system
believe	heaven	popular	sun
center	hero	prove	telescope
change	important	reach	time
civilize	joint	return	universe
climb	leave	reusable	war
discover	moon	rich	weather
Earth	money	round	world
famous	name	sail	
favorite	new	science	
flat	ocean	sea captain	
flight	own	ship	

Academic Courses

Yes-or-no questions can be made in three ways.

1. With **to be**, the subject follows the verb.

   Is *economics interesting?*   *(Yes.)*

2. With all other verbs, the simple form of the verb follows the subject, and the question begins with the auxiliary verb **do** (does, did).

   Do *I need economics?*   *(Yes.)*

3. With all auxiliaries, including **do**, the question begins with the auxiliary followed by the subject.

   Did Jane take algebra?   *(Yes.)*
   Will you take it next term?   *(No.)*
   May I see your algebra book?   *(Yes.)*
   Should Jack ask for help?   *(Yes.)*
   Can we sign up for History?   *(No.)*
   Must all seniors pass American History?   *(Yes.)*

A. Make these sentences into yes-or-no questions. Use the auxiliary **do (does, did)** if necessary.

Geometry is your very best subject.

Is geometry your very best subject?

Sarah hates biology!

Does Sarah hate biology?

1. French 520 is at 7:30 am.

   _____

2. Physics is fun!

   _____

3. Economics is easy.

   _____

4. Philosophy is difficult.

   _____

5. Biology, chemistry, and physics are called the natural sciences.

    _____

6. Our Language Department gives a course in Chinese.

    _____

7. Mary takes French twice a week.

    _____

8. You take German from Mrs. Doppfeldorf.

    _____

9. June wants to study Chinese.

    _____

10. We signed up for algebra in room 609.

    _____

B. Make these sentences into yes-or-no questions.

    You will help me with my homework.
    Will you help me with my homework?
    I may have your notebook.
    May I have your notebook?

1. A freshman can take Bookkeeping.

    _____

2. My advisor will let me take typing.

    _____

3. John should study physics.

    _____

4. Geometry is a prerequisite for modern art.

    _____

5. Anyone can get credit for physical education.

    _____

6. Philosphy and history are called social sciences.

    _____

7. Political Science 421 met in Keller Hall today.

    _____

8. Maria failed the geography exam.

    _____

C. Circle the mistakes; write the correct sentences. Not all the sentences are wrong.

(Are) you like high school? (Do you are) happy there now? Are you in Mr. Mack's history class? Can you take computer science? Is difficult algebra? Was Veronica in your math class last week? She did be the best student? All students must take physical education? Passes everyone English? Did you fail?

Do you like high school? Are you happy there now?

_____

_____

_____

Vocabulary Summary

advisor	economics	lessons	physics
algebra	fail	math	political
biology	French	modern art	science
bookkeeping	freshman	natural sciences	prerequisite
Chinese	geometry	notebook	sign up
chemistry	German	pass	social sciences
credit	history	philosophy	term
computer science	homework	physical	typing
course	language	education	

Extra Exercise

Write at least eight yes-or-no questions about courses you are taking now or courses you will take. Use the verb **to be**, the auxiliary **do**, and other auxiliaries. Parts of some sentences have been given to you. Answers for those sentences are given at the back of the book, but they are only possible answers. They are correct, but they are not **your** answers about your courses. Compare them to your answers, and be sure you understand the differences. Ask someone to mark your mistakes, and then write the correct sentences.

     Am I in your *English* class?

     Will you take *algebra* next year?

1. _____ pass _____ this term?
2. _____ sign up for _____ next term?
3. _____ my _____ course meet at _____ o'clock?
4. _____ we have _____ on Tuesday?
5. _____ I get to _____ class on time?
6. _____ I like this _____ course?
7. _____
8. _____

Short answers 4

Transportation costs

We often answer affirmative, yes-or-no questions with short answers, particularly in conversation.

1. We simply answer **yes** or **no**.

   Do you want to ride? **Yes**. *(Thank you, or Please.)**
   No. *(Thanks.)*

2. With the verb **to be**, we can use the verb **to be** in the answer.

   Are you the driver? Yes, *I* **am**.
   No, *I'm* **not**. *(I* **am** *not!)***

3. With all other verbs, we can answer using the same auxiliary we used in the question.

   Do you have a car? Yes, *I* **do**.
   No, *I* **don't**. *(I* **do** *not.)***
   Can he drive a motorcycle? Yes, he **can**.
   No, he **can't**. *(He* **cannot**.)

*Polite expressions are usually added after simple yes-or-no answers if the question is a request or invitation.

**Negative short answers are generally contracted except in anger or for emphasis. (See lesson 8, contractions.)

A. Answer these questions only with **yes** or **no** and, if the question is an invitation or a request, add the polite forms (**thank you, please, I'm sorry**).

	Is Jack's car blue?	*Yes.*
	Do you like Jack's car?	*Yes.*
	Do you want to buy Jack's car?	*No, thank you.*
	Can you give me money to buy it?	*No, I'm sorry.*
1.	Are Cadillacs small?	
2.	Do Cadillacs burn coal?	
3.	Do Cadillacs burn gasoline?	
4.	Can Cadillacs burn wood?	
5.	May I give you an old VW?	
6.	Do you want to buy my old car?	

7. Can I give you my father's Cadillac? _____
8. Is your father's car new? _____
9. Is your father's car big? _____
10. Can I buy your father's car? _____
11. Will you buy his car for me? _____
12. Is his car expensive? _____

B. Write all the possible short answers to the questions in A. above using **to be** or the proper auxiliary. When contraction is possible, write both the full and the contracted form.

a. Is Jack's car blue?
b. Do you like Jack's car?
c. Do you want to buy Jack's car?
d. Can you give me money to buy it?

	Yes	No	Contraction
a.	Yes, it is.	No, it is not.	No, it isn't.
b.	Yes, I do.	No, I do not.	No, I don't.
c.	Yes, I do.	No, I do not	No, I don't.
d.	Yes, I can.	No, I cannot.	No, I can't.
1.			
2.			
3.			
4.			
5.			
6.			
7.			
8.			
9.			
10.			
11.			
12.			

C. Look at the chart on the next page and answer the questions with short answers.

Are we going to Washington tomorrow? — Yes, we are.
Do you want to drive your car? — No, I don't.
Is driving your car expensive? — No, it isn't.
Does driving take too long? — Yes, it does.

TRAVEL FROM BOSTON, MASSACHUSETTS, TO WASHINGTON, D.C.
455 miles

Vehicle	Time	Cost	Other
Car	8 hours	$45	food
Bus	10 hours, 20 minutes	$57	food, taxi, subway
Train	7 hours	$95	taxi, subway
Airplane	1 hour, 20 minutes	$180	taxi, subway

1. Can we drive to Washington in 8 hours? _____
2. Will a train get us there faster? _____
3. Does a train take longer than a bus? _____
4. Does a train ticket cost more than a bus ticket? _____
5. Does a bus cost more than a car? _____
6. Is a train faster than a car? _____
7. Can we get to Washington in less than 7 hours? _____
8. Is an airplane faster than a train? _____
9. Is a plane ticket cheaper than going in your car? _____
10. Will a train be cheaper than a plane? _____
11. If we drive, will we need to buy food? _____
12. If we take a bus, can we buy food? _____
13. If we take a plane, can we buy food? _____
14. Are the costs listed above the only costs for this trip? _____
15. Do you pay for tolls when you go by bus? _____
16. Do you need a taxi from the airport? _____
17. Do you need a taxi from the train or bus station? _____
18. What is the best way to travel on this trip? Why? _____

Vocabulary summary

airplane	coal	invitation	take time
airport	cost	I'm sorry	taxi
available	drive	listed	ticket
burn	expensive	motorcycle	tolls
bus	fast	pay	train
bus station	food	polite	train station
buy	gasoline	request	travel
car	get there	ride	trip
cheaper	included	subway	wood

5 Subject question words

Work in the office

The question words **who**, **what**, **which** and **whose** can be used as the subject of a sentence.

Subject	Verb	Complement
Jackson	*answers*	*the telephone.*
Who	*answers*	*the telephone?*

Who refers to people.
What refers to things.
Which and **whose** refer to either people or things.

What, **which**, and **whose** can be used alone or with a noun.

Who is calling?
What company has hired Janet Johnson?
What is her job at Communitronics?
Which days will be good for the meeting?
Which is better for us?
Whose secretary will make the reservations?
Whose will type the new contract?

What used with a noun asks for general information. **Which** used with a noun asks for a choice. The meaning is very similar.

What company has hired her now?
Which company has hired her now, IBM, Communitronics, or ATT?

A. Read this paragraph. Add the question words **who** and **what** to the questions below.

Janet Johnson starts to work for **Communitronics** today. There is a new desk in her office with a telephone and a typewriter on it. The typewriter doesn't work. She needs a secretary and a new typewriter immediately. She needs to write a contract, and she wants a secretary to type it. The contract is needed in the morning. Marie Rosen is the best typist in the office, but she is on vacation.

Who starts work today?

What is in Janet Johnson's office?

1. _____ needs a secretary?

2. _____ will write a contract today?

3. _____ doesn't work?

4. _____ wants a typist?

5. _____ is on the desk?

6. _____ is the best typist in the office?

7. _____ needs a new typewriter immediately?

8. _____ needs a telephone?

9. _____ is on vacation?

10. _____ will type the contract?

11. _____ is needed in the morning?

12. _____ is Marie Rosen?

B. Read the paragraph and then add the question words **who, what, which,** or **whose** to the questions below. More than one answer may be correct.

All the secretaries at **Commutronics** are busy. Jim Block has a lot to do, but he works very fast. He has some free time today. Jim works for Sam Paulson. Sam is out of town helping **Blackwell and Barns** install a new **Commutronics** system. Janet Johnson needs a contract typed fast. She wants a word processor not a typewriter. She likes new machines. Marie Rosen's word processor is available. Sandra Peabody's is not. Jim Block does not have a word processor, but he can use one.

Who is busy today?

Which secretaries are busy?

Whose secretary is Jim Block?

1. _____ works fast?

2. _____ secretary has a lot to do, Marie or Jim?

3. _____ works for Mr. Paulson?

4. _____ company is out of town?

5. _____ machine will type a contract fast?

6. _____ word processor is available?

7. _____ word processor is not available?

8. _____ word processor is available, Marie's or Sandra's?

9. _____ company is installing a new system?

10. _____ has some free time today, Jim or Sandra?

11. _____ secretary works for Sam?

12. _____ will work for Janet today?

13. _____ will help Janet's secretary type fast?

14. _____ doesn't have a word processor?

15. _____ likes fast machines?

16. _____ typist is Ms. Peabody?

C. These are the answers. You write the questions. Use subject question words for the subjects underlined. Ask more than one question when you can.

Who works for Communitronics now?

<u>Janet Johnson</u> works for Communitronics now.

What is broken?

Whose typewriter is broken?

<u>Her</u> <u>typewriter</u> is broken

1. _____

<u>The desk in her office</u> is new.

2. _____

<u>She</u> sells computer software.

3. _____

_____

_____

<u>Her</u> <u>new</u> <u>customer</u> needs to see her immediately.

4. _____

<u>A new contract</u> must be typed for Manning and Company.

5. _____

<u>Typing</u> is not part of Janet Johnson's job.

6. _____

<u>She</u> doesn't have the necessary time.

7. _____

_____

_____

The Manning & Company <u>contract</u> must be ready by tomorrow.

8. _____

<u>It</u> should be perfectly typed.

Vocabulary summary

available	free time	phone	telephone call
busy	hire	ready	type
company	install	refer	typewriter
computer	job	reservations	typist
contract	meeting	software	vacation
customer	office	system	word processor

Extra Exercise

Read this memorandum and then fill in the question words.

```
                                        4/19    11:30 am

MEMO to:  J.R. Block

From:  Janet Johnson

Jack Williams tells me you have some free time.  If you don't he can free up some for
you.  I have just been hired to handle the Manning account.  I worked with them when
I was with Businetronics, so I know their operation.  However, the system here at
Commutronics is new to me.

What I need is some experienced short-term help until Jack can get me an administrative
assistant.  I know you have a background in contract development and account management
and that you have typing and word processing skills as well.

Jack has assigned you to me starting after lunch today.  Please check in with him first
and then report to Room 14B as soon as you get back to your desk.  I'll need contract
forms and form letters B-109-67 and JD-39.  Please bring the necessary floppy disks.
We'll be working late this evening.  Manning must have their contract in the a.m. tomorrow.
I hope you can work overtime.  Thanks.
                                              Janet

cc.  Jack Williams, Personnel
```

COMMUNITRONICS

1. _Who_ says Jim Block has free time?
2. _____ needs some short-term help?
3. _____ of Jim's skills will be helpful to Janet Johnson?
4. _____ assigned Jim to work with Janet Johnson?
5. _____ secretary will bring the floppy disks to Room 14B?
6. _____ operation does Janet Johnson know?
7. _____ form letters will be necessary?
8. _____ background will be useful to Janet Johnson?
9. _____ company needs their contract in the morning?
10. _____ company is Janet working for, Communitronics or Businetronics?
11. _____ will get Janet Johnson an administrative assistant?
12. _____ is going to work late this evening?
13. _____ system is new to Janet Johnson?
14. _____ account has been assigned to Janet Johnson? Is it Blair and Son?
15. _____ executive has been hired to handle the Manning account?
16. _____ will be paid overtime tonight?

Americans and their pets

When we ask about the object of a verb or preposition, we use the question words **whom** (**who**), **what**, **which**, and **whose**. (See 5 Subject question words.)

Subject	Verb	Object of the verb
Jim	*buys*	*fish*

O/QW	Auxiliary	Subject	Verb
What	*does*	*Jim*	*buy?*

In normal usage, we use the objective form **whom** only when it follows the verb or preposition. At the beginning of a sentence most Americans use **who**, even when writing.

Object of the preposition

*Jim buys fish **for***		*his cat Sam.*	
*Jim buys fish **for***		*whom?*	
	Who	*does Jim buy fish **for**?*	(normal usage)
	For	*whom*	*does Jim buy fish?* (very formal)

Object of the verb

*Jim **spoils***		*Sam*	*terribly.*	
*Jim **spoils***		*whom?*		(normal usage)
	Who	*does Jim **spoil**?*	(normal usage)
	Whom	*does Jim **spoil**?*	(very formal)

A. Write questions for these answers using the object question words for the objects underlined. Ask more than one question when you can.

Who does Jim spoil with food?

Whose cat does Jim spoil with food?

Jim spoils <u>his</u> <u>fat</u> <u>cat</u> with food.

What does Sam love?

Sam loves <u>fish</u>.

1. _____

_____

He is very fond of <u>Jim's</u> <u>breakfast herring</u>.

2. _____

For lunch Sam likes <u>fresh trout</u>.

3. _____

He adores <u>shrimp and lobster</u>.

4. _____

Jim gives shrimp to <u>Sam</u> for Sunday dinner.

5. _____

_____

He shares <u>his own</u> <u>lobster</u> with Sam.

6. _____

Sam likes his <u>lobster</u> for dessert.

7. _____

When given a choice, Sam always prefers <u>lobster</u>.

8. _____

Sam eats well at <u>Jim's</u> house.

9. _____

However, he loves to come to <u>my</u> house.

10. _____

_____

His very favorite food in the world is <u>my</u> <u>goldfish</u>.

11. _____

He likes to eat <u>them</u> fresh.

12. _____

Sam sits patiently next to <u>the fish bowl</u>.

13. _____

_____

He closes his green eyes and dreams about <u>my fish</u>.

14. _____

I am not fond of <u>Sam</u>.

B. Write questions for these answers using the object question words <u>who</u> and <u>whom</u> for the underlined words.

1. *Who did I get together with during the holidays?*

I got together with <u>all my relatives</u> during the holidays.

2. _____

On Christmas Day I saw <u>Aunt Flossie</u>.

3. _____

She showed her new Pekinese puppy to <u>me</u>.

4. _____

Aunt Flossie gave <u>her puppy</u> the name Poopsie.

5. _____

The next day she went with <u>Poopsie</u> to The Doggy Beauty Salon.

6. _____

She had <u>the Pekinese</u> tinted pink.

7. _____

They put gold nail polish and Puppy Perfume on <u>the dog</u>.

8. _____

Flossie bought a new rhinestone collar for <u>him</u>.

9. _____

You should see <u>poor pink Poopsie, the pampered Pekinese</u>.

10. _____

All the ladies love <u>him</u>.

11. _____

They feed <u>him</u> candy all day long.

12. _____

When they cuddle him, Poopsie loves <u>the ladies</u>.

13. _____

Flossie says to <u>him</u>, "Poopsie, darling, you're a new dog!"
She's right. He <u>is</u>.

14. _____

Brave little Poopsie is afraid of <u>the dog in Flossie's mirror</u>.

C. Complete the questions about this children's nursery rhyme. Then give the shortest answer possible.

Old Mother Hubbard	_____*Who*_____ did she want a bone for?
went to the cupboard	_____*Her dog.*_____
to get her poor dog a bone,	_____ dog did she want a bone for?
but when she got there	_____
the cupboard was bare,	_____ did she find in the cupboard?
and so the poor dog had none.	_____
She went to the butcher's	To _____ did she go to buy tripe?
to buy him some tripe,	_____
but when she got back	_____ did she find when she got home?
he was smoking her pipe.	_____
She went to the grocer's	_____ did she buy at the grocer's shop?
to buy him some fat,	_____
but when she got back	_____ was he feeding?
he was feeding the cat.	_____
She went to the barber's	_____ did she do at the barber's?
to buy him a wig,	_____
but when she got back	_____ kind of dance was he dancing?
he was dancing a jig.	_____
She went to the baker's	To _____ shop did she go for bread?
to buy him some bread,	_____
but when she got back	_____ dog was dead?
her poor dog was dead.	_____

Vocabulary summary

afraid	butcher	dream	mirror	prefer
aunt	cat	fat	nail	puppy
baker	child	favorite	pampered	relative
barber	collar	fish	patiently	rhinestone
bare	cupboard	fond	Pekinese	salon
beauty	cuddle	fresh	perfume	shrimp
bird	dance	goldfish	pet	smoke
bone	darling	grocer	pig	tinted
bowl	dead	holiday	pipe	tripe
brave	dessert	jig	polish	trout
bread	dog (doggy)	lobster	poor	wig

Extra Exercise

Write at least ten questions about this paragraph. Use object question words only. Some possible answers are given at the back of the book.

Americans love pets. We give our pets human names and talk to them in English as if they were children. They live with us in our homes. Most of us have dogs or cats. People who like fancy dogs prefer poodles, cockers, police dogs, and retrievers. People who like fancy cats prefer pure breds like the American shorthair, Persian and Siamese cats. Most people have mutts and alley cats for pets. Many Americans also keep rodents. Children keep cages of mice, rats, guinea pigs, rabbits, and hamsters. Many people also keep fish. Children enjoy owning goldfish. Adults often keep tropical fish. Lots of people also enjoy having reptiles and birds. Some people keep ants, spiders, and other insects. A few rich Americans have exotic animals in their homes like leopards, wolves, and bears. A lot of boys and girls enjoy keeping horses and ponies. Children on farms raise lambs, pigs, chickens, and other farm animals. These are not really pets. Americans don't eat their pets.

1. *What do Americans love?*
2. _____
3. _____
4. _____
5. _____
6. _____
7. _____
8. _____
9. _____
10. _____
11. _____
12. _____
13. _____
14. _____
15. _____
16. _____
17. _____
18. _____

Love

In questions using the question words **when**, **where**, **how**, and **why**

1. with the verb **to be**, the subject follows the verb.

Question word	Verb	Subject	Complement
Why	*is*	*Joe*	*so happy?*
Where	*are*	*the women?*	

2. with all other verbs, we use an auxiliary and this word order:

Question word	Auxiliary	Subject	Verb	Complement
When	*did*	*they*	*meet*	*for the first time?*
Where	*will*	*they*	*go*	*on their date?*
How	*can*	*he*	*pay*	*for it?*
Why	*do*	*they*	*like*	*each other?*

A. These sentences are scrambled. Write the questions putting the parts of the sentences in the correct order.

do   want   when   to meet me, Sally   you

When do you want to meet me, Sally?

can   pick you up   I   where

Where can I pick you up?

1. you   where   be waiting   will

   _____

2. do   why   to go out so early   want   you

   _____

3. the movie   is   when

   _____

4. be over   when   the movie   will

   _____

5.   be dressed   you   how   will

_____

6.   where   want   do   you   to eat supper

_____

7.   want   you   to go dancing   do   why

_____

8.   the dance   is   where

_____

9.   we get to the dance   can   how   on time

_____

10.   is   so important   the dance   why

_____

11.   I dress   how   for the dance   should

_____

12.   this party   why   so expensive   is

_____

13.   to go home   how   you want   do

_____

14.   when   again   we   can   go out

_____

B.   Read the answers and then write the questions using the question words.

In 1982 Molly moved to Portland

When   *did Molly move to Portland ?* _____

Where   *did Molly move to ?* _____

1.   She was unhappy in Portland because she didn't know anyone.

Why _____

Where _____

2.   After two weeks, her brother Bill took her to a party at Tommy's house.

When _____

Where _____

3.   At the party she met Mike and Tommy.

Where _____

When _____

4.   Tommy joked a lot to make her laugh.

     Why _____

     How _____

5.   Mike seemed very serious at the beginning of the party.

     How _____

     When _____

6.   Molly felt pleased because Mike talked to her seriously.

     How _____

     Why _____

7.   By the end of the party at Tommy's house Molly and Mike became good friends.

     When _____

     Where _____

8.   After the party, Molly began to date Mike.

     When _____

     Why _____

9.   By the end of the year Mike and Molly fell in love, married, and lived happily
     ever after.

     When _____

     How _____

Vocabulary summary

dance	friends	move	serious
date	get to (arrive)	movie	suggest
dressed	go out	on time	supper
early	joke	party	wait
ever after	laugh	pay	
expensive	meet	pick up	

Extra Exercise

This is a cartoon by the great French cartoonist Sempé. It tells a love story
called the The Loser. Write 8 or more questions about the pictures using the
question words **when, where, how,** and **why.** Compare your questions to the questions
in the back of the book.

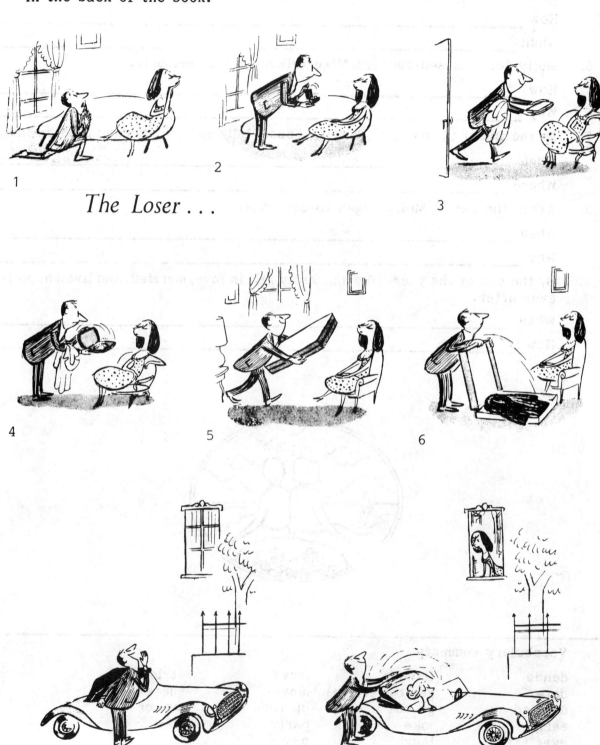

The Loser . . .

Marriage

In spoken and informal written English, we often use contractions. These **negative contractions** are common:

do not	> don't	are not	> aren't
does not	> doesn't	is not	> isn't
did not	> didn't	was not	> wasn't
will not	> won't	were not	> weren't

> *Bob was not married.* > *Bob **wasn't** married.*
> *Bob is single, is he not?* > *Bob is single, **isn't** he?*   (notice word order)

Modals are often contracted with not. (See Lessons 34 and 35, Modals)

cannot > can't	would not > wouldn't	must not > mustn't

We often use the following **affirmative contractions** with **to be** and **will**, particularly in speech.

I am > I'm	Jack is > Jack's	he will > he'll
you are > you're	we are > we're	she will > she'll
he is > he's	they are > they're	it will > it'll
she is > she's	I will > I'll	we will > we'll
it is > it's	you will > you'll	they will > they'll

> *The wedding will be lovely!* > *The **wedding'll** be lovely!*

We use two kinds of **negative contraction** with **to be**

> *He **isn't** in love.*   *He's **not** in love*
> *You **aren't** in love.*   *You're **not** in love.*

but **am** can only be contracted as **I'm not**. You may often hear **I ain't** or **I amn't** in some parts of the United States, but these forms are not generally considered to be "good English."

Have is also often contracted as an auxiliary.

> *She has been married before.* > ***She's** been married before.*
> *They have seen the bride.* > ***They've** seen the bride.*

A. In the following dialogue make all the possible contractions.

Ralph: Jack and ~~Jill are~~ *Jill're* getting married.

~~I am~~ *I'm* going to the wedding.

1. Bob is going too.

Willie: 2. I think I will go too.

3. It is on Saturday, is it not?

Ralph: 4. Yup. They are having a traditional wedding.

5. They have invited lots of family and friends.

6. Jack will have a bachelor's party on Thursday night.

7. The rehearsal is on Friday afternoon.

8. Then they will have a formal bridal dinner.

Willie: 9. They do not want to wait long after graduation.

10. We will all graduate June 6th,

11. and wedding bells are ringing for Jack and Jill June 13th!

Ralph: 12. Jill sure does not believe in wasting time.

Willie: 13. They are taking a honeymoon, are they not?

Ralph: 14. Sure. They have got tickets to Niagara Falls.

Willie: 15. You have got to be kidding. Even Jill would not pick Niagara Falls!

Ralph: 16. No, she would not. We are not supposed to know where they are going.

17. I know, but I cannot tell you. It is a big secret.

Willie: 18. I see. Well, I have got a pretty good idea anyway.

19. I bet Jack could not resist Disney World!

Ralph: 20. Willie, you are not old enough to get married. You are still a little kid!

Willie: 21. You can say that again!

22. I will not marry until I am at least thirty!

B. Use contractions in this letter to Jimmy from his mom.

April 1

Dear Jimmy,

You know your cousin Mary and your old friend
~~Joe're~~
~~Joe are~~ still in love. Now *they're* ~~they are~~ saying ~~they are~~
going to get married in the spring! ~~Is~~ that ~~not~~ great
news! She ~~does not~~ know when her ~~father will~~ be back
from Spain. ~~He will~~ probably be back in May, so ~~they~~
~~are~~ planning to have the wedding in June. ~~We are~~
~~not~~ going to be here in August, so ~~I am~~ hoping ~~it~~
~~will not~~ be postponed. ~~You will~~ be able to go in
August, but ~~I do not~~ want to miss Mary's wedding!
~~They are not~~ having a big wedding. ~~Mary will~~
have a maid of honor and only one bride's maid. ~~Joe~~
~~is~~ having a best man and ~~that is~~ all. ~~It is~~ possible
that ~~they will~~ change their plans, but ~~I am~~ sure,
if ~~they are~~ going to get married, ~~they will~~ end up
with a small, family wedding and an informal reception
outdoors, that is, if it ~~does not~~ rain as ~~it is~~ raining
today! And ~~do not~~ worry, Joe's ~~mother is~~ going to
bake the wedding cake, no matter what happens, so
~~you will~~ be there, ~~I am~~ sure.
~~Do not~~ forget to write!

Love,

Mom

Vocabulary summary

bells	cake	kid	party	resist
best man	formal	kidding	plan	ring
bridal dinner	graduation	love	postpone	traditional
bride	honeymoon	maid of honor	reception	waste time
bride's maid	invite	married	rehearsal	wedding

Extra Exercise

This story is difficult, but the contractions are easy. Underline the words you want to contract and then write the contractions on the lines below the story.

<u>It is</u> going to be a big month for the family and for Grandma and Grandpa MacIntosh. <u>They are</u> having their golden wedding anniversary. They will have been married fifty years on March 4th. Imagine! We will all be there, of course. We would not miss it.

They would have been married longer, you know, but the 1930's were not good years for weddings. Your Grandpa was not going to marry if he could not support his wife. "We will just have to wait 'til the cows come home," he would say to Grandma. "As soon as my ship comes in, we will get hitched." Grandma did not like waiting. "We are not getting any younger, Dearie!" she would say. They were not, of course. Then she added, "You must not miss your chance." You can hear her, can you not?

They finally got married when your Grandpa went off to war. I am a war baby. I did not see Grandpa until I was four. He had been in a prison camp. Aunt Sally was not born until after the end of the war. Your Grandma must have been in her early thirties when Sally was born, but that did not stop her. By her forty-fifth birthday she had had six more kids. I cannot imagine how she raised us!

In those days, Grandma and Grandpa were not happy together, but with eight children they could not get a divorce. Luckily, they did not. After we had grown up, they fell back in love. You will not find a couple of any age happier than your grandparents are now, as they are celebrating fifty golden years.

It's , They're _____
_____
_____
_____

Tag questions 9

Baseball

> We use **tag questions** in English when we expect the listener to agree with us. We expect confirmation of our statement.
>
> Tag questions have two parts, a statement and a tag. The answer usually agrees with the statement.
>
> 1. **Affirmative** tag questions = affirmative statements + negative tags. They expect affirmative answers.
>
> > *Americans love baseball, don't they?   Yes, they do.*
> > *Baseball is played in the Spring and Summer, isn't it?   Yes, it is.*
>
> 2. **Negative** tag questions = negative statements + affirmative tags. They expect negative answers.
>
> > *Americans don't play cricket, do they?   No, they don't.*
> > *Baseball isn't a winter sport, is it?   No, it isn't.*
>
> 3. Disagreement is possible.
>
> > *All Americans love baseball, don't they?   No, they don't.*

A. Study the roster of baseball teams on the next page. Make the statements below into affirmative tag questions. Then write the expected short answers agreeing with the questions.

The Brewers are in the American League.

The Brewers are in the American League, aren't they? Yes, they are.

The Atlanta Braves play in Georgia.

The Atlanta Braves play in Georgia, don't they? Yes, they do.

1. The Tigers come from Michigan.

_____

2. Seattle is the home of the Mariners.

_____

3. Ray saw the Astros in Chicago.

_____

4. Jon is a Red Sox fan.

_____

5. The Cleveland Indians play good baseball.

_____

6.   The St. Louis Cards are a great team too.

_____

7.   So is Baltimore.

_____

8.   The Angels play home games in Los Angeles.

_____

9.   Luis wants to be a Met someday.

_____

10.   Molly can get tickets for the Expos' game.

_____

11.   The Phillies are from Philly.

_____

12.   The Red Sox are the world's best team!

_____

A ROSTER OF THE NORTH AMERICAN PROFESSIONAL BASEBALL TEAMS

THE AMERICAN LEAGUE		THE NATIONAL LEAGUE	
Baltimore Orioles	Maryland	Atlanta Braves	Georgia
Boston Red Sox	Massachusetts	Chicago Cubs	Illinois
California Angels	California	Cincinnati Reds	Ohio
Chicago White Sox	Illinois	Houston Astros	Texas
Cleveland Indians	Ohio	Los Angeles Dodgers	California
Detroit Tigers	Michigan	Montreal Expos	Quebec, Canada
Kansas City Royals	Missouri	New York Mets	New York
Milwaukee Brewers	Wisconsin	Philadelphia Phillies	Pennsylvania
Minnesota Twins	Minnesota	Pittsburg Pirates	Pennsylvania
New York Yankees	New York	St. Louis Cardinals	Missouri
Oakland A's	California	San Diego Padres	California
Seattle Mariners	Washington	San Francisco Giants	California
Texas Rangers	Texas		
Toronto Blue Jays	Ontario, Canada		

B.   Study the roster of baseball teams. The following statements are all affirmative. Make them into negative tag questions.

The Oakland A's are not from Michigan, *are they?*

The St. Louis team is not Roman Catholic, *is it?*

1.   The Royals come from Kansas.

2.   The Boston team wears white socks.

3.   You remember the Brooklyn Dodgers.

4.   An American team will always win the World Series.

5.   The Milwaukee Brewers sell beer.

6.   Yoshi is a Rangers fan.

7.   Pierre is nuts about the Expos.

8.   Your grandfather thinks the Braves are from Boston!

9.   The Cubs beat the Pirates yesterday.

10. The A's are going to lose in the tenth inning.

C.   Study the roster of baseball teams. The following are all affirmative statements.
     Write negative (–) or affirmative (+) tag questions as indicated, and then give
     the correct answer. Don't give the expected answer unless it is correct.

     The Twins are from Houston.
     (–) *The Twins aren't from Houston, are they? No, they aren't.*
     All the Giants are over 7 feet tall.
     (+) *All the Giants are over 7 feet tall, aren't they? No, they aren't.*

1.   Both leagues have the same number of teams.
     (+) _____

2.   Chicago has more teams than any other city.
     (–) _____

3.   Fourteen states in the U.S. have teams.
     (+) _____

4.   The Atlanta Braves were the American League champions in 1983.
     (+) _____

5.   The Pirates are in the National League.
     (–) _____

6.   Four teams have the names of birds.
     (+) _____

7.   Three teams are named for animals.
     (+) _____

8. The Mets are from Pennsylvania.

   (+)_____

9. There are two teams from Texas.

   (+)_____

10. There are three teams from Missouri.

    (-)_____

11. There is a good team from Arizona.

    (+)_____

12. Canada has two teams in the American League.

    (-)_____

13. California has more teams than Canada.

    (-)_____

14. The Yankees are the most famous team in the world.

    (+)_____

Vocabulary summary

beat	great	play	ticket
beer	home game	roster	wear
champions	inning	sell	win
cricket	league	sock	
famous	lose	sport	
fan	nuts about	team	

Compound sentences 10

Going out on the town

English sentences can be connected together

1. with **and**, when one thought is added to another.

   *Mom cooks dinner, **and** Dad does the dishes.*

2. with **but**, when one thought is contrasted with another.

   *Sally wants to go shopping, **but** she has no money.*

3. with **or**, when one idea is the alternative to another.

   *I can go to the bar, **or** I can go home.*

A **comma** (,) is used between the two thoughts (parts of the new sentence).

A. Connect these thoughts (short sentences) into one long sentence using **and.** Add commas **(,)** and periods **(.),** and rewrite the first word of the second short sentence using a small letter, unless it is a name.

Mom and Dad came home from work, ~~Then~~ *and then* they got dressed to go out. They went out for dinner, *and they* ~~They~~ left me at home babysitting for Bobby.

1. First Mom had some wine   Dad had a beer
2. Then they had salad   Dad had some soup
3. Dad ordered a jumbo steak and a baked potato   Mom ordered spaghetti
4. They both drank wine with dinner   They had coffee with dessert
5. Mom enjoyed fresh strawberries   Dad finished a big fudge sundae with nuts
6. The bill was forty dollars   They left a six dollar tip
7. Dinner took a long time   They almost missed the movie
8. Dad bought the tickets   Mom bought the popcorn
9. They missed the beginning of the movie   Dad was mad
10. It was an old Bogart film   Mother loved it
11. She cried and cried   Dad fell asleep
12. He had seen it before   He had eaten too much dinner

B. Rewrite these short sentences making one longer sentence. Use **and** or **but** and a **comma**.

Sally and Suzie are sisters. They like to do things together.

Sally and Suzie are sisters, and they like to do things together.

They want to go out tonight. They have different plans.

They want to go out tonight, but they have different plans.

1. Sally is sixteen. Suzie is nineteen.

_____

2. Sally wants to go roller skating. Her friends will meet her there.

_____

3. Sally wants a ride from Suzie. Suzie doesn't want to go roller skating.

_____

4. She likes roller skating. Tonight she has other plans.

_____

5. Bob called her. He has invited her to go to Riverside Park.

_____

6. Riverside is an amusement park. Suzie loves amusement parks.

_____

7. She likes Bob a lot. She doesn't want to disappoint him!

_____

8. Sally likes Riverside too. Suzie doesn't want her to go along.

_____

9. It's fun to do things with your kid sister. This will be her first date with Bob.

_____

10. Suzie likes the Haunted House. Bob likes the roller coaster.

_____

11. Bob also wants to ride the parachute. Suzie is afraid of heights.

_____

12. She doesn't even like the Ferris wheel. She will go with Bob.

_____

13. They will pick up hot dogs for dinner. Later they will share a banana split.

_____

Vocabulary summary

amusement park	dinner	kid sister	soup
babysitting	Ferris wheel	movie	spaghetti
baked potato	fresh	parachute	steak
banana split	fudge	raspberries	sundae
bar	fun	ride	tip
beer	haunted house	roller coaster	wine
bill	heights	roller skating	
cook	hot dog	salad	
date	invite	shopping	
dessert			

Extra Exercise

Connect these sentences using **but** or **or** and a **comma**.

Alfredo Palladio just bought Pop's Bar and Grill on Flat Street, *but* he paid too much for it. I go to Pop's for lunch at noon, *or* I go at five after work for a beer. I love Pop's   I am not sure I will like Alfredo's. He will not change the Bar and Grill now   he is planning big changes before Christmas. He says he will make more profits from Pop's   he will sell it or close it. Maybe he will make Alfredo's Palace into an elegant, expensive cocktail lounge   he will make it into a gourmet restaurant. I like the sound of the Palace Bar better than Alfredo's Fine Dining

I don't like fancy bars. I like a working man's bar   I like to drink my beer at home. I guess a gourmet restaurant can make money in this town   I like plain, simple food. I eat pizza   I eat hamburgers. I like good food   I never like to spend money on it. Either it's cheap   I eat at home.

Alfredo has another plan. He will change Pop's into a night club with live music   he will make it into a disco dance hall. "OK," I said to Alfredo last night, "Good luck to you   don't count on my business!" I like music   I don't like Alfredo's loud rock. I like classical music, opera   folk music. I even like Country and Western   Alfredo doesn't. He likes rock. Dancing! I like to dance   Alfredo's idea is awful. He wants to attract lots of teenagers   he will lose me, that's for sure.

Things around the house

Nouns are usually made plural by adding **s**.

    tool > tools   toy > toys   table > tables

With nouns ending in **s**, **x**, **z**, **ch**, and **sh**, we add **es**.

    glass > glasses   mailbox > mailboxes   match > matches
    dish > dishes

With nouns ending in **y** preceded by a consonant, we change the **y** to **i** and add **es**.

    pantry > pantries   utility > utilities

With nouns ending in **o** preceded by a consonant, we add **es**.

    tomato > tomatoes

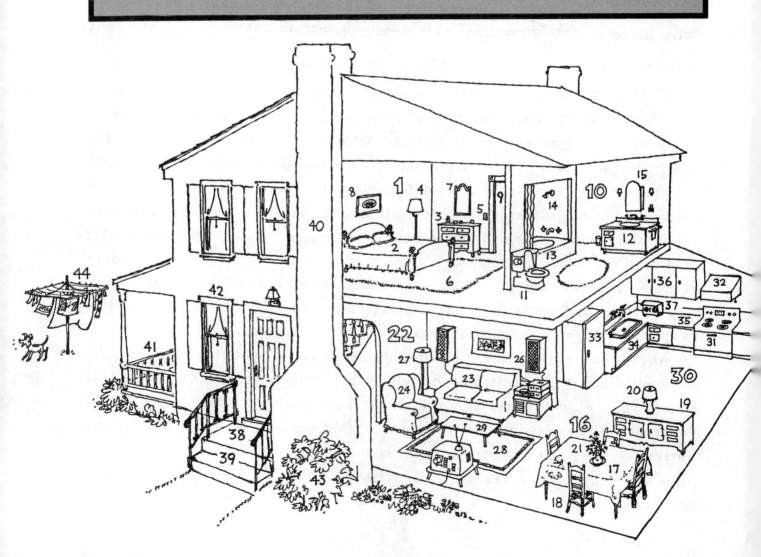

A. Study the illustration of a typical American house. Numbers 1, 10, 16, 22, and 30 are the rooms in the house. The rest of the numbers are furnishings or parts of the house. Name as many as you can from memory and write the names in the spaces below. When there are two common names for something, there are two spaces. Check your answers with the list at the end of the lesson and write in the names you didn't know. Then write the plural of each noun.

Number	Singular	Plural	Number	Singular	Plural
1.	*bedroom*	*bedrooms*	24.		
2.	*bed*	*beds*			
3.			25.		
4.			26.		
5.			26.		
6.			27.		
			28.		
7.			29.		
8.			**30.**		
9.			31.		
10.			32.		
11.			33.		
12.			34.		
			35.		
13.			36.		
14.					
15.			37.		
16.			+++		
17.			38.		
18.			39.		
19.			40.		
20.			41.		
21.			42.		
22.			43.		
23.			44.		
			45.		

B. This is a letter from Sam to Mike. Sam has made some mistakes. Correct the plurals. The correct singular forms are given in the vocabulary summary.

Dear Mike,

Are you sure you left the ~~bottlees~~ *bottles* of cleaner here or at Jack's? I've looked everywhere. I'll be specific. I looked in both ~~atties~~ *attics*, in all the closets, in the medicine cabinetes, under the bathroom basines, in the kitchen cupboards, under the kitchen sinkes, in the pantrys, the back halls, and the porchs. I checked around the utilitys, the dryers, the washers, on top of the electric switchs, around all the windowes and behind all the doores.

Then I searched the breezeways to the garages. In the cellares, I checked the bases of the chimneyes, the bulkheads, the workshoppes, the storage boxs and the trunkes. I found paintes, staines, varnishes, cleaner for brushs, thinneres, soapes, bleaches, detergentes, waxes, floor cleaneres, spot removeres, cleaneres for kitchenes and toiletes, and even cleaneres for stoves. I found lotes of lubricantes and oiles. I even found cannes of stewed tomatos and peachs. But, my friend, I didn't find the bottles you say we have. I'm sorry.

Good luck,

Sam

Vocabulary Summary

attic	chimney	lot	stove
base	cleaner	lubricant	switch
basin	closet	oil	thinner
bleach	cupboard	pantry	toilet
bottle	detergent	paint	tomato
box	door	peach	trunk
breezeway	dryer	porch	utility
brush	electric	sink	varnish
bulkhead	floor	soap	washer
cabinet	garage	spot remover	wax
can	hall	stain	window
cellar	kitchen	storage	workshop

Word list of exercise A. A typical house.

1. **bedroom**
2. bed
3. bureau
   dresser
   chest of drawers
4. floor lamp
5. light switch
6. rug
   carpet
7. mirror
8. picture
9. doorway
10. **bathroom**
11. toilet
12. basin
    sink
13. bathtub
14. shower
15. medicine cabinet
16. **dining room**
17. table
18. chair
19. side board
20. table lamp
21. vase of flowers
22. **living room**
23. couch
    sofa
24. easy chair
    arm chair
25. television
    TV
26. stereo
    speaker
27. floor lamp
28. rug
29. coffee table
30. **kitchen**
31. stove
32. vent
    hood
33. refrigerator
    ice box
34. kitchen sink
35. counter
36. cabinet
    cupboard
37. radio
    +++
38. front porch
    front stoop
39. front steps
40. chimney
41. porch
42. window
43. bush
44. laundry
    clothes line
45. _____

A children's story

In English many very common nouns have irregular plural forms. It is necessary to memorize them. Here are some typical examples:

		Singular	**Plural**
Type A	f > v	life	lives
Type B	vowel change	man	men
Type C	-en suffix	child	children
Type D	no change	fish	fish
Type E	no change, nationalities	Japanese	Japanese
Type F	"a pair of ___" no singular form	—	pants
Type G	no singular form	—	clothes
Type H	foreign words	thesis	theses

To learn the irregular verbs, first you study the types of changes and then you learn a lot of vocabulary. There is a lot of vocabulary in this lesson because it is a vocabulary lesson. Memorize the words you want to know.

A. Column I gives the singular of nouns; you give the plural. Column II gives the plurals; you give the singular. Write in the type of plural. Check your answers and fill in any spaces you didn't know and correct your answers.

Column I			**Column II**		
goose	*geese*	*B*	*half*	halves	*A*
foot	_____	___	_____	shorts	___
woman	_____	___	_____	sheep	___
calf	_____	___	_____	stimuli	___
index	_____	___	_____	wolves	___
tooth	_____	___	_____	crises	___
loaf	_____	___	_____	Chinese	___
species	_____	___	_____	pajamas	___
deer	_____	___	_____	series	___
medium	_____	___	_____	mice	___
child	_____	___	_____	scissors	___

B. Read this story. The singular forms of some of the nouns are given in (parenthesis) *parentheses* . Sometimes related singular nouns are given as clues to other words. ("pant") pants. Write the correct plural forms of these nouns on the lines which follow. Then check your plurals against the list of answers given in the (appendix) *appendices* .

A (Child's) *Children's* Story

Once upon a time, there was an old man, a farmer, who lived alone. In his youth he had three (wife) _____ and twelve (child) _____. Now he had none. He told travellers that he did not want (woman) _____ in his house. He did not want ("person") _____ around him at all. He perferred (animal) _____. In his house he lived with a large dog and six _____. He kept the (cat) _____ to catch (mouse) _____, but he said to travellers, "(Cat) _____ are not much better than (woman) _____, but you can throw a cat out when you want to be alone." The old man also kept (ox) _____ for plowing, (cow) _____ for milk, (calf) _____ for meat, (sheep) _____ for wool, (duck) _____, (goose) _____, and (chicken) _____ for (egg) _____, and in two quiet (pool) _____ filled with cold water, beautiful, fat (trout) _____, (bass) _____, (salmon) _____, and other (fish) _____ for fishing.

One hot summer, four Swiss (student) _____, who were hiking in the (mountain) _____ near the old man's farm stayed with him for two (day) _____, watching him and his (beast) _____. Then they walked on to the nearest village and reported to the ("person") _____ in the tavern that they had found a "wild man."

"He doesn't wear ("trouser") _____ or (shirt) _____ or (shoe) _____ on his (foot) _____ ," the (man) _____ explained. "At night he is naked! He goes without ("pajama") _____! In summer, all he wears is ("short") _____ . For winter, he has two great (coat) _____ to keep him warm. He has no other ("cloth")_____!"

The four (Swiss) _____ continued with excitement, "His hair and beard are long and dirty, and his (tooth) _____ are all yellow and sharp. He is thin and old, but he doesn't seem to be poor because he is so strong and healthy!"

In the tavern there were two (thief) _____ listening to the story. They said to each other, "(Wildman) _____ usually have (bag) _____ of gold hidden in their (house) _____ . Maybe this man isn't poor! Let's take our (knife) _____ and our (club) _____ and attack him. Crazy old ("person") _____ don't need silver. (Fool) _____ don't need gold. Let's go and help (ourself) _____!"

When the (thief) _____ came to the old man's mountain farm, they didn't find anyone at home, only the (cat) _____ and farm (animal) _____ . They searched everywhere, but all they found were the poor old man's ("scissor") _____ and (eye glass) _____ and some (pot) _____ and a pair of ("tong") _____ by the fire. On the (shelf) _____ there were two (tin) _____ of tobacco, three (pipe) _____ , some strange (nut) _____ and (leaf) _____ , and two (loaf) _____ of black bread broken into (half) _____ which the (mouse) _____ and (squirrel) _____ had been eating, in spite of the (cat) _____ .

It was getting dark inside, but outside there was enough light to search the barn yard for (sign) _____ of buried treasure. They stopped and looked. Then one of the (thief) _____ noticed that there were no (footprint) _____ in the dust. Only (paw) _____ and (hoof) _____ had left their _____ . Just then from the surrounding (hill) _____ , the strange (echo) _____ of (wolf) _____ and (dog) _____ singing together broke the silence. Then this wild music started all the (farm animal) _____ moaning and jabbering. The (thief) _____ never stopped running until they reached the tavern.

No travellers ever bothered that old farmer again. Isn't that strange?

Vocabulary summary

animal	dog	leaf	people	tavern
attack	duck	life	pipe	thesis
bag	dust	light	plowing	thief
barn yard	echo	loaf	pool	time
bass (fish)	egg	man	poor	tin
beard	eye glasses	meat	pot	tobacco
beast	fish	milk	salmon	tong
bother	fool	mountain	scissors	tooth
bread	foot	mouse	sheep	traveller
broken	footprint	music	shelf	trousers
buried	gold	naked	shirt	trout
treasure	goose	notice	shoe	village
calf	hair	nut	shorts	watch
chicken	hike	ox	sign	water
child	hill	pair	silence	wife
clothes	hoof	pajamas	silver	wolf
club	in spite of	pants	squirrel	woman
coat	keep	paw	surround	
cow	knife	person	Swiss	

Extra Exercise

The scrambled words below are all in the vocabulary summary above. Unscramble them and then put their plurals in the crossword puzzle.

Across

a. GAB   *BAG*
1. WAP   _____
4. MEIT   _____
7. XO   _____
8. FEINK   _____
10. PHESE   _____
12. LIHL   _____
13. OPELEP   _____
15. OSEUM   _____
16. FLESH   _____
17. OSEH   _____

Down

b. OTOF   *FOOT*
1. TOP   _____
2. NOWAM   _____
3. ISSETH   _____
5. WOC   _____
6. OSOEG   _____
9. SROERUTS   _____
11. EIPP   _____
12. FOOH   _____
14. ELFI   _____
15. AMN   _____

Shopping list

Non-count nouns do not have a plural form. There are two types.

1. **Mass nouns**. Matter which is measured because it cannot be counted.

    water   bread   gold

The units of measurement or sale can be counted.

    two cups of water   one loaf of bread   a bar of gold

2. **Abstract nouns.** These include:

emotions	greed, rage	**fields of study**	botany, engineering
qualities	beauty, peace	**sports**	hockey, swimming
generic terms	cereal, metal	**recreation**	dance, gardening
concepts	liberty, liberalism		

Most non-count nouns can be used in a countable sense, but the meaning is different when the noun is countable. Some examples:

I love coffee.   (in general)
I need a coffee!   (a cup of coffee)
The Gourmet Shop sells 20 different coffees.   (types of coffee)

Democracy means government by the people.   (the general concept)
Our village is a true democracy.   (an example of democracy)

Time is money.   (in general)
I fell four times.   (on four occasions)
At one time I was young.   (at one period of time)

A. Study Andy's shopping list. Then in the space below, list the **countable** and **non-countable** nouns.

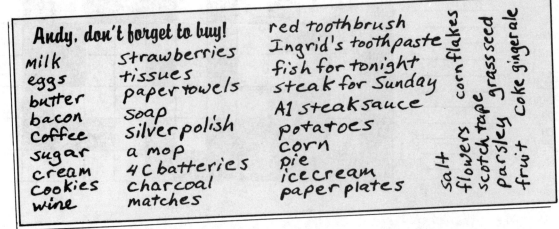

Andy, don't forget to buy!

milk
eggs
butter
bacon
coffee
sugar
cream
cookies
wine

strawberries
tissues
paper towels
soap
silver polish
a mop
4 C batteries
charcoal
matches

red toothbrush
Ingrid's toothpaste
fish for tonight
steak for Sunday
A1 steak sauce
potatoes
corn
pie
ice cream
paper plates

corn flakes
scotch tape
grass seed
parsley
coke gingerale
salt
flowers
fruit

COUNTABLE NOUNS	NON-COUNTABLE NOUNS
eggs	*milk*

What difference do you notice between the countable and non-countable nouns in these lists?

_____

_____

B. Use your lists above to give the common units of sale for each item. One or more units for each are given in the answers at the back.

a carton of *eggs, milk* _____

a dozen *eggs* _____

a quart of _____

a gallon of _____

a pound of _____

a package of _____

a pint of _____

a box of _____

a bar of _____

a bottle of _____

a bag of _____

a tube of _____

a piece of _____

a bouquet of _____

a roll of _____

C. Sort out the following list of count and non-count nouns.

geology	money	fun	traffic
joke	pavement	economics	glory
groceries	hunting	propaganda	Mohammedism
industry	dancing	garbage	calendar
dollar	furniture	youth	poverty
rage	happiness	computer	knowledge
baseball	truth	cooking	laughter
fear	philosophy	space	date
luggage	literature	hope	automobile
stationery	law	art	education
chair	slang	history	laugh
emotion	book	wealth	French
vocabulary	garden	joy	map
physics	leaf	paper	

COUNT NOUNS	NON-COUNT NOUNS
joke	*geology*

Possessive forms 14

Clothing

There are three ways of showing possession in English.

1. **possessive adjectives** and **pronouns.** (See Lessons 18 and 19.)

2. add **'s** to nouns not ending in **s.**

   girl**'s**   people**'s**

   add (**'**) to nouns ending in **s.**

   Charles**'**   girls**'**

3. **of** may also be used to show possession.

   the style **of** Winston Churchill

's is generally used when people or animals are the possessors, except when the length of the sentence makes this awkward.

   The girl's coat is blue.
   The dog's collar is broken.

of is often used when the possessor is a thing or when the "possessive" relationship indicates association or origin.

   The buttons of the coat are blue.
   The jeans of the Levi Strauss Company are the toughest.
   The lace of Belgium is world famous.

A. Here is a picture of some clothes. Try to name each piece of clothing. When you have named all you can, check the vocabulary summary at the end of Exercise C.

1. *dress*
2. _____
3. _____
4. _____
5. _____

6. _____
7. _____
8. _____
9. _____
10. _____
11. _____

12. _____
13. _____
14. _____
15. _____
16. _____

B. Match the clothes in the picture with the names given in the exercise and make sentences using the possessive **'s** or **s'**. If you want more practice, add the names of friends or classmates and write sentences about them.

1. Sam   *Sam's shirt is pink.*
2. the policeman _____
3. Susan _____
4. Bill _____
5. James _____
6. the mailman _____
7. Joan _____
8. the nurse _____

9. Ellen _____

10. the Balls _____

11. Lou _____

12. Thomas _____

13. Joy _____

14. the monkeys _____

15. _____ _____

16. _____ _____

17. _____ _____

18. _____ _____

C. Join the two phrases below into a single possessive phrase.

size	*the size of my hat*	my hat
length	_____	this sleeve
sole	_____	his shoes
handle	_____	my umbrella
buckle	_____	that old belt
fashions	_____	my favorite designer
style	_____	his new outfit
taste	_____	my brother Frank
pockets	_____	my new pants
buttons	_____	these fancy shirts
clothes	_____	today's teenagers
trends	_____	the 1980's
stripes	_____	that red shirt

Vocabulary summary

1. dress 2. skirt 3. blouse (woman's shirt) 4. T-shirt 5. shirt 6. belt
7. socks 8. jeans, pants 9. gloves 10. mittens 11. sweater, pull-over
12. boots 13. cap, hat 14. shorts 15. shoes 16. umbrella

buckle	fancy	length	stripes
button	fashion	mend	style
clothes	favorite	outfit	taste
coat	gold	pocket	trend
collar	handle	size	
color	heel	sleeve	
designer	hole	sole	

Extra Exercise

Write two sentences using possessives for each sentence below. Put a star (*) in front of the sentence which sounds better to you. Compare your choices with those in the answers. If both the sentences are equally easy to say, don't put a star.

The buckle is broken. (Mary's belt)

* The buckle of Mary's belt is broken.
Mary's belt's buckle is broken.

The right sleeve is torn. (my pull-over)

The right sleeve of my pull-over is torn.
My pull-over's right sleeve is torn.

Her shorts are too tight. (Jackie's girlfriend)

* Jackie's girlfriend's shorts are too tight.
The shorts of Jackie's girlfriend are too tight.

1. The legs are too short. (these pants)

    _____

    _____

2. The handle is leather. (my umbrella)

    _____

    _____

3. What's the size? (her skirt)

    _____

    _____

4. There's a hole in the sole! (this shoe)

   _____

5. I don't like the color. (your umbrella)

   _____

6. The laces are always untied. (old Mrs. Wilson's shoes)

   _____

7. The boots are his pride and joy. (an urban cowboy)

   _____

8. The stitching on the pocket is in gold. (his designer jeans)

   _____

9. The outfits are always stylish. (Frank)

   _____

10. The stripes match his tie and his socks. (his shirt)

   _____

11. There's a stain on my sleeve. (shirt)

   _____

12. Can you mend the right leg? (pants)

   _____

15 Subject pronouns

TV, radio, and phonograph

Pronouns are words which replace nouns. The subject pronouns are:

I	we
you	you
he, she, it	they

The noun subject of a sentence is replaced by a subject pronoun.

My TV isn't working.   *It isn't working.*

Note that the first person singular subject pronoun **I** is always capitalized.

Last summer I sold my stereo.

A. Rewrite these sentences replacing the noun subjects with pronouns.

Everyone (including you and me) enjoys being entertained.

We enjoy being entertained.

TV and radio are the major entertainment media.

They are the major entertainment media.

1. Movies are also popular,

   _____

2. but the average person doesn't go to the movies very often.

   _____

3. My sister is typical.

   _____

4. All day long, her television is going.

   _____

5. Yesterday I said, "Laurie, _____ watch too much TV.

   _____

6. She answered, "My set is on most of the time,

   _____

7. but my family and I don't watch it much.

   _____

8.   <u>Television</u> is like radio.

_____

9.   <u>Television and radio</u> are good company."

_____

10. <u>Most Americans</u> listen to TV or radio for hours everyday.

_____

11. <u>Laurie</u> also listens to CDs, tapes, and her old records on her stereo.

_____

12. <u>Some people</u> even listen to CDs and cassette tapes while they are walking.

_____

13. Of course, <u>the Japanese</u> invented that pleasure.

_____

14. <u>America</u> may be known for its entertainment media,

_____

15. but <u>constant noise</u> isn't unique to America.

_____

16. <u>You and I</u> can find TV's and radios everywhere.

_____

B. Rewrite these sentences using the phrases and nouns below in place of the subject pronouns. Use each phrase or noun only once.

the turntable on my stereo	the Japanese
the instructions	TV Guide (magazine)
the knob marked "on/off"	May and I
Joe	Channels 2 and 13
UHF channels	adult listeners

They are public broadcasting stations.

Channels 2 and 13 are Public Broadcasting stations.

1.   It is published once a week.

_____

2.   They often prefer FM radio.

_____

3.   It is German.

_____

4.   They come with the set.

_____

5.   We listen to FM radio all the time.

_____

6.   They are numbered 14 and higher.

_____

7.   He lives with his AM rock station on.

_____

8.   It is also marked "volume."

_____

9.   They made both my FM receiver and amplifier.

_____

C. Rewrite the following letter of instructions from Mike to Mr. and Mrs. Tafawa, who will be staying in his apartment while he is away. The subjects of the sentence are underlined. Use all the subject pronouns you can, but be sure the Tafawas can understand what each pronoun refers to.

A Note from Mike

Dear Mr. and Mrs. Tafawa,

These are instructions for using the TV and radio. These *They* instructions will be on the TV set. Mr. and Mrs. Tafawa *You* may have questions which these instructions don't answer. If Mr. and Mrs. Tafawa do, ask my neighbor, Jane Duncan. Jane Duncan will be glad to help. Jane and I have the same kind of TV.

My TV gets fourteen channels. The channels are both VHF and UHF. My set has two tuning dials. The dials are at the right of the screen. The one with the big numbers, 1 to 13, is for VHF (Very High Frequency). The other one is for UHF (Ultra High Frequency). I have subscribed to TV Guide. TV Guide comes in the mail every week.

To turn my set on, Mr. and Mrs. Tafawa must pull out the knob below the channel selectors. The knob is marked "On/Off — Volume." If Mr. and Mrs. Tafawa turn the knob, the knob makes the TV louder or softer. <u>The knob</u> comes off easily, so don't pull it too hard.

   <u>My radio</u> is a stereo. <u>My radio</u> has two On/Off switches. One is for the tuner. <u>The other</u> is for the amplifier. <u>Mr and Mrs. Tafawa</u> can choose either the AM band or the FM band. There is a switch marked AM-FM-Phono on the tuner. <u>The switch</u> is to the left of the On/Off switch.

   Please don't use the automatic turntable (the record player) or the tape deck. <u>The turntable and the tape deck</u> are difficult to use and the <u>turntable and the tape deck</u> need fixing.

   If you have any problems with the stereo, Sam Johnson lives on the other side of Jane. <u>Sam and Jane</u> can both help with the TV, but <u>Sam</u> is better with the radio. <u>Sam's</u> a nice guy as well. <u>Sam</u> said <u>Sam</u> would be glad to look after you, so feel free to call on him. <u>Sam and I</u> are good friends, too.

                              Good luck,

                              Mike

Vocabulary summary

AM/FM (band)	listener	rock	tape deck
amplifier	louder	screen	tuner
automatic	media	selector	turn on
channel	movies	set	turntable
come off	pull out	softer	TV set
dial	programs	station	UHF/VHF
entertain	radio	stereo	volume
fix	receiver	subscribe	work (use,
instructions	record	switch	operate)
knob	record player	tape	

Toiletries and cosmetics

The object pronouns are:

me   us
you   you
him, her, it   them

Object pronouns may replace the direct object of a verb.

Subject	Verb	Direct object
Pete	*sees*	*the drugstore.*
Pete	*sees*	**it**.
He	*meets*	*Grace Fairfax.*
He	*meets*	**her**.

Object pronouns may replace the object of a preposition.

Subject	Verb	Preposition	Object of the preposition
Her store	*is*	*near*	*the pharmacy.*
Her store	*is*	*near*	**it**.
Pete	*walks*	*towards*	*the prettiest sales clerk.*
Pete	*walks*	*towards*	**her**.

Object pronouns may replace the indirect object of a verb. (See Lesson 17.)

A. In these sentences, replace the subject pronouns and the names in parentheses with the correct object pronouns.

Jack sees (he) _**him**_ in the drugstore.

Does your mother have shampoo for (you and I) _**us**_ ?

1. John wants (he) _____ to come into the store.

2. Pete introduces (she and me) _____ to Mr. Perkins.

3. Mr. Perkins is sitting next to (she) _____.

4. That's the cosmetics counter. Molly watches (it) _____.

5. She also watches (I) _____.

6. I like (she) _____.

7. Molly, do you like (Grace and I) _____ best,

8. or do you prefer (Jack and Pete) _____.

9. Why are you looking at (Jack and Pete and Mr. Perkins) _____?

10. Please put (it and it) _____ in front of (she and them) _____.

11. That is Perkins' Drugstore. Grace opens (it) _____ every morning.

12. Mr. Perkins trusts (she) _____ to open the store before he comes in.

B. In these sentences, replace the nouns and the names in parentheses with the correct pronouns. If you use a subject pronoun, put an **S** in the brackets at the end of the sentence. If you use an object pronoun, put an **O**.

Mr. Perkins runs (Perkins' Drugstore on Oak Street) __*it*__. [O]

(The store) __*It*__ was started by his uncle in 1927. [S]

1. John needs to buy (medicine and Band-Aids) _____. [ ]

2. He rides his bike down to (Perkins' Drugstore) _____. [ ]

3. He wants to see (Molly Perkins) _____. [ ]

4. (John and Molly) _____ are old friends. [ ]

5. Mr. Lee is talking with (Molly) _____. [ ]

6. "My wife thinks (my wife) _____ is pregnant," Mr. Lee says. [ ]

7. "Do you sell (pregnancy test kits) _____? [ ]

8. "Yes," Molly says. "(The kits) _____ cost $6.99 to $14.99." [ ]

9. "We want (the best kit you have) _____." [ ]

10. "Mr. Lee, (this $10.99 kit) _____ is the same as the $14.99 kit." [ ]

11. At the back of the store, (Sam and Pete) _____ are talking to Grace Fairfax. [ ]

12. Grace says, "(Sam and Pete), are _____ going to buy something? [ ]

13. "Grace, please tell (Sam and me) _____ how much these cost." [ ]

14. "Why do you want (those expensive perfumes) _____, Pete?" [ ]

15. "We want (the perfumes) _____ for _____, (Grace)." [ ]

16. Grace blushes and laughs at (Sam and Pete) _____. [ ]

17. Mr. Perkins comes up to (John) _____. [ ]

18. "Johnny, can I help you or do you want to wait for (Molly) _____? [ ]

19. "Thanks, Mr. P, I need (a box of Band-Aids) _____." [ ]

20. "Here (the Band-Aids) _____ are, Johnny. Anything else?" [ ]

21. "Some cough medicine for (my dad) _____." [ ]

22. "OK, I have (the cough medicine) _____. Anything else?" [ ]

23. No thanks. Just a minute with (your daughter) _____." [ ]

24. With a laugh, (her father) _____ lets Molly take over helping John. [ ]

25. Mr. Lee says "This is an exciting day for my wife and (I) _____ . [ ]

26. (My wife and I) _____ are praying for a positive result." [ ]

27. "I hope (you and Mrs. Lee) _____ get the result you want," Molly says. [ ]

28. "Let (Mr. Perkins and Grace and me) _____ know. Good luck."

Mr. Lee says, "I sure will, Molly. Thanks. Bye bye, now."

Molly waves to him. "See you later." Then she turns to talk to John.

"You" The teacher	"I"	Mr. Perkins The druggist	Molly Perkins The clerk	Grace Fairfax	Joe The barber

Bruce	Ernie	Mrs. Taylor	Sally		

C. These are the people in Perkins' Drugstore yesterday. Fill in your name, your teacher's name, and the names of two of your friends. If you want to, draw in the missing faces.

Study this list of merchandise for sale at Perkins' Drugstore. Be sure you understand all the vocabulary.

after shave lotion	facial soap	pregnancy test kit
Band-Aid bandages	hair brush	razor
cold medicine	hair dye	razor blades
comb	hand cream	scissors
condoms	Kleenex facial tissues	shampoo
cough medicine	lipstick	shaving cream
cream rinse	mascara	sun tan lotion
dental floss	mirror	toilet paper
deodorant	perfume	tooth brush
deodorant bath soap	prescription medicine	tooth paste
eye shadow	pills	vitamins

Rewrite the following sentences substituting the people and merchandise above for the pronouns. Possible answers are given at the back of the book.

<u>She</u> buys <u>it</u> from <u>her</u>.

Mrs. Taylor buys shampoo from Grace.

<u>She</u> pays Mr. Perkins for two <u>of them</u> in cash.

Sally pays Mr. Perkins for two combs in cash.

1. Could <u>you</u> give <u>them</u> to Miss Curry, please?

2. Please take <u>it</u> to the Thompsons' house.

3. <u>She</u> needs <u>it</u> now.

4. Mrs. Taylor gave three <u>of them</u> to <u>you</u>.

5. Buy <u>me</u> some <u>of them</u>, please.

6. Bruce will need <u>them</u> tonight.

7. <u>You</u> found <u>it</u> for us.

8. <u>He</u> met <u>her</u> in the drugstore.

9. <u>He</u> wants a new <u>one of them</u>.

10. <u>He</u> wants <u>it</u> to be a good one.

11. <u>I</u> saw an ad for <u>it</u>.

12. <u>She</u> takes <u>them</u> every day.

13. Please use some <u>of them</u>.

14. <u>She</u> buys <u>them</u> every week.

15. <u>He</u> used <u>one of them</u> last time.

16. Take <u>it</u> after supper.

_____

17. <u>He</u> bought <u>it</u> for Sally.

_____

18. Can <u>she</u> afford to buy <u>them</u> tonight?

_____

19. <u>They</u> told us that the store was out of <u>them</u>.

_____

20. <u>You and I</u> put <u>them</u> in front of <u>him</u>.

_____

D. Fill in the blanks in this story with names, nouns, and subject and object pronouns. Possible answers are given at the back of the book.

A boy ____*I*____ know named _____ met his girlfriend _____ yesterday at Perkins' Drugstore. _____ had planned to meet _____ at six o'clock, but _____ was late. _____ wanted to buy _____ a _____ for a present. When _____ got to the store, _____ looked for _____, but _____ couldn't find _____. _____ asked _____, the druggist. _____ found _____ right away, and _____ bought _____ for _____. Then _____ sat down at the counter of the snack bar and _____ bought _____ a soda.

When _____ left the _____, _____ took _____ to the _____. A Tarzan picture was showing. _____ had seen _____ before, but _____ didn't care. _____ saw _____ anyway. I was at the _____ too, and _____ sat together. _____ didn't like the film, but _____ did. _____ loved _____! _____ were just happy being together. Love is wonderful, isn't it?

Business

The indirect object of a verb is the person to whom or for whom something (the direct object) is given, made, sold, taken, etc. The object pronouns (See Lesson 16) may replace names or nouns as indirect objects.

1. We use **to** or **for** before the noun or pronoun indirect object when the direct object comes before the indirect object.

Subject	Verb	Direct Object	Indirect Object
The clerk	*sold*	*this notebook*	**to** *Jake.*
The clerk	*sold*	*this notebook*	**to** *him.*

2. We do not use **to** or **for** when the indirect object comes before the direct object.

Subject	Verb	Indirect object	Direct object
The clerk	*sold*	**Jake**	*this notebook.*
The clerk	*sold*	**him**	*this notebook.*

3. When pronouns are used for both the indirect object and the direct object, we always put the direct object first and use **to** or **for** before the indirect object.

Subject	Verb	Direct object	Indirect object
The Clerk	*sold*	**it**	**to him**

4. The use of verbs with indirect objects is a little complicated. Most verbs can be used with **to** or **for** or without a preposition (∅). However, a few verbs cannot be used with **to**, a few cannot be used with **for**, and a few cannot be used without a preposition.

bring (to, for, ∅)	**to**	*I will bring the checkbook* **to her.**
	For	*I will bring the checkbook* **for her.**
	(∅)	*I will bring* **her** *the checkbook.*
borrow (for)	**For**	*I will borrow the checkbook* **for her.**

The partial list below includes all the other verbs in this lesson.

buy (for, ∅)	get (to, for, ∅)	pass (to, for, ∅)	send (to, for, ∅)
cash (for, ∅)	give (to, for, ∅)	pay (to, for, ∅)	take (to, for, ∅)
deliver (to, for, ∅)	loan (to, for, ∅)	read (to, for, ∅)	tell (to, for, ∅)
describe (to, for)	make (for, ∅)	return (to, for, ∅)	write (to, for, ∅)
explain (to, for)	offer (to, for, ∅)	say (to, for)	
fix (for)	owe (to, ∅)	sell (to, for, ∅)	

A. Rewrite each of these sentences, using the preposition **to** or **for** and the indirect object from the list.

1. **Rayco Manufacturing, Inc.**   5. **Yolanda, the receptionist**
2. **Wayne, a salesman**   6. **James, a new file clerk**
3. **Henrietta, a salesperson**   7. **Radio Shack, a retail customer**
4. **Henry, the office manager**   8. **Mr. Phillips, the buyer**

Please read this order over the phone.

(to, 2) *Please read this order over the phone to Wayne.*

Wayne describes the equipment.

(for, 8) *Wayne describes the equipment for Mr. Phillips.*

1. Return this package to Rayco, please.

   (for, 3) _____

2. Send the model R 211.

   (to, 7) _____

3. Ask Henry to fix that disk drive.

   (for, 6) _____

4. Mr. Phillips will give the message.

   (to, 5) _____

5. Pass on the instruction manual.

   (to, 8) _____

6. Wayne tells everything he hears.

   (to, 5) _____

7. This repair manual was written.

   (for, 7) _____

8. Today Henrietta sold the complete product line.

   (to, 8) _____

9. Pay $2,575 for this shipment.

   (to, 1) _____

10. Mr. Phillips buys Rayco products every Tuesday.

    (for, 7) _____

11. Wayne needs to borrow a company car.

    (for 3,) _____

12. Rayco offers a special discount.

    (to, 4) _____

B. Rewrite the sentences below using the words in the parentheses.

The salesman delivered a new PC to Yolanda.

(to her)	*The salesman delivered a new PC to her.*
(it)	*The salesman delivered it to her.*

1. (the calculator) _____
2. (them) _____
3. (to Mr. Phillips) _____
4. (a package) _____
5. (for Henry) _____
6. (got) _____
7. (a receipt) _____
8. (it) _____
9. (for me) _____
10. (loaned, to James) _____
11. (the manual) _____
12. (to him) _____
13. (it) _____
14. (sold) _____
15. (her, the typewriter) _____
16. (us) _____
17. (to you) _____
18. (gave) _____
19. (him) _____
20. (it, to her) _____

C. These are scrambled sentences. First, correct the order. Then, where you can, without changing the meaning, rewrite the sentence without using a **to** or **for** phrase.

for   an appointment   the salesman   made   the receptionist

The receptionist made an appointment for the salesman.
The receptionist made the salesman an appointment.

Jonathan   please   the new policy   explain   to

Explain the new policy to Jonathan, please.

1. sold   my broker   for   some stock   me

_____

_____

2. its stockholders   big dividends   to   IBM   pays

_____

_____

3. for   this check   will you   me   please   ?   cash

_____

_____

4. more money   us   to   your company   owes

_____

_____

5. for   a receipt   the bookkeeper   get

_____

_____

6. her   did   say   the manager   ?   to   anything

_____

_____

7. the salesman   to   delivered   them   the new model

_____

_____

8. us   secretary   office supplies   his   for   buys

_____

_____

9. on   April 15th   the shipment   I   them   sent   to

_____

_____

10.   to   offered   the calculator   Mary   the new owner

_____

_____

11.   this   receipt   please   to   take   her

_____

_____

12.   the Wilcox file   to   right now   get   !   the president

_____

_____

13.   will   the cash   to   the bank   you   loan

_____

_____

14.   three   us   her accountant   for   checks   wrote

_____

_____

15.   Sharp   this calculator   can   for   fix   Elise   ?

_____

_____

16.   them   Pat   all the office supplies   buys   for

_____

_____

_____

Vocabulary Summary

accountant	clerk	model	repair manual
appointment	company	notebook	retail
bank	customer	office	right now
broker	discount	order	salesman
business	disk drive	owner	salesperson
buyer	dividends	package	shipment
calculator	equipment	policy	stock
cash	file clerk	product line	stockholder
check	manager	receipt	supplies
checkbook	message	receptionist	typewriter

Sports

The possessive pronouns are:

mine	ours
yours	yours
his, hers, its	theirs

Possessive pronouns replace possessive nouns or noun phrases. They can be used alone as subjects or objects. (See Lesson 14.)

Subject: *Jack's bike is American.*   ***His** is American.*
Object: *Wong can't play his favorite game.*   *Wong can't play **his**.*

A. Answer the questions using possessive pronouns and the word "too."

My game is softball. And yours?

Mine is softball too.

Joe wants Fritz's motorcycle. And Mary's?

Joe wants hers too.

1. New Yorkers' favorite sports are football and baseball. And Californians'?

   _____

2. The favorite of foreign students is soccer. And yours and mine?

   _____

3. Tennis is Chris Evert's favorite sport. And Jimmy Connors'?

   _____

4. Mohammed Ali watches my favorite team on TV. And yours?

   _____

5. You need clubs to enjoy George Bush's best sport. And Nancy Lopez'?

   _____

6. Bronco busters risk their lives in rodeos. And rodeo clowns?

   _____

7. The Cubs' stadium is in Chicago. And the White Sox'?

   _____

8. My Brother Bill and I have lost our tournament. And you two?

   _____

9. Fran's golfball is in the water. And Jane's?

_____

10. Mark Spitz worked out in our local pool. And yours?

_____

11. I'd like to play nine holes with Jack Nicklaus' clubs. And Arnold Palmer's?

_____

12. Every surfer has his favorite beach. And Bob?

_____

13. Weight lifters' bodies are strong. And gymnasts'?

_____

14. Jesse Owen's achievments in track and field were remarkable. And Carl Lewis'?

_____

15. The baseball career of Lou Gehrig was cut short. And Harry Agannis'?

_____

16. Sally shot her arrow but missed by a mile. And you?

_____

17. Her arrow's point is missing. And your arrow's?

_____

B. In this story, cross out the phrases which <u>should be</u> replaced by possessive pronouns. Possessive pronouns should only be used when it is clear what they refer to. Write the pronouns over the phrases you cross out.

Wanda and Phil and I have <u>our homes</u> in San Francisco. <u>My home</u> *Mine* is in the city. *Theirs* <u>Their home</u> is in the suburbs. They both love all kinds of sports. <u>Their life</u> is a good life. <u>Their jobs</u> pay well and leave them time for athletics. <u>Wanda's job</u> is with a medical laboratory; Phil's is with the administration <u>of the university's library</u>. Both jobs are from nine to five. After work Wanda meets Phil as <u>the university's gym</u>. When they work out separately, <u>his exercise</u> is lifting weights and <u>her exercise</u> is swimming. <u>My exercise</u> is swimming, too, so I see Wanda in the pool sometimes. <u>Their training schedule</u> is tougher than <u>my schedule</u>, so I don't see her often. This month, when they play together, <u>their sport</u> is racquetball.

Why don't you come to <u>our gym</u> with me next time? <u>Your physical condition</u> is not the best physical condition, but we can challenge Phil and Wanda to <u>my new favorite game</u>, volley ball. <u>Their choice</u> would be tennis or racquetball, but <u>our choice</u> doesn't have to be that strenuous. If <u>our choice</u> is volleyball, we might even win! <u>My experience</u> with the game isn't much, but it's more than <u>Wanda's experience</u>. And <u>your experience</u> is a lot better than <u>Phil's</u>, even if he could beat you wrestling with one of <u>his hands</u> tied behind his back. In tennis, their chances of beating us are fantastic, but <u>our chances</u> are better in volleyball. Come on. Let's try.

Vocabulary summary

achievement	experience	physical condition	team
arrow	favorite	racket	tennis
ball	football	racquetball	tournament
baseball	game	rodeo	track and field
beach	golfball	schedule	training
beat	gym	soccer	volleyball
body	gymnast	softball	weightlifter
bronco buster	hole	sport	work out
career	horse	stadium	wrestling
clown	miss by a mile	strenuous	
club (golf club)	motorcycle	surfer	
exercise	pool	swim	

The body

> The possessive adjectives are:
>
> | my | our |
> |----|-----|
> | your | your |
> | his, her, its | their |
>
> Possessive adjectives modify nouns. They cannot be used alone.
>
> ***My** head hurts.*
> *He looked sadly at **his** big feet.*

A. First label this illustration. Fill in all the words you can remember, and then check your list and fill in the rest of the words using the list in the vocabulary summary box.

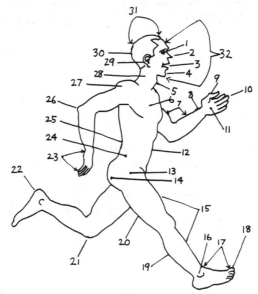

Parts of the body.

1. *eye*	9. _____	17. _____	25. _____
2. _____	10. _____	18. _____	26. _____
3. _____	11. _____	19. _____	27. _____
4. _____	12. _____	20. _____	28. _____
5. _____	13. _____	21. _____	29. _____
6. _____	14. _____	22. _____	30. _____
7. _____	15. _____	23. _____	31. _____
8. _____	16. _____	24. _____	32. _____

Fill in the sentences below and then rewrite them using possessive adjectives.

Mary Lou's (27) <u>*shoulders*</u> are broad; she's powerful.

Her shoulders are broad; she's powerful.

Watch out for Mohammed Ali's right (23) <u>*hand*</u>! It could kill you.

Watch out for his right hand! It could kill you.

Kitty poked (she) (26) *elbow* into (I) (12) *stomach*.

Kitty poked her elbow into my stomach.

1. I like Sally's (2)_____; it's cute.

    _____

2. Look at Mike's (12)_____; it's a beer belly.

    _____

3. Have you seen Aaron's (17)_____; they're huge.

    _____

4. Beth Anne's (10)_____are unusual; she has twelve.

    _____

5. When I look into Jack's (1)_____, my heart pounds.

    _____

6. The (13)_____of that wrestler are wide; he's built like a tank.

    _____

7. Children love to sit on Santa's (21)_____.

    _____

8. He tore the diamond choker from around Liz's (28)_____.

    _____

9. Spiderman's (2)_____ can smell trouble a mile away.

    _____

10. There were stars in Marie and Harold's (1)_____.

    _____

11. Joe put (Joe's) (17)_____ in (Joe's) (3)_____ by saying what he said.

    _____

12. Manuel has a long, pointed beard on (Manuel's) (4)_____.

    _____

13. Let's shake. I agree. Give me (you) (23)_____.

    _____

14. Mary and Jan's (29)_____must have been burning; Bill said such nice things about them.

_____

15. Lady Godiva's (30)_____ was quite famous.

_____

16. Betty Grable's (15)_____ were insured for $10,000,000.

_____

17. William Tell shot an apple off of (Tell's) son's (31)_____.

_____

18. Big Mike put (Mike's) (23)_____completely around Sandra's (24)_____.

_____

19. Who put Little Jack Horner's (9)_____ into a Christmas Pie?

_____

20. Helen's (32)_____ launched a thousand ships and started a war.

_____

21. You should have seen (his and my) (32)_____ when she tripped.

_____

22. He confessed, "We just lost (her and my) (31)_____."

_____

23. His Lordship looked so funny when Charlie kicked him in (His Lordship's)
     (14)_____.

_____

24. There once was a lady from Niger
     Who smiled as she rode on a tiger.
        They returned from the ride
        With the lady inside
     And the smile on the (32) _____ of the tiger.

B. Add the possessive adjectives which match the subjects of these sentences or which make sense.

        My head hurts. I have a headache.
        His heel hurts. Juan has a sore heel.
        Her chest hurts. Maybe she is having a heart attack.
1.   _____ throat hurts. He has a sore throat.
2.   _____ back hurts. Mable has a backache.
3.   _____ ear hurts. You have an earache.

4. _____ feet hurt. We have sore feet.

5. _____ finger hurts. She has a sore finger.

6. _____ leg hurts. It has a sore leg.

7. _____ tooth hurts. I have a toothache.

8. _____ stomachs hurt. The kids have stomachaches.

9. _____ head hurts. Bill has a hangover.

10. _____ chest hurts. You are having chest pains.

11. _____ heart hurts. Mark's in love. That's heartache.

12. _____ knees hurt. Will and I have sore knees.

13. _____ ankle hurts. Jennifer twisted it and it aches.

14. _____ eyes hurt. You've been reading too much, and they ache.

15. _____ toe hurts. Nureyev stubbed it and it's sore.

16. _____ arms hurt. Both our pitchers have sore arms.

17. _____ skin hurts. Margo has a little sunburn.

18. _____ pride is hurt. The director laughed at us.

19. _____ hair is hurt. She bleached it too often.

20. _____ nose hurts. Melinda punched me right in the face.

21. _____ feelings are hurt. The girls ignored us.

22. _____ ears hurt. I boxed them when he talked back to me.

23. _____ butt hurts. My kid brother's just a pain in the butt to me.

24. _____ belly aches. Next time Anders won't eat so much candy.

Vocabulary Summary

1. eye 2. nose 3. mouth 4. chin 5. throat 6. chest 7. arm 8. wrist
9. thumb 10. finger 11. palm 12. stomach, belly 13. hip 14. buttocks,
butt 15. leg 16. ankle 17. foot 18. toe 19. calf 20. thigh 21. knee
22. heel 23. hand 24. waist 25. back 26. elbow 27. shoulder 28. neck
29. ear 30. hair 31. head 32. face

ache	director	lose my head	sore
beard	feelings	pain	stars
beer belly	funny	pointed	stub
bleach	hangover	powerful	sunburn
box your ears	heart attack	pride	tooth
broad	huge	punch	tripped
burning	hurt	shake	twist
candy	kick	skin	wide
cute	kill	smell	wrestler
diamond	launch	smile	

Expletive IT 20

Weather/time/distance

The impersonal subject **it** is used in expressions of weather, time, distance, and identification.

weather	*It is hot.*	*It will be getting dark.*
	It is stormy.	*It is too cold to swim!*
	It was raining.	*How hot is it?*
time	*What time is it?*	*How much time does it take?*
	It is Wednesday.	*It's dinner time.*
	It was late.	*It's time for work.*
	It is two o'clock	*It will be time to go.*
	It was evening	*It takes two hours.*
distance	*How far is it to Houston.?*	
	It is thirty miles.	
	It is half an hour to Houston by car.	
Identification	*Is that Jane? Yes, it is.*	
	Who is it? It's I (or me), Jane.	

Other typical structures are:

It's fun to travel.
How much is it?   It's one hundred dollars.
It was Shakespeare who wrote Othello.
It was in Cairo that they met.
It might be exciting.

In speaking and informal writing **it is** and **it will** are often contracted to **it's** and **it'll**. **It would** and **it had** are contracted to **it'd** in speaking only.

A. The expletives are missing from this story. Read the story, put in all the expletives, and study the different structures they are used in. The answers are not given at the back of the book. **It** is very difficult to make a mistake on this exercise.

It was the middle of the night. I heard something. What was *it*? *It* was a knock at the door. Who was __? A stranger. __ was a woman. I saw her face. __ was white as a sheet. Was __ a ghost? "Who is __?" I asked through the door. "__ is Marie. You don't know me, but __ doesn't matter. __ is cold out here.

__ is dark and __ is stormy." "__'s very early," I said. "What time is __?" I asked myself as I looked at my watch. __ was 3:34 by my watch. "__'s just before four o'clock!" I said. "__ is early, I know __, but please let me in," she said. I opened the door and let her in. "Thank you," the woman said, "__ was terrible out there. My car is over there. __ is icy, and I am stuck in the snow. __ is too far to walk to town." "__ is three miles," I put in. "Yes, and __ is ten degrees outside. May I use your phone?" She called a tow truck. "__ will be an hour before they come. May I stay here?" she asked. "__ is so nice and warm, and __ was frightening being alone." "Sure, you can stay as long as you like," I answered. "Please have a seat and some nice hot coffee. __ isn't every night I can rescue a lovely lady in distress." She smiled, and _ was a beautiful smile.

B. In the spaces below write all the sentences and clauses that are about time, weather and distance.

1. *It was the middle of the night.*
2. _____
3. _____
4. _____
5. _____
6. _____
7. _____
8. _____
9. _____
10. _____
11. _____
12. _____
13. _____
14. _____

C. Write simple questions and answers on these subjects using the expletive **it**.
Make your answers true if you can. The answers at the back are examples.

book (the book you are reading)

What book is it? It's a grammar book.

century

What century is it? It's the 20th Century.

1. date

    _____

2. day of the week

    _____

3. year

    _____

4. temperature

    _____

5. weather

    _____

6. time of day (early morning?)

    _____

7. time (time to study math?)

    _____

8. distance to Chicago (in miles from where you are)

    _____

9. distance to Chicago (in hours by car or plane)

    _____

10. time in Chicago

    _____

11. time in Chicago (time for breakfast?)

    _____

12. distance to San Diego (in miles from where you are)

    _____

13. distance to San Diego (time by car, etc.)

    _____

14. time of day in San Diego

    _____

15. time and date in San Diego

    _____

16.   temperature in Chicago

_____

17.   weather in Chicago

_____

18.   more about weather in Chicago (dark, windy?)

_____

19.   weather in San Diego

_____

20.   more about weather in San Diego (foggy, freezing?)

_____

21.   time (in your home country)

_____

22.   temperature and weather (in your country)

_____

23.   distance (in miles to your home)

_____

24.   distance (in time by plane to your home)

_____

Vocabulary Summary

century	early	late	temperature
cold	evening	middle	time
dark	frightening	miles	tow truck
date	ghost	raining	warm
degrees	hot	rescue	weather
distance	icy	stormy	
distress	knock	stuck	

Expletive THERE IS / ARE

The "Great Melting Pot"

The expletive **there** takes the singular forms of the verb **to be (is, was)** when it is used with singular nouns.

> *There is a large Irish community in Boston.*
> *There was a large Pennsylvania Dutch population before 1776.*

There takes the plural forms of the verb **to be (are, were)** when it is used with plural objects.

> *There are many Scandinavians in Minnesota.*
> *By 1870 in New York City, there were large neighborhoods of non-English speaking immigrants.*

When forming questions, we use **there** as the subject of the sentence. (See Lessons 3 and 9).

> *Is there anyone here who speaks German? There isn't, is there?*

In negative sentences using **there,** we usually use contractions with the verb **to be,** particularly with negative questions. (See Lessons 2, 8, and 9).

> *There aren't many Indians in Indianapolis.*
> *Isn't there a big Portuguese minority in New England?*
> *There's a good reason for everyone to learn English, isn't there?*

There is also used with modals and with these verbs: **appear, come, go, happen, remain, seem.**

> *There may be a cultural melting pot in the USA, but there seem to be many "unmelted" cultural minorities here.*
> *There remain strong ethnic groups in many places around the country, but there comes a time in every family when the children forget.*

We usually use the expletive **there** when explaining the location of something.

> *There is a big Chinatown in San Francisco.*

A. All the sentences describing things in this picture of 3rd Avenue are grammatical, but they sound better if they are rewritten using the expletive **there.** Look at the picture and rewrite the sentences following the examples.

Lots of people are on 3rd Avenue today.

There are lots of people on 3rd Avenue today.

A house is at 56 3rd Avenue.

There is a house at 56, 3rd Avenue.

1. Steps are in front of the house.

_____

2. An elevated train, the L, is above the house.

_____

3. Below the house is a subway.

_____

4. Two restaurants are next door to 56 3rd Avenue.

_____

5. First is a Chinese restaurant.

_____

6. A Jewish delicatessen is next to that.

_____

7. A taxi is stopped in front of Fong's Fast Food.

_____

8. In the taxi is a fat woman.

_____

9. Through Fong's window, a Chinese man is watching.

_____

10. A woman is in Gottlieb's doorway.

_____

11. A pleased expression isn't on her face.

_____

12. Lots of noises are on 3rd Avenue today.

_____

13. Something appears to be wrong on 3rd Avenue.

_____

14. "Peace and quiet" goes!

_____

B. These sentences all describe progressive actions. Rewrite them using the expletive **there.**

A lot seems to be happening on 3rd Avenue today.

There seems to be a lot happening on 3rd Avenue today.

1. Trains are rumbling by.

   _____

2. A fat woman is paying her taxi driver.

   _____

3. Between Mrs. Gottlieb and Mr. Fong, tension is growing.

   _____

4. A fight is brewing on 3rd Avenue.

   _____

5. A dog is barking at Mrs. Gottlieb's cat; it is Fong's.

   _____

6. In front of number 56, a boy is sitting on the steps.

   _____

7. A boy is watching the excitement build.

   _____

8. Nothing unusual is happening here.

   _____

9. A battle is always coming between the Fongs and the Gottliebs.

   _____

10. Now only one hope for peace remains.

    _____

C. Rewrite your first five answers in exercise A above making them into incorrect negative statements. Then correct the statement with "Oh, but there is/are..."

Lots of people are on 3rd Avenue today.

There aren't lots of people on 3rd Avenue today.
Oh, but there are.

1. _____

   _____

2. _____

   _____

3. _____

_____

4. _____

_____

5. _____

_____

D. Rewrite your second five answers in exercise A above making them into questions. Then answer the question with "You bet there is/are!"

A house is at 56 3rd Avenue.

Is there a house at 56 3rd Avenue?
You bet there is!

6. _____

_____

7. _____

_____

8. _____

_____

9. _____

_____

10. _____

_____

E. Using this chart of population statistics from the U.S. Census, complete the sentences on the next page using the expletive <u>there</u>. Then write a question for which your statement is the answer. Several questions are possible.

POPULATION STATISTICS
by Race and Hispanic Origin
from the 1991 World Almanac from the U.S. Census Bureau

	Total	White	Black	Asian	Hispanic
Atlanta GA	425,022	138,235	283,158	2,001	5,750
Chicago IL	3,005,078	1,512,411	1,197,174	73,745	423,357
Detroit MI	1,203,339	420,529	758,468	7,614	28,466
Honolulu HI	762,565	262,604	17,203	463,117	54,619
New York NY	7,071,639	4,348,605	1,788,377	245,759	1,406,389
San Antonio TX	785,809	621,679	57,566	5,821	421,808
Washington DC	638,333	174,705	448,370	6,883	17,777

There are   758,468 _Black Americans_ living in Detroit.

How many Black Americans are there living in Detroit?

There is   a total population of 762,565 in _Honolulu._

What is the total population of Honolulu?

1. _____ a bigger Asian population than _____ or _____ in Honolulu.

2. _____ more Hispanics in New York than _____ in San Antonio.

3. In Detroit _____ more _____ than Whites.

4. _____ a large Asian _____ in Honolulu.

5. In Atlanta _____ only 5,750 _____

6. In _____ an _____ population of only 7,614.

7. _____ almost as many Blacks in Chicago as _____ .

8. _____ about the same number of _____ in San Antonio as in _____

Vocabulary Summary

appear	ethnic	minority	seem
community	groups	neighborhood	steps
cultural	happen	population	subway
delicatessen	immigrants	remain	taxi
elevated train	location	restaurant	you bet there is!

Note: In this lesson there are many words used for nationality, ethnic, and racial groups. It is important to learn about them and use them with cultural sensitivity. What educated people in the U.S. consider to be the "correct term" varies from one situation to another, from one region of the country to another, and from one year to the next. For example, in Exercise E, the terms used for "race" are those used by the 1991 U.S. Census. However, many North Americans no longer like the term "black." Some Black leaders advocate going back to the term "Negro-American." Others prefer "African-" or "Afro-American," while others prefer the broader term "people of color."

The terms used in this lesson are Irish, Pennsylvania Dutch, Scandinavian, German, (American) Indian, Portugese, Chinese, Jewish, White, Black, Asian, and Hispanic. In the Census, Hispanic refers to people who identify themselves in that way. They may be of any race. Some are immigrants from Spanish or Portugese speaking countries; others feel that their family origins are primarily Hispanic.

Extra Exercise

F. = Fun. These are popular sayings and proverbs. In the blank spaces add the correct form of the verb **to be**. The vocabulary in this extra exercise is not included in the vocabulary summary. If you have trouble understanding the saying or want to know how we use it, ask a friend for help.

1. There _____*is*_____ never enough time.
2. There _____ a pot of gold at the end of the rainbow.
3. There will never _____ another you.
4. There _____ no place like home.
5. In every cloud, there _____ a silver lining.
6. There _____ no flies on Jack.
7. There _____ no need to hurry.
8. There _____ a sucker born every minute.
9. There _____ many ways to skin a cat.
10. There _____ no business like show business.
11. Where there _____ smoke, there _____ fire.
12. There _____ little time to lose.
13. There _____ no hope.
14. There _____ no teaching an old dog new tricks.
15. Where there _____ life, there _____ hope.
16. There _____ days when I should have stayed in bed.
17. There must _____ a way out of this mess.
18. There ought _____ a law.
19. There _____ always tomorrow.
20. There _____ never enough hours in a day.
21. There must _____ something we can do.
22. There _____ always a chance.
23. There _____ something rotten in the state of Denmark.
24. There _____ lots of good fish in the sea.
25. There _____ no turning back.

Human qualities

The present tense of the verb **to be** is:

I am   we are
you are   you are
he is
she is   they are
it is

*I **am** a teenager.*   *He **is** too.*
*We **are** bored.*

A. Fill in the blanks using the correct forms of the verb **to be** in the present tense.

Jane *is* thirteen and proud of it.

Many of her classmates *are* still little kids and act like it,

but I *am* happy to say that Jane *is* quite grown up for her age.

1. She _____ a hard-working student at Lincolnfield Junior High.
2. I know a lot about her because her parents ____ our next door neighbors.
3. They think she ____ special, a model teen, and I ____ sure they are right.
4. Jane and I ____ friends.
5. In fact, I ____ her boyfriend, although we ____ not going steady.
6. Her parents think she and I ____ too young.
7. I ____ confused by their thinking.
8. Jane ____ dependable, courteous, intelligent, and attractive.
9. And I ____ almost fifteen. Why ____ we too young?
10. Jane's brother's name ____ Jack.
11. Jane and Jack ____ twins.
12. Of course, they ____ the same age, but she ____ much more mature.
13. Now Jack ____ one of my best friends,
14. but I must admit he ____ a dumb nut.
15. Everyone loves him because he ____ such a clown, but he ____ a bit immature.
16. In fact, at times when he and I ____ just fooling around, he ____ quite insane.

17. But that's all right because he'____ only thirteen,

18. and boys his age ____ kind of wild sometimes.

19. Yesterday I got an awful shock. Jane said, "You know, Billy, Mom'___ right.

20. You ____ as crazy as Jack ___ . Sometimes you'____ all sophisticated,

21. and the next minute you'____ a goofy comic or a droopy lover.

22. It'____ OK with me though, 'cause we ____ three of a kind!"

B. Rewrite the sentence substituting the word in parentheses. Make any other necessary changes.

Why is that woman so rude?

(some people)   *Why are some people so rude?*

(shy)   *Why are some people so shy?*

(very)   *Why are some people very shy?*

(affirmative statement) *Some people are very shy.*

1. (Mr. Bowers)   _____

2. (negative statement)   _____

3. (ugly)   _____

4. (affirmative statement)   _____

5. (too)   _____

6. (industrious)   _____

7. (we)   _____

8. (I)   _____

9. (friendly)   _____

10. (Texans)   _____

11. (complacent)   _____

12. (conceited)   _____

13. (you three)   _____

14. (greedy)   _____

15. (crazy about Patty)   _____

16. (we)   _____

17. (up-tight)   _____

18. (Susan)   _____

19. (studious)   _____

20. (stuck up)   _____

Vocabulary Summary

awful	fooling around	kind of	sophisticated
bored	friend	lover	special
classmates	friendly	mature	stuck up
clown	going steady	model	student
comic	goofy	neighbor	studious
complacent	greedy	nut	teenager (teen)
conceited	grown up	parents	Texans
confused	happy	proud	three of a kind
courteous	hard-working	quite	twins
crazy	immature	right	ugly
crazy about	industrious	rude	up-tight
dependable	insane	sexy	young
droopy	intelligent	shock	wild
dumb	just a little	shy	

Extra Exercise

This letter has many errors in it. Correct the verb **to be**. The grammar in this
exercise is easy; the vocabulary is more difficult. The words are not included
in the vocabulary summary, so underline those you want to remember.

Dear Frank,

    This letter ~~are~~ *is* an answer to your questions about the two men we met from Iowa. Senator MacLane and Bob O'Brien ~~is~~ *are* both politicians. Now don't say all politicians is crooks. Some are and some aren't. It am the same with doctors and plumbers. The senator is an old-timer, while Bob is a newcomer. The senator's record are good and clean. It is too soon to tell about Bob. You know that Betsy and I am both Democrats. So is Bob O'Brien and the senator. Both's loyal to the party. Now you know that in Iowa the Democrats is the best for the people. They are mostly trustworthy and generous and very concerned with the common man. The Iowa Republicans, on the other hand, are not for the working people. It am the party of greed and aggression. Betsy and I am not prejudiced, but we's very unhappy when the Republicans is in office.

    I am for all the Democrats. Betsy are more particular. She are for O'Brien. She says he am young and energetic and his ideas is the ideas of the future. I think she also thinks he's sexy. She doesn't like Senator MacLane. He am a bit ugly and up-tight, but he are honest and bright, so I is for him. He isn't at all sexy, but he are no stuck up wheeler-deeler like Bob O'Brien. It am sad, but I is more comfortable with a reserved, sane old work horse like the senator. Betsy says, "He's so very boring!" "OK, you is right," I tell her, "but he am honest, and he are a tried and true Democrat, so I am for him!"

                                                        Best wishes,
                                                            Tom

U.S. Presidents

> The past tense of the verb **to be** is:
>
> | I was | we were |
> |---|---|
> | you were | you were |
> | he was | |
> | she was | they were |
> | it was | |
>
> *In 1942, Franklin Roosevelt **was** the President.*
> *I **was** a great supporter of his.*
> *The Democrats **were** in control of Washington.*

A. Fill in the blanks will the correct forms of the verb **to be** with the past tense.

In 1963, you *were* two years old.

John Kennedy *was* the President of the United States.

Our parents *were* Kennedy Democrats.

1. We _____ too young to know about politics or government.

2. Lyndon Johnson of Texas _____ Vice President.

3. My father _____ not happy about the Vice President; he loved Kennedy.

4. The day _____ November 22, 1963.

5. President and Mrs. Kennedy _____ in Dallas, Texas.

6. A crazy gunman named Lee Harvey Oswald _____ out to get Kennedy.

7. Kennedy knew there _____ danger, but he _____ brave.

8. Kennedy and his friend Connally _____ in an open car.

9. It _____ Oswald who shot them both.

10. Many people _____ certain Oswald _____ not alone.

11. My dad _____ certain that Oswald _____ part of a conspiracy.

12. My granddad said Oswald _____ a Russian spy.

13. Other people _____ certain the Mafia _____ behind the murder.

14. Even we little kids _____ very sad to hear that Kennedy _____ dead.

15. Then two days later Oswald ___ on TV when another madman gunned him down.

16. Mr. Johnson, who _____ now the new President, came from Texas.

17. It _____ a frightening time.
18. You didn't understand, but you _____ very frightened too.
19. This _____ the fourth successful assassination of an American President,
20. and before 1963, four other Presidents _____ almost assassinated.
21. We Americans _____ really worried that our nation was going crazy,
22. but worse times _____ still to come.

B. In many of these sentences, the past tense form of the verb **to be** is not correct. Underline the incorrect forms and write the correct forms in the blanks at the ends of each line. If two verbs are needed put down two. If none, put X.

George Washington <u>were</u> the first President of the United States. *was*

John Adams <u>am</u> Washington's Vice President. *was*

It <u>is</u> when Adams <u>are</u> President that party politics *was*, *was*

Jefferson was the head of the opposition party.   *X*

1. Washington, Jefferson, and Andrew Jackson was famous early Presidents. _____
2. It were Washington who put the Constitution into practice. _____
3. Jefferson is a political philosopher. _____
4. Jackson am the first Democrat. _____
5. He was the leader of the common people against the rich and powerful. _____
6. Three war-time Presidents was very famous. _____
7. The first was Abraham Lincoln during the Civil War. _____
8. Lincoln be the first Republican President. _____
9. His father was a poor, hard-working farmer. _____
10. Lincoln is an intelligent and powerful lawyer and politician, but also a very honest one. _____
11. His years as President are war years, _____
12. but he were planning to have peace with justice after the war. _____
13. He was shot before peace came. _____
14. The next years was years of injustice and corruption in politics. _____
15. Woodrow Wilson and Franklin Roosevelt are also war Presidents. _____
16. Like Lincoln, Wilson were working hard for a just peace during the war. _____
17. Wilson is too sick at the end of the war to win the peace. _____
18. After Wilson too, there am years of injustice and corruption. _____
19. Franklin Roosevelt are President for the longest time in U.S. history. _____
20. His first years are the Great Depression. _____
21. Personally, he were conservative; he came from a rich, powerful family. _____
22. His cousin, Theodore Roosevelt, is a famous Republican President. _____

23. Franklin am a Democrat. _____

24. The U.S. were weak in 1933 and needed a strong Federal Government. _____

25. Roosevelt's policies was both capitalist and socialist. _____

26. The last years of Roosevelt's presidency is during World War II. _____

27. He too was sick and died during the war, _____

28. but this time there is a wiser and more just peace after the war. _____

29. The next Presidents, Truman, Eisenhower, and Kennedy were honest, _____

30. and their presidential terms is good years for most Americans. _____

C. Using the information on these five Presidents, write ten sentences. Use the verb **to be** in the past tense. Try to use as many different forms of the verb as you can. Some possible sentences are given at the back of the book.

Lyndon B. Johnson
1908–1975
Party: Democrat
Term: 1963–1969
Born in Texas
Teacher
Representative
Senator
Vice President

Richard M. Nixon
1913–
Party: Republican
Term: 1969–1974
Born in California
Lawyer
Representative
Senator
Vice President

Gerald R. Ford
1913–
Party: Republican
Term: 1974–1977
Born in Nebraska
Lawyer
Representative
Vice President

Jimmy Carter
1924–
Party: Democrat
Term: 1977–1981
Born in Georgia
Navy Physicist
Peanut Farmer
Governor

Ronald Reagan
1911–
Party: Republican
Term: 1981–1989
Born in Illinois
Actor
Labor Leader
Governor

Johnson and Carter were Democrats.
I was twelve when Ford became President.

1. _____
2. _____
3. _____
4. _____
5. _____
6. _____
7. _____
8. _____
9. _____
10. _____

Vocabulary Summary

assassinate	famous	peace	spy
born	farmer	physicist	strong
capitalist	governor	politics	successful
certain	gunman	poor	teacher
conspiracy	honest	powerful	term
constitution	intelligent	president	vice president
corruption	just (justice)	representative	war
cousin	labor leader	Republican	weak
crazy	madman	rich	win
dead	murder	senator	wiser
Democrat	nation	shot	
died	navy	sick	
early	party	socialist	

Simple present

Cops and robbers

The simple form of the verb is used for the simple present tense except in the third person singular.

Simple form: telephone.

I telephone	we telephone
you telephone	you telephone
he telephones	
she telephones	they telephone
it telephones	

*In an emergency, she **dials** "O".*

We add **s** to the simple form to make the third person singular

dial > dials   radio > radios   pay > pays

except when

1. a verb ends in **o** preceded by a consonant.

   I **go** > he goes   We **do** > She does

2. a verb ends in **sh, ch, s, x,** or **z.** You cat**ch** > It cat**ches**
3. a verb ends in **y** preceded by a consonant. We s**py** > He sp**ies**

The simple present is used for everyday actions and general truths.

*The watchman **walks** his rounds every night.*
*The police always **protect** the people.*

The simple present is also used for the future with an adverb of time. (See Lesson 29, Future—going to.)

*The court **opens** at 9 am. **tomorrow**.*

A. Fill in the blanks with the correct forms of the verbs given in parentheses.

(hide)   They *hide* from the police.

(come)   He *comes* when a house is on fire.

1. (use)   You _____ the telephone to call for help.

2. (sell)   He _____ drugs.

3. (steal)   She _____ clothes.

4. (commit)   They _____ robbery.

5. (watch)   He _____ our property every night.

6. (know)   Art thieves _____ a lot about art.

7. (stop)   We _____ prostitutes from walking the streets.

8. (start)   The alcoholic _____ to drink again.

9. (happen)   It _____ every time he stops.

10. (die)   When drunks drive, innocent people _____ .

B. Fill in the blanks with the correct forms of the verbs given in parentheses.

(watch)   A watchman *watches* other people's property.

(try)   Policemen always *try* to catch thieves.

1. (belong)   Crooks _____ in jail.

2. (steal)   That thief _____ at least $2000 of silver each week.

3. (stop)   Traffic cops _____ lots of drunk drivers.

4. (commit)   Those crooks _____ many kinds of crime.

5. (use)   Drug dealers often _____ their own drugs.

6. (help)   Our local policeman _____ people with all kinds of problems.

7. (hide)   The killer _____ his gun.

8. (kill)   Guns _____ .

9. (sell)   Burglars _____ their stolen goods.

10. (sentence) Judge Williams _____ most burglars to jail.

11. (need)   Our policemen _____ a new car.

12. (find)   The police rarely _____ runaway children.

13. (collect) The FBI _____ information about crooks.

14. (happen)   Robberies _____ every night in some neighborhoods.

15. (need)   The government _____ help from the people to fight crime.

16. (become)   The public _____ more aware of crime every year.

17. (turn)   Blackmail _____ people guilty of small crimes into victims.

C. Use the correct forms of the verbs below in the sentences. Some verbs are used more than once. There may be more than one possible correct answer for some of the sentences.

blackmail	radio	steal
catch	rush	try
kill	snatch	happen

A burglar *steals* jewelry.

Firemen *rush* to put out fires.

1. The police _____ some burglars.

2. Blackmailers _____ people who have done something wrong.

3. The fire truck _____ down the street.

4. The police department _____ to stop crime before it _____

5. These burglars _____ valuable art.

6. A policeman _____ criminals.

7. That blackmailer _____ shoplifters.

8. A fireman _____ to the fire.

9. A patrolman in trouble _____ the police station for help.

10. The court _____ criminals of all kinds.

11. A killer _____ his victim with a weapon or with his hands.

12. The fire chief _____ to the police for help at a fire.

13. A policeman _____ never to use his gun.

Vocabulary summary

alcoholic	drink	kill(er)	start
art	drunk	local	steal
belong	drugs	police(man)	stolen
blackmail(er)	fight crime	police station	stop
burglar	find	public	telephone
catch	fire(man)	property	thief
chief	firetruck	prostitute	traffic
come	guilty	protect	try
commit	gun	radio	use
cop	happen	robbery	valuable
court	help	runaway	victim
crime	hide	rush	walk
criminal	innocent	sell	watch
crook	jail	sentence	weapon
dealer	jewelry	shoplifter	wrong
die	judge	silver	

Extra Exercise

In this story about Sherlock Holmes, there are many errors in the use of the simple present tense. Write the correct forms over the errors.

                               uses   *reads*

Sherlock Holmes always use the same method. He read the newspapers day and night. He never miss news stories about crimes. He like strange crimes. If the explanation in the paper makes no sense, he become interested. Often the police brings difficult cases to him. Sometimes the victim finds his way to Holmes' Baker Street apartment.

24   Simple present tense

98

Holmes generally ask his friend Dr. Watson to join him. They listens while the victim or the policeman explains the story of the crime. The story seem to be a complete mystery. Holmes and Watson pay very close attention to detail, but little facts which Watson overlook start Holmes thinking. The great detective also watch the victim very carefully while he talks. He observes the man's speech, gestures, and clothes. Holmes try not to miss anything, and he forget nothing. He develop several theories, but, before he tells anyone, he go to the scene of the crime and looks for evidence. The men from Scotland Yard always miss the important details, but Holmes find lots of clues - a bit of tobacco, a bloody finger print, a useless bellpull.

Then Holmes try to trap the criminal. The police think they understands the crime, but Scotland Yard usually fixes the blame on the wrong man. The detectives collects lots of evidence to prove their theory are right. The chief inspector laugh at Holmes, but Holmes work like a bloodhound. Nothing can distract him. He stay on the trail of the crooks. The police investigators wants to talk to him, but he ignores them. The police and Dr. Watson never understand until suddenly Sherlock catch the villian or at least solves the mystery. At the end of the story, the solution seem very simple. Sherlock say, "Elementary, my dear Watson. It was elementary." Then he lights his famous pipe or play his violin while he waits for the next knock on the door.

Polls and questionnaires

The simple present is used to express everyday actions, general truths and the future (See Lesson 24, Simple present.)

The simple present is also used to express **non-action** states or conditions. When verbs do not express action, they are **stative**
Here are a few stative verbs. A longer list is given below.

1. Verbs of perception: **see, hear, feel, taste, smell**

   *I **hear** that the government is collecting information.*

2. Verbs of emotion or mental state: **love, hate, know, believe, guess, want**

   *I **guess** the government want's to collect this information.*

3. Verbs of measurement: **weigh, measure, cost, value, equal**

   *I **value** my privacy.*

All of these verbs can be used in the present progressive. (See Lesson 26.) When they are in the present progressive they express action and the meaning is different.

Stative Verb List

agree	have	measure	suppose
ask	hear	need	taste
believe	hesitate	prefer	tend
belong	hold	promise	think
consider	hope	realize	trust
cost	imagine	regard	value
enjoy	indicate	remember	want
equal	know	require	weigh
fear	laugh	say	wish
feel	like	see	
guess	love	seem	
hate	mean	smell	

A. In the blanks, put the correct simple present forms of the verbs given in parentheses.

       (feel)   The American often _feels_ strange about questionnaires.

       (seem)   Our culture _seems_ very impersonal.

       (think)   The individual often _thinks_ he is unimportant.

1. (like)   Therefore he _____ to answer questionnaires about himself.
2. (want)   If a polling company _____ information about him,
3. (consider) it _____ him to be important.
4. (ask)   If someone _____ his opinion about something,
5. (value)   that person _____ his ideas.
6. (need)   Since we all _____ to be valued,
7. (enjoy)   we _____ answering questionnaires.
8. (realize) Everyone _____ that surveys are impersonal,
9. (imagine) but he _____ that
10. (believe) someone _____ he is important enough to be counted.
11. (hesitate) At the same time, the American _____.
12. (promise) Our Constitution _____ the right of privacy.
13. (trust)   He _____ his government,
14. (hate)   but he _____ to give it necessary information about himself.
15. (fear)   He _____ that,
16. (know)   if the government _____ all about him,
17. (hold)   it _____ him in its power.
18. (like)   If he _____ to give information to his government,
19. (feel)   he _____ more uncomfortable giving information to strangers.
20. (equal)   In America, privacy _____ freedom.

B. This is a questionaire about your father, brother, or friend. Fill in the blanks with the simple present form of the verb given in parentheses and then circle the correct answer to finish the sentence. For example,

    (put)   He _puts_ all questionnaires in   the mail.

                                                  his pocket.

                                               (the wastepaper basket.)

                                             (no more questionnaires.)

    (want)   He _wants_ to get   lots of questionnaires.

                                              one questionnaire every day.

1.   father's
   My brother's name is _____.
   friend's

2.   (love)   He _____
   to answer questionnaires.
   to throw away questionnaires.
   to drink Coke.

3.   (hate)   He _____
   to answer silly questions.
   to throw away anything.
   to eat sandwiches.

4.   (consider) He _____ questionnaires to be
   interesting.
   a waste of time.
   dangerous.

5.   (wish)   He _____ he had
   never seen a questionnaire.
   one questionnaire every week.
   more questionnaires to answer.

6.   (hesitate) He _____ before answering
   advertising surveys.
   government surveys.
   political surveys.

7.   (prefer)   He _____
   census forms.
   tax forms.
   death.

8.   (realize)   He _____ that some surveys are
   necessary.
   stupid.
   a waste of time.

9.   (laugh)   He _____ at
   political opinion polls.
   sex research surveys.
   bad jokes.

10.   (believe)   He _____ his opinions are
   important.
   never read.
   valuable.

Vocabulary summary (not included in the verb list above)

advertising	government	poll	survey
census	impersonal	privacy	stupid
collect	information	questionnaire	tax
cultural	necessary	research	throw away
dangerous	opinion	the right to	waste of time
forms	political	silly	

C. Exercises C and D are vocabulary lessons. The words are not included in the summary vocabulary. Circle the words you want to learn so you can review them later.

Exercise C gives the instructions for D. Fill in the blanks with the simple present of the verbs in **bold type.** These verbs are given in the past form. (See lessons 27 and 28.)

Instructions for Exercise D

The following questionnaire **was** _is_ from a new store in Phillipsburgh. The store **said** _says_ it **needed** _needs_ information about the community. It **wanted** _____ people to feel that Mannings Department Store is interested in them. Mr. Manning **believed** _____ people **liked** _____ to shop in a store which **showed** _____ them that they are important, that the store **valued** _____ their business.

Study the questionnaire. It **seemed** _____ to ask for information, but it really **told** _____ you about the store. It **was** _____ a form of advertising. Notice that the form **used** _____ the simple present tense and a lot of stative verbs. Questionnaires **asked** _____ about general truth and everyday activities, about perceptions, feelings, opinions, and measurements. People who **wrote** _____ questionnaires generally **liked** _____ the feeling of the present tense.

For the following exercise (D), we **gave** _____ you Mr. Manning's questionnaire. He **had** _____ his questions put into type. Then to save you time, he **wrote** _____ part of your answers for you. He **thought** _____ this **made** _____ it easier for you to answer the questions. To make this exercise, we **underlined** _____ the verb in the question and **left** _____ a blank for the verb in the answer. Fill in the blanks with the simple present of the verbs.

If you **wanted** _____ to answer the questions, finish the answers with the information about yourself. Do you enjoy doing this? Or do you feel uneasy?

MANNINGS

Dear Friends,

   My wife Darla and I open our new Mannings Department Store next month on May 25th. Before the GRAND OPENING, we want to get to know you. What interests you? What can we do for you? Please finish the answers on our little questionnaire so that we know you and can serve you and our community better. Thanks,   *Herb Manning*

What is your name? _____   What is your wife or husband's name?_____

Where do you <u>live</u>? *I* _____

What credit cards do you <u>prefer</u> to use? *I* _____

What shopping center do you <u>like</u> best now? *I* _____

What department store do you <u>shop</u> at now? *I* _____

Where does your husband/wife <u>prefer</u> to shop? _____

What does he/she really <u>enjoy</u> shopping for? _____

What do you <u>enjoy</u> shopping for? *I* _____

When do you and he/she <u>go</u> shopping together? *We* _____

When you go shopping at Mannings
     do you <u>intend</u> to use our laundromat or 1-hour dry cleaning service?

     We _____
     do you <u>expect</u> to enjoy our "3-Square-Meals-Cafe" or our "Take-a-Break Cocktail Lounge?"

     We _____

When you and your husband/wife shop for clothing, what do <u>you consider</u> to be most important, style, price, quality, variety, or designer?

     We _____

When you buy hardware, housewares, or auto parts, do you <u>regard</u> style, price, quality, or brand names to be most important?

_____

When your husband/wife buys gifts for you does he/she <u>tend</u> to buy you clothing, jewelry, flowers, gourmet foods or wine, books, or what?

_____

Does he/she <u>remember</u> your birthday and anniversary?

_____

Do you <u>feel</u> he/she would appreciate a reminder from Darla?

     I _____

Personal information about you:

Weight: *I* _____

Height: *I am* _____ *tall.* _____

Waist <u>measurement</u>: *My waist* _____

My birthday is _____ My anniversary is _____

What holidays does your family celebrate? *We* _____

Do you <u>agree</u> that we need a FIRST CLASS department store in Phillipsburgh?

_____

If you agree, Darla and I hope you will come and see us. Plan to take advantage of our GRAND OPENING SALE. And please accept our personal invitation to our OPENING WINE AND CHEESE TASTING GALA all day on May 26th.

See you there and thanks!   Herb

These are the words of a famous old Black American spiritual. What do they mean?

> There's a man goin' 'round takin' names*,
> There's a man goin' 'round takin' names.
> He has taken my brother's name,
> An' he's cleft my heart in twain**.
> There's a man goin' 'round takin' names.

* There is a man going around taking names

** And he has cut my heart in two

Present progressive

Travel

We <u>form</u> the present progressive by using the present of the verb **to be** (See Lesson 22.) and the present participle (the **-ing** form) of the verb.

>   **Present:**   travel
>   **Present participle:**   traveling
>   *Herman is traveling.*

We <u>use</u> the present progressive to

1. express action in the present

>   *Herman is traveling **now**.*

2. express an action in the future using an adverb

>   *Herman is traveling **next week**.*

Notice the formation of questions and negative sentences.

>   *Is Herman traveling?*
>   *Herman is not traveling.*

A. Fill in the blanks with the correct form of the verb given in parentheses.

	(drive)	Sally *is driving* to Denver.
	(stay)	I ___*am*___ not ___*staying*___ in that hotel again!
1.	(fly)	Next week we _____ to Moscow.
2.	(talk, ride)	While we _____, I _____ in my car.
3.	(sail)	_____ you _____ with me at five o'clock?
4.	(ride, rain)	You _____ not _____ your bike! It _____!
5.	(leave)	The bus _____ in ten minutes.
6.	(arrive)	_____ her ship _____ tomorrow?
7.	(walk)	This week they _____ from Wichita to Kansas City.
8.	(take off)	My plane _____ right now.
9.	(run)	Mrs. Wilson ____always _____from one meeting to another.
10.	(take)	You _____ the airport limousine in an hour.
11.	(try)	_____ they _____ to catch a taxi?

12. (go) _____ she _____ by train to L.A.?
13. (stay) We _____ not _____ in a Stay-a-Day Motel again.
14. (travel) These folks _____ first class.
15. (rent) When I arrive, I _____ a Chevy from Hertz.
16. (eat out) She _____ every night this week.
17. (sightsee) _____ you both _____ all day tomorrow?
18. (tour) _____ Miss Patterson _____ Virginia now?
19. (take) Bob _____ the express train to the Loop.
20. (be, spending) We _____ tourists: we _____ our time sightseeing.

B. These are scrambled sentences. Unscramble them.

     Gate   looking   for   am   9A   .   I

     I am looking for Gate 9A.

     Omaha   is   bus   why   Henry   to   the   ?   taking

     Why is Henry taking the bus to Omaha?

1. leaving   your   is   train   ?   when

_____

2. car   aren't   by   traveling   ?   you

_____

3. all   Ali   the   Reno   hitch-hiking   to   's   !   way

_____

4. is   in   hotel   tonight   she   again   sleeping   .   that

_____

5. Interstate   Gwen   95   Jacksonville   is   Highway   into   . taking

_____

6. tonight   you   sleeping   I   and   are   where   ?   Jack

_____

7. Mickey   is   Wednesday   for   the   leaving   ?   Coast

_____

8. Vail   are   for   skiing   we   in   going   a   . vacation

_____

9. is   train   at   departing   our   ?   six

_____

10. customs   in   waiting   immigration   line   is   or   ?   for   he

_____

C. Fill in the blanks in these sentences with the verbs below. In some sentences, more than one verb may make sense. Use all the verbs only once. The verbs are given in the infinitive form; put them into the present progressive.

to buy	**to window shop**	**to rent**	**to tick**	**to race**
to ride	**to pick up**	**to run**	**to fly**	**to walk**
to sail	**to check in**	**to stay**		

Melissa *is buying* her tickets at Lyon Travel Agency.

Caroline *is window shopping* on fashionable North Michigan Avenue.

1. _____ they _____ at the Hyatt House Hotel?

2. Max _____ his ticket at the airport.

3. The trains _____ on time this evening.

4. The Abbotts _____ United Airlines out to Hawaii.

5. She _____ not _____ horseback to Phoenix, believe me!

6. _____ you _____ a camper to go to Yellowstone or not?

7. Elsie _____ her Mazerati at 158 miles per hour!

8. The taxi meter _____ away while you keep on talking to Mom.

9. My girl _____ on the Queen Elizabeth for Barbados.

10. _____ we _____ or grabbing a cab because it's late.

11. I'm too tired to drive so I _____ at the next motel.

Vocabulary Summary

arrive	express	limousine (limo)	sightsee	tired
bike	fashionable	make	skiing	tour
bus	first class	meet	sleep	tourist
buy	fly	motel	stay	train
camper	gate	plane	take	travel
catch	go	race	take off	travel agency
check in	hitch-hiking	rent	taxi	try
customs	horseback	ride	taxi meter	vacation
depart	hotel	run	tick	walk
drive	immigration	sail	ticket	window shop
eat out	leave	ship		

Two nursery rhymes:

London Bridge is falling down, falling down, falling down.
London Bridge is falling down, My fair lady.

Christmas is coming, the goose is getting fat.
Please to put a penny in the old man's hat.
If you haven't got a penny, a ha'penny will do.
If you haven't got a ha'penny, then God bless you.

We <u>form</u> the simple past by adding **-ed** to regular verbs.

Present:	borrow
Past:	borrow**ed**

We <u>use</u> the past tense to express a completed action in the past.

*Nan **borrowed** only a hundred dollars yesterday.*

Notice the formation of questions and negative statements.

*Did she **borrow** enough?*
*No, she didn't **borrow** enough.*

Spelling rules:

1. If a regular verb ends in **e**, we only add **-d**.

   balance > balance**d**   agree > agree**d**

2. If a regular verb ends in **y** preceded by a consonant, change the **y** to **i** and then add **-ed.**

   t**ry** > tr**ied**   de**ny** > den**ied**

3. If a regular verb ends in a single consonant preceded by a single vowel, double the final consonant and then add **-ed**

   a. with words of one syllable

      stop > stop**ped**

   b. with words accented on the last syllable

      omit (o **mit'**) > omit**ted**

   c. but not with words accented on other syllables

      debit (**deb'** it) > debit**ed**
      deposit (de **pos'** it) > deposit**ed**

A. Fill in the blanks with the correct form of the verb in parentheses. Use the simple past.

	(balance)	Ruth *balanced* her checkbook.
	(submit)	Our lawyer *submitted* his bill to us for 16 hours of work.
	(count)	The clerk *counted* my money carefully.
1.	(accept)	The teller _____ my personal check.
2.	(cash)	Eloise _____ her paycheck.
3.	(loan)	The bank _____ Max the money for his new car.
4.	(borrow)	My sister _____ money to pay for her son's school.
5.	(insure)	Luckily, I _____ my watch.
6.	(deposit)	Mr. Wong _____ half his paycheck in savings.
7.	(endorse)	You _____ your check incorrectly.
8.	(debit)	Sulafa _____ $16.28 from her checking account.
9.	(open)	Sylvie _____ a new account.
10.	(save)	She _____ $756.00 last year.
11.	(sign)	Jerome _____ the loan agreement.
12.	(unlock)	In private, Mrs. Van der Pool _____ her safe-deposit box.
13.	(explain)	The receptionist _____ the bank's interest rates.
14.	(deposit)	Mort _____ my check.
15.	(check)	The teller _____ the balance of our account.
16.	(charge)	Henry _____ too much on his Visa card.
17.	(close out)	The Olsen Rug Company _____ its accounts.
18.	(cash)	Horace _____ a check for $12,000.
19.	(bounce)	Anges Smith's check _____!
20.	(stop)	We _____ payment on that lost check.
21.	(borrow)	I _____ $150.00 to buy a $2,500.00 certificate of deposit.

B. Change the sentences given in the simple present into simple past affirmative statements (+), then into simple past questions (?), and then into simple past negative statements (−).

Sue Ann saves forty-seven dollars weekly.

(+) *Sue Ann saved forty-seven dollars* last week.

(?) *Did Sue Ann save forty-seven dollars last week?*

(−) *Sue Ann didn't save forty-seven dollars last week.*

I ask the teller for a receipt on Wednesdays.

(+) _I asked the teller for a receipt_ last Wednesday.
Did I ask the teller for a receipt last Wednesday?
I didn't ask the teller for a receipt last Wednesday.

1. Bill cancels his credit cards.

_____ last May.

_____

_____

2. Miss Pickering endorses all of the checks.

_____

_____

_____

3. The bank accepts traveler's checks.

_____ last week.

_____

_____

4. Felinda receives a receipt for her payment.

_____

_____

_____

5. Ralph always charges everything he wants.

_____ last year.

_____

_____

6. My children try to pay with half of a dollar bill.

_____

_____

_____

7. Our bank closes promptly at three every afternoon.

_____ this afternoon.

_____

_____

8. That damned bank charges a service charge for everything!

_____

_____

_____

9. The 1st National Bank cancels a check for us.

                                                                      on May 6th.
    _____

    _____

    _____

10. I deny that this is my signature on this check.

    _____

    _____

    _____

11. Humphrey uses the drive-in teller every day.

                                                                      last Friday.
    _____

    _____

    _____

12. You apply for a car loan from the Merchant's Bank.

    _____

    _____

    _____

13. Butch cancels his appointment at the bank.

    _____

    _____

    _____

Vocabulary summary

accept	charge	drive in	safe-deposit
account	check	endorse	box
agree	checkbook	insure	save
agreement	checking	interest rate	savings
appointment	account	lawyer	service charge
balance	clerk	loan	sign
bank	close out	paycheck	signature
bill	count	payment	stop
borrow	credit card	personal	submit
bounce	debit	promptly	teller
cancel	deny	omit	try
cash	deposit	open	unlock
certificate	dollar	receipt	
of deposit	dollar bill	receptionist	

Extra Exercise

Correct the verbs in this story. Put them into the simple past.

At two yesterday afternoon, I ~~open~~ *opened* the front door of the Florida Trust Company on Orange Blossom Avenue and ~~walk~~ *walked* into the lobby. I look around for a withdrawal slip. On a desk behind the door, I spot one. I pick it up, fill it out carefully, and carry it up to a pretty blond teller. The name plate on her window calls her Frankie. She smiles sweetly and asks if she can help me. I answer that I need to take out some money from my savings account.

Just then a fat man in a pink T shirt pushes me aside and shoves a note in front of the teller. She grabs the note and turns white. "Hurry up, Sister," he whispers.

She replies, "I can't. I don't have the key."

The man whips out a big black gun and waves it in her face. "So get it and quick!" he hisses. I try to walk away, but he stops me. "Hey you, Buster. You're next in line. Stay here. You stay put." I stay. He laughs at me. I feel sick, and I probably look sick too. I smile weakly. The man straightens his dark glasses and taps his fake mustache nervously. Then he points the gun right at me.

Just as I faint, the bank's alarm sounds. The bank robber shouts angrily and fires his gun at the alarm. The tellers all duck. He runs and escapes through the front door.

When I pull myself up from the floor, Frankie asks politely, "Now, may I help you?" She waits for my answer. I drop my withdrawal slip in front of her. With a smile she picks it up, checks my savings balance on her computer, and hands me my money. "Bye," she laughs. As I step back out into the sunshine, I wonder if I am dreaming.

Irregular past forms

28

Tools and trade

In English some very common verbs are irregular in the past tense.

Present: **give** *She gives me the wrench.*
Past: **gave** *She **gave** me the wrench yesterday.*

Notice the formation of questions and negative statements.

*Did she **give** me the wrench?*
*She didn't **give** me the wrench.*

A summary of the verbs used in this exercise is given below. Memorize the irregular past tense forms of the verbs you are interested in.

Vocabulary

blow – blew	forget – forgot	make – made	stand – stood
break – broke	fly – flew	meet – met	steal – stole
build – built	get – got	pay – paid	swear – swore
buy – bought	go – went	put – put	sweep – swept
catch – caught	grow – grew	quit – quit	swim – swam
come – came	have – had	read – read	take – took
cost – cost	hear – heard	ride – rode	teach – taught
cut – cut	hit – hit	run – ran	tear – tore
do – did	hold – held	say – said	tell – told
fall – fell	keep – kept	sell – sold	think – thought
feed – fed	lead – led	shake – shook	throw – threw
feel – felt	leave – left	sing – sang	weep – wept
fight – fought	light – lit	sit – sat	
find – found	lose – lost	speak – spoke	

A. These are common tools used by tradesmen. See how many you can identify and then check your work against the list given in the summary vocabulary.

a. *hammer*   f. _____   k. _____

b. _____   g. _____   l. _____

c. _____   h. _____   m. _____

d. _____   i. _____   n. _____

e. _____   j. _____

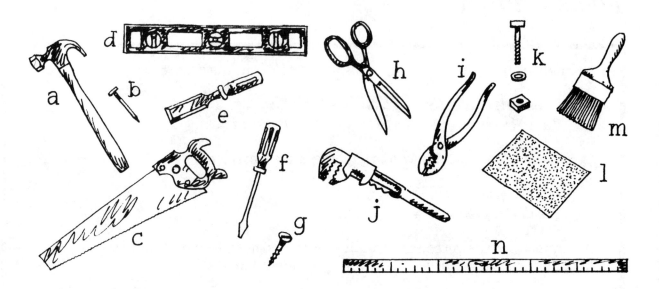

Fill in the blanks with the names of the tools indicated and then rewrite each sentence putting it into the past tense.

Mary leaves one (g) *screw* in the box.

Mary left one screw in the box.

Jake hit his thumb with a (a) *hammer*.

Jake hit his thumb with a hammer.

1. The electrician holds the (f) _____ carefully.

   _____

2. Does my (c) _____ cut as well as yours?

   _____

3. She sells me her best (i) _____.

   _____

4. The carpenter comes up with a bag of (b) _____.

   _____

5. The barber cut my hair with dull (h) _____.

   _____

6. She keeps her (n) _____ in my tool box.

   _____

7. Mr. Maloney has the sharpest (e) _____s in the shop.

   _____

8. "I pay a lot of money for a good (d) _____; it's worth it."

   _____

9. Cynthia loses (g) _____ all over the place.

    _____

10. As I throw my weight on it, the (j) _____ breaks.

    _____

11. Butch sings and plays music on an old (c) _____ .

    _____

12. Kathy builds it without one (k) _____ , _____ or _____ .

    _____

13. Johnny leaves his worn out (l) _____ on the floor.

    _____

14. Willie puts his dirty (m) _____ in turpentine.

    _____

B. Rewrite these sentences in the simple past and then transform them into questions (?) or negative statements (−) as indicated.

The plumber comes quickly in an emergency.

The plumber came quickly in an emergency.

(?) *Did the plumber come quickly in an emergency?*

Fritz catches enough fish to sell to Max's restaurant.

Fritz caught enough fish to sell to Max's restaurant.

(−) *Fritz didn't catch enough fish to sell to Max's restaurant.*

1. The painter falls off his ladder.

    _____

    (−)_____

2. Farmer Cobb feeds her pigs.

    _____

    (−)_____

3. You pay the electricians.

    _____

    (?)_____

4. The secretary gets very angry.

    _____

    (?)_____

5. The cashiers have to count the money carefully.

    _____

    (−)_____

6. The police officer rides around all night in his car.

_____

(?)_____

7. The meter reader reads Sally's meter every two months.

_____

(-)_____

8. The priest takes time to talk to the old and sick.

_____

(?)_____

9. The teachers teach five days a week.

_____

(?)_____

10. The night watchman goes to work at midnight.

_____

(?)_____

11. Lawyers cost too much.

_____

(-)_____

12. Mary gives the grocer thirty dollars.

_____

(?)_____

13. The janitor sweeps the rugs.

_____

(?)_____

14. The farmer grows tomatoes.

_____

(-)_____

15. The librarians read a lot.

_____

(?)_____

16. The hotel doorman blows his whistle for a taxi.

_____

(-)_____

Vocabulary summary
This list does not include the verbs from the beginning of the lesson.

a. hammer   e. chisel   i. pliers   l. sandpaper
b. nail   f. screwdriver   j. wrench   m. paint brush
c. saw   g. screw   k. bolt, washer,   n. rule
d. level   h. scissors   nut

angry	electrician	officer	taxi
bag	emergency	painter	teacher
barber	farmer	pig	thumb
box	fish	play	turpentine
carpenter	floor	plumber	watchman
cashier	grocer	police	weight
count	hair	priest	whistle
cut	hotel	restaurant	worth
dirty	janitor	rug	worn out
dollar	ladder	sale	
doorman	lawyer	secretary	
dull	librarian	sharp	
dust	meter reader	shop	

Extra Exercise

Put the following letter into the past tense.

Judy Sweetie,
   This *is* (was) a day to remember! First I *walk* (walked) to Dixwell Avenue
in the rain and *get* all wet and *catch* a cold. The rain *falls*
in sheets, and the wind *blows* in a great gust and *tears* my
umbrella inside out and *steals* the hat right off my head. At
Murray's on Dixwell I *take* the bus. What *does* it *do*? It *breaks*
down after two blocks. As soon as we *stop*, one of those crazy
taxi drivers *hits* us sideways and the traffic *gets* blocked for
a mile in every direction. It only *takes* a minute.
   I say, "I quit." So I put my hat on and throw myself
into the crowd getting off the bus, and I push and fight until
I escape. Then I run two blocks north and fly four blocks east
and get to the railroad station and make my train! Whew, at
last, Good Luck! Right? So I ride along for ten minutes, buy
a paper, light a cigarette, read for a bit, notice the Handsome

Devil who is sitting across from me and who is definitely noticing me. I feel ashamed of looking like a drowned rat - although he clearly finds me attractive. And then that dumb, stupid train loses power. We hear this great sigh, and the air conditioner quits.. The train groans and shudders and stands still.

Of course, inside me I swear and weep, but, believe, me, outside I sit there and smile in an amused, superior sort of way to Handsome. Our eyes meet and he loses no time. No fooling. He smiles - he finds the right sort of smile - he speaks in this real husky voice, and stands up, and takes my hand, and leads me to the door. My head swims. I think I am dreaming. An old song sings in my ears, and I forget all my troubles, my rush to get to the office, my big appointment.

We get off the train, find a tiny but clean trackside cafe right there by the train - really! Amazing! Gorgeous

buys me coffee and then leaves me for a minute to call his office. Then we sit and drink coffee and make small talk and tell a couple of funny travel stories. Then his driver comes with a spiffy silver grey car.

After half an hour getting oh-so-comfortable chitchatting with Mr. Right, we get to my office. The Hunk leaps out of the car and holds the door for me to get out, and then he says in his sweet husky way, "I would invite you to lunch, Lurene, but I'm having lunch with my wife."

"Thanks anyway," I say, "for the idea and for the ride." We shake hands and he leaves me standing on the curb with my mouth open. A day to remember. Some days it doesn't pay to get up.

I'll see you soon, *Lurene*

Future — GOING TO 29

Cooking

We <u>form</u> the future in three basic ways in English. We use **going to, will,** and adverbs. (See Lessons 24, 26, and 30.)

1. **going to**   *She **is going to** bake cookies.*

2. **will**   *She **will** bake cookies.*

3. the simple present   *Tomorrow she **bakes** cookies.*
   form with an adverb

   the present progressive   *Tomorrow she **is baking** cookies.*
   form with an adverb

When we form the future with **going to,** we use **to be + going to +** the simple form of the verb.

> *They **are going to bake** a cake.*

Notice the formation of questions and negative statements.

> *Are they **going to** bake a cake?*
> *They are not **going to** bake a cake.*

A. Fill in the blanks in these sentences with the **going to** future of the verbs given in parentheses.

	(chop)	Frank *is going to chop* some onions.
	(make)	We *are going to make* stew for dinner.
	(bake)	Tomorrow Buddy *is going to bake* a blueberry pie.
1.	(boil)	Mrs. Williams _____ six potatoes.
2.	(roast)	When _____ they _____ the leg of lamb?
3.	(mince)	Joanne _____ the garlic very fine.
4.	(squeeze)	Then she _____ four lemons.
5.	(melt)	Alison _____ half a stick of butter.
6.	(mix)	First we _____ a cup of milk into the flour.
7.	(stir)	Then we _____ in two eggs.

8.   (spoon)   Next we _____ the batter on the griddle.

9.   (turn)   In a minute, you _____ over the pancakes.

10.   (cook)   When _____ they _____ more pancakes?

11.   (grind)   I _____ the pepper at the last minute.

12.   (measure) Bobby _____ out two teaspoons of salt.

13.   (need)   Ralph _____ 2/3 cup of vinegar.

14.   (add)   Last, she _____ a pinch of red pepper.

B.   First change these sentences into affirmative statements (+) in the **going to** future. Then rewrite them as negative statements (−). Finally, rewrite them as questions (?).

Sally tosses the salad.

(+) *Sally is going to toss the salad.*

(−) *Sally isn't going to toss the salad.*

(?) *Is Sally going to toss the salad?*

Becky roasts a chicken.

(+) *Becky is going to roast a chicken.*

Becky isn't going to roast a chicken.

Is Becky going to roast a chicken?

1.   Andy is spreading on lots of peanut butter.

_____

_____

_____

2.   Sue slices the bread.

_____

_____

_____

3.   The old cook mashes lots of potatoes.

_____

_____

_____

4.   Ingrid licks the mixing bowl clean.

_____

_____

_____

5.   Harold barbecues steaks next Sunday.

_____
_____
_____

6.   Kitty is spooning out big bowls of ice cream.

_____
_____
_____

7.   Paula is beating two egg yolks.

_____
_____
_____

8.   Ralph chills the wine before dinner.

_____
_____
_____

9.   Elise fries her eggs sunny side up.

_____
_____
_____

10.   You whip the cream first.

_____
_____
_____

C.   Rewrite this recipe using **you** and the **going to** future.

Ice

Pour water in an ice tray.
You are going to pour water in an ice tray.
Freeze the water.
You are going to freeze the water.

A Common Hamburger

Divide the ground meat.

_____

Make round balls.

_____

Flatten the meatballs.

_____

Fry the meat patties.

_____

Put the cooked hamburger on a hamburger bun.

_____

Add ketchup, mustard, and a slice of onion.

_____

Extra Exercise

Rewrite this recipe as a paragraph using **I**, the **going to** future, and such adverbs as **next, first, after that, following that,** and **finally.**

The World's Greatest All-American Hamburger

Mince 1 small onion.
Saute the onion in butter until golden.
Put the onion into a bowl.
Add 1 lb of lean ground beef to the onions.
Pour in 1/4 cup of milk.
Shake 1/3 cup of seasoned bread crumbs over the meat.
Add 1 tablespoon of A1 or some other rich steak sauce.
Sprinkle 1/4 teaspoon of thyme over the meat mixture.
Mix the meat mixture thoroughly with your hands.
Shape it into 4 large hamburger patties.
Split 4 English muffins in half with a fork.
Toast the muffins.
Fry the patties over medium heat in a pan or on a grill
or broil them under a broiler or over a charcoal fire.
Turn the burgers after two minutes.
Cook them on the 2nd side for 2 more minutes (for rare) or 4 (for well done)
Melt a slice of Swiss or American cheese on the top of each muffin.
Lay the burgers on the muffins.
Top each burger with a slice of tomato.
Serve the burgers with a mixed salad and a good beer.

Predictions

For a general explanation of the future tense in English, See Lesson 29.

When we form the future with the modal **will,** we use *will* + the simple form of the verb.

> *When we grow up I **will learn** to fly.*
> *I **will be** an aviator.*

Notice the formation of questions and negative statements.

> ***Will** I learn to fly?*
> *I **will** not learn to fly.*

Shall is sometimes used in place of **will,** especially when we want to express determination, too. In modern American English, **shall** and **will** mean the same thing.

> *I **shall** go whether it rains or not! = I **will** go whether it rains or not!*
> *You **will** not say a word. = You **shall** not say a word.*

When **shall** and **will** are used in questions, their meanings are different. **Will** is asking for a prediction of the future. **Shall** is an invitation or request for permission or approval.

> ***Will** it rain tomorrow?*   Prediction
> ***Shall** we go to the movies?* Invitation
> ***Shall** I sing for you?*   Asking approval or permission

Will and **shall** are often contracted in informal speech and writing. (See Lesson 8)

> I will go. = I shall go. > **I'll** go.
> I will not run. = I shall not run > **I won't** run.

A. When they graduate from school, Americans often make predictions about their classmates. Look over this list of 6th grade children. Next to their names are predictions of what they will do when they grow up. Then finish filling out the list on the next page using the **will** future.

Bobby - architect   **Carol** - work in hospital as a nurse   **Larry** - fireman   **Kenneth** - make millions of dollars as a movie star   **Daisy** - painter   **Gloria** - study to be a lawyer   **Stu** - play as a football star for the Los Angeles Raiders   **Wally** - star as a ballet dancer   **Ginny** - the mayor   **Ted** - become a famous newspaper reporter **Joy** - President   **Walt** - box Mohammed Ali   **Anita** - mother   **Mandy** - drive a big truck   **Clark** - accountant   **Mr. Moran** - tennis star, millionaire, inventor, famous author, and daddy.

Wishes   The Class of '94   Dreams

Mr. Moran's 6th Grade — Room 213
Sunnyside Elementary School

When we grow up:

Bobby *will be an architect.*

Carol *will work in a hospital as a nurse.*

Larry

Kenneth

Daisy

Gloria

Stu

Wally

Ginny

Ted

Joy

Walt

Anita

Mandy

Clark

Mr. Moran

B. Use **will** in these sentences. Then rewrite them with contractions. Then rewrite them as questions. Finally, write them as contracted negative sentences.

You _will_ get married this year.

You'll get married this year.
Will you get married this year?
You won't get married this year.

1. Bruce _____ play baseball in college.

2. She _____ finish <u>War and Peace</u> next week.

3. The job _____ be done soon.

4. Victoria _____ study architecture.

5. It _____ rain forever.

6. They _____ both be doctors.

7. I _____ always remember you.

8.   Bob and I _____ be lawyers.

_____

_____

_____

C.   Using your dictionary, make up a list of predictions like the list in exercise A, but list your own classmates in your ESL class or other friends. There are no answers for this exercise in the back of the book.

MY PREDICTIONS

In the year 2002 A.D.:

Extra Exercise

Q. What **will** life be like in the year 2002 A.D.?   Rewrite this story with the **will** future and find out.   Or write your own predictions (with the **will** future) and have an American friend check your work.

In the year 2002, we are *will be* all wearing tiny "headphones" like necklaces around our necks.   They are *will be* connected to the receiver which we keep in our pockets or wear strapped to our arms like watches.   The receivers are called communications packets or "Compacs" for short.   We listen to radio or watch TV on the Compacs or we use them as mini computer terminals.   If we want music, we slip disks the size of quarters into the Compacs and we have hours of stereo.   Since the sound comes through the beautiful necklaces, we are still able to hear with our ears. The Compacs are also programmable to monitor our hearts and so they help prevent heart attacks.   The most amazing thing about these Compacs is that they allow telecommunications wherever we are.   All we have to do is push a code into the compac.   This code puts us into a communications mode or "Commode."   We then tell the automated operator who we want to speak to, our own personal international ID code ("I-code") and the other person's code.   If the person we are calling is awake and willing, the commode system puts us through immediately.   If not, our compac keeps trying the call until it gets through.

The other wonderful thing about 2002 is the new types of transportation. People still have cars but they use them mostly for short trips.   They run on miniaturized power cells ("Minibats") and "Sinfuel."   This (synthetic synergistic polybiofuel) is invented by an unknown chemist in the small national university of a very small third world country.   He is now called just Mr. E and he owns all of Megacorp, the world's largest employer.   Megacorp has established intercity and international containerized carriers ("piggies") to move the new minicars around while their drivers enjoy luxurious mobile lounges which provide work, play or sleep spaces and facilities.   The Piggies have made automobile commuting almost obsolete.   Most people work at home using their home computer terminals ("I-terms") or home manufacturing systems ("Miniman Kits").   Those who must commute to work use the Piggies with or without their minicars.   We usually leave our cute little Ford Darter at home when we have to go to the city, because the public transport systems ("Zippers") in Great Kalamazoo are so terrific.   Admittedly, the facilities in the new megalopolises are better than in the historic urban centers like Atlanta, New York, or Houston where early urban overdevelopment makes modernization and growth difficult.

Advertising

> Imperatives express a command or request. The subject you is understood.
>
> > *(You)* **Buy** now.
> > **Fly** *Northwest to Florida.*
>
> We use **do not** or **don't** to form the negative.
>
> > **Don't miss** *this offer.*
>
> **Please** makes imperatives more polite.
>
> > **Please come** *in.*
> > **Come** *in,* **please.**

A. Here is a collection of advertising slogans. First rewrite them making them more polite. Then rewrite them as negative commands or requests.

Buy one while they're hot.

Please buy one while they're hot.
Don't buy one while they're hot.

Elect Thomas O'Shay, a good man for Congress.

Elect Thomas O'Shay, a good man for Congress, please.
Do not elect Thomas O'shay, please.

1. Take one free.

    _____

    _____

2. Buy two for the price of one.

    _____

    _____

3. Try it. You'll like it.

    _____

    _____

4. Put your money on Mike's.

    _____

    _____

5. Ride the rails.

_____

_____

6. See the World at Woolsey's Opticians.

_____

_____

7. Buy American.

_____

_____

8. Get a dozen while they last.

_____

_____

9. Take her home, you Macho, you.

_____

_____

10. Eat at Joe's.

_____

_____

11. Fly me to Tahiti.

_____

_____

12. Think small.

_____

_____

13. Come up and see me some time.

_____

_____

14. Send it Speedexpress to get it there on time.

_____

_____

15. Be a man. Smoke a Mule.

_____

_____

16. Taste one, I dare you.

_____

_____

B. Here is a page of advertising copy. How many imperatives can you find? Take your time. Study it carefully, and then count them. If you want to, list them.

How many imperatives are in the instructions above? ___4___

How may imperatives are in the copy below? _____

SAVE $20
sale 99.99 Plus shipping
Reg. 119.99
AM/FM dual cassette stereo records 4 ways:
from the AM/FM radio, cassette to cassette,
8 track to cassette and from built in mikes.
With auto stop and continuous play. #39599.

SALT EATS CARS
burton CAR WASH
STOP RUST HERE
"THE CAR WASH PROS"
107 Canal Street, Brattleboro, Vt.
802-254-2086
Open 8 to 6 Monday to Saturday
8 to 5 Sundays & Holidays. 8pm Fri. Nights
Other Locations at:
124 Northside Drive   131 So. Main Street
Bennington, Vt.   Rutland, Vt.
We Are Open All Winter
PUT YOUR CAR ON A SALT FREE DIET

**Sound Your Trumpet!
with a Town Crier
Classified Ad**

It's worth the trip
Because you'll find more
than warehouse prices –
you'll find what you're
looking for.
Edwards food warehouse
Winchester St., Keene
New Hampshire

GET AUTOMATIC TRANSMISSION AT NO EXTRA COST!
Order This Horizon Special Value Package:
• 2.2. liter engine   • Center arm rest
• Power steering   • Rally wheels
• AM/FM stereo   • Dual remote mirrors
• Console
— And the Automatic
Transmission is Yours —
NO CHARGE!
Plus Get Chrysler's 5/50 Protection Plan

Starts Friday!
IF NANCY
DOESN'T
WAKE UP
SCREAMING,
SHE WON'T
WAKE UP
AT ALL.
A Nightmare ON ELM STREET
New Line Cinema

Dirty Datsun?
Clean it up!

Gulf
Saveway
214 Canal Street
Brattleboro, Vermont
Self Car Wash
Barrows Coal Company

Volunteer.
American
Red Cross

NEW DIMENSIONS
*Chase Away
The Winter Blues
with New Color
or a Perm!!*
At 10% OFF
our regular price.
Through January 31
*Watch for our
"New Location"!*
254-9291
Landmark Hill, Brattleboro

Just leave everything to us...
Advertise
in the
Town Crier.

SHOP COMPARE AND SAVE
NAME BRAND PRODUCTS
Appliances • Heating
Plumbing • Electrical
SHOPPING HOURS:
Thursday 10-8, Friday 10-8
Saturday 10-6. Sunday 12-6
Rte. 12, No. Swanzey, N.H.
1 ½ Miles South of Jct. 101

Take Care of Yourself.
Women's Health Care
Call for an appointment
257-0534

Planned Parenthood
of Northern New England
208 Canal St., Brattleboro

THIS IS A TEST
We are testing the effectiveness of this advertising space. If you bring this ad with you we will
offer you: (1) our most popular Waterbed with
Bookcase and fully equipped for $128.20 or (2)
our heavy Solid Pine Bunk Beds for $76.50 or
(3) our best selling Posture Firm Bedding, Mat-
tress and Foundation, both pieces for $96.50.
Limited Quantities. Offer good for 7 days only.

KAL Nutritional Supplements
BUY 1 GET FREE!
45 Cap.
E-400 +
400 I.U. of natural unesterified
Vitamin E as d-alpha tocopherol,
beta, gamma and delta tocopherols.

CALL US TODAY FOR A FREE, INTRODUCTORY CONSULTATION.

 VISA

**Diet Center.®
Lite Years Ahead.™**

**205 Main St.,
Brattleboro**

HOW TO WIN AT THE LOSING GAME
DIET CENTER

 master card

**Ellyn Portnoy Mgr.
802•257•1953**

Say you saw it in the Town Crier 1/30

Imperative — LET'S 32

Leisure activities

> In English, we introduce suggestions and invitations with the expression **let us**.
>
> If the person (or people) addressed is to be involved in the activity with the speaker, we almost always use the contraction **let's**. Let us is used to emphasize the formality of an invitation.
>
> > ***Let's*** *go for a run together (you and I).*
> > *Ladies and gentlemen, it is now time for dinner.* ***Let us*** *sit down.*
>
> If the person addressed is not being invited to be involved but is being asked for permission, the contraction is never used. When permission is being asked, pronouns other than **us** may be used.
>
> > *Dad, please* ***let us*** *(Mary and me) borrow the car.*
> > *Mom, will you please* ***let me*** *go to the dance with Mary?*
> > *Mom and dad, won't you please* ***let her*** *(Mary) wear jeans to the dance?*

A. Use **let's** or **let us** in the following sentences. If permission is being asked, use **let us**. If not, use **let's**.

Hey, Bud, there's a great movie in town. _Let's_ go.

Dad, Bud and I want to go to the movies. _Let us_ go, ok?

1. _____ swim across the lake. I'll beat you to the other side.

2. _____ go skiing at Haystack. I have an extra pass for you.

3. Mr. Smith, please _____ leave early. Sam and I have a date.

4. _____ all go to Jamaica together for vacation.

5. Dad, Joe and I can pay our own way, so _____ drive out to Denver.

6. Next time you and I meet in the city, _____ go to Radio City Music Hall.

7. If we can get permission, _____ go to the zoo together.

8. Mick and I both have ID cards, so _____ buy some beer, Mr. Frank.

B. Read this play aloud adding **let us** or **let's** where they are appropriate. If you have a tape recorder, tape your performance. Work on your own or with friends.

Boring, Boring!

A Play about Summer Vacation

PLACE: *Jimmy's living room and kitchen.* TIME: *Afternoon, late summer.*
CHARACTERS: **Jimmy**, *age 13.* **Gerry**, *Jimmy's friend, age 13.*
Mom, *Jimmy's mother.* **Dad**, *Jimmy's father*
Ruthy, *Jimmy's little sister, age 7.*

Jimmy: I'm bored! *Let's* do something. _____ go swimming. Nobody's at your pool, right?

Gerry: Right, no one's there. They're all out shopping, except Dad. He's working.

Jimmy: Well? _____ go, ok?

Gerry: No, _____ not. It's no fun.

Jimmy: Aw, come on, _____ do it anyway. We can stop by Sue Ellen's and pick her and Franny up. I bet they're bored like we are. Your mom won't mind. She'll _____.

Gerry: She may _____ but Sue Ellen's mom won't.

Jimmy: Well, _____ do something.

Gerry: I don't feel like it. It's too hot.

Ruthy has been sitting listening to the boys.

Ruthy: Hey, I know. You guys could take me to the park.

Gerry: Bug off, kid.

Jimmy: Yeah, bug off. Get lost, Ruthy.

Gerry: Hey, I know what, Jimmy. _____ catch Ruthy and lock her up in the shed. _____ get her!

*The boys jump up to their feet, and **Ruthy** squeals and runs from the living room into the kitchen where **Mom** is fixing supper. The boys chase her.*

Ruthy: Mommy! Help! Jimmy's after me! Stop them!

Mom: What's all this? Stop it. Ruthy, stop that squealing! Boys, you quit it! Come on you guys, stop picking on her. _____ cut it out. _____ have some peace around here. It's too hot. _____ quiet down. Ruthy, quiet!

Jimmy: Ok, Mom. You're right.

Gerry: Hey, Jimmy. _____ get out of here.

Jimmy: Yeah, _____ go. See you, Mom.

Mom: Where are you two off to?

Jimmy: We don't know. That's the whole problem. It's too boring. There is nothing to do.

Mom: Right! *(she says ironically)* You have nothing to do. "_____ go running." "Nope, it's too hot." "_____ go swimming." "Nope, it's too cold." "_____ go over to Helen's house!" "Nope, it's too late." "_____ go fishing." "Nope, it's too early." "_____ take Ruthy to the park." "Nope, too many people." "_____ go over to Gerry's pool." "Nope, there's nobody there!"

Gerry: Hey, Jimmy, your mom's got an idea. _____ go fishing. Mrs. G, will you _____ borrow Jimmy's dad's fishing rod?

Mom: I can't. He's got them.

Dad comes into the kitchen.

Dad: No, I haven't. I'm back. Do you guys want to catch a fish?

Gerry: Sure, if you'll _____ have your fishing stuff.

Jimmy: No, Gerry, _____ not. It's boring. Boring! Who wants to sit there for hours in the sun watching for some stupid little fish?

Gerry: Aw, come on, Jimbo, old Buddy. _____ go do it.

Ruthy: Hey, Gerry, I'll go with you. Jimmy can stay here. I know where there is a big bass! _____ go get it.

Gerry is suddenly enthusiastic. He speaks to Mom and Dad.

Gerry: Is it ok? _____ go and we'll come back with that big bass.

Dad: Sure, Gerry. The rod's out on the porch. Just look after Ruthy. Don't let her get wet.

Jimmy: Ok. OK! I'll go! _____ go and catch that bass, all three of us. Come on Ruthy. _____ all three get out of here. Gerry and I are in a hurry!

C. Put **let us** or **let's** into the blanks in these suggestions and requests. Then on the next line write in one of these responses or one of your own.

Responses:

OK
No
Sure. When?
OK, I'd love to.
No, sorry. Not today.

Thanks a lot. That sounds great!
No. Thanks anyway. I'm busy.
I'd really love to, but I just can't.
That sounds great, but I'm not up for it.
No thanks. Another time, maybe?

Let's go for a walk.
OK, I'd love to.

Please, *let us* use your bicycle for our trip.
No, sorry. Not today.

1. _____ go hunting.

   _____

2. _____ borrow your car.

   _____

3. Please, _____ go swimming.

   _____

4. Please, _____ have $30 for dinner.

   _____

5. _____ go jogging together.

   _____

6. Frank and I want to go canoeing. Please _____ go.

   _____

7. _____ go on a hike.

   _____

8. _____ go hiking.

   _____

9. _____ go for a bike ride. OK?

   _____

10. Ginny, _____ go fishing.

    _____

11. _____ go bowling, Mrs. Smith.

    _____

12. It's starting to snow! _____ go skiing.

    _____

Polite expressions

Invitations and requests

We form polite expressions in many ways in English. They all mean approximately the same thing and they are all used to request something from the person addressed or to invite that person to do something. The following are a few of the common polite expressions.

Requests:
    Please, pass the salt.
    Would you (please) pass the salt?
    Will you (please) pass the salt?
    Could you (please) pass the salt?
    Won't you (please) pass the salt?
    May I (please) have the salt? (Also see lesson 35)
    Can I (please) have the salt? (Also see lesson 35)
    Would you mind passing the salt? (please)?

Invitations:
    Please, come to dinner.
    Would you come to dinner (please)?
    Will you come to dinner (please)?
    Could you come to dinner (please)?
    Won't you come to dinner (please)?
    Would you like to come to dinner?

With the exception of **would you mind** and **would you like to, please** can be used next to the polite expressions (see the requests above). It can also be separated from them (see the invitations above), or omitted.

    *Will you **please** repeat that?*
    *Will you repeat that, **please**?*
    Please, will you repeat that?
    Will you repeat that?

All of these expressions are often introduced with polite expressions to get the attention of the person addressed.

    Excuse me,
    Pardon me,
    Mr. Jones,   *could you please pass the salt.*
    If I may interrupt,

    Excuse me, Mr Jones, if I may interrupt, could you please pass the salt.

A. These sentences are all simple imperatives or demands in the form of statements. They do not use polite expressions. They could be said very nicely and politely to avoid being rude, but in writing they seem very rude or impolite. Rewrite each sentence using one of the polite forms. Possible answers are given at the back of the book.

Give me the corn.

Would you mind giving me the corn?

Give the children more to eat.

Would you please give the children more to eat?

1. Go to Maxim's with us.

   _____

2. Buy me a drink.

   _____

3. Hand Mary the gravy.

   _____

4. Ask the waitress for our check.

   _____

5. Get me some ice water.

   _____

6. I want apple pie à la mode.

   _____

7. Dance with me.

   _____

8. Follow me to your table.

   _____

9. Find us another fork.

   _____

10. Bring us some more rice.

    _____

11. Take me out to dinner tomorrow.

    _____

12. Catch the waiter's eye.

    _____

13. We are out of salt.

    _____

14. Pick me up at six thirty-five.

    _____

15. Fix me another cocktail.

_____

16. Take the meat.

_____

17. Pour the wine.

_____

18. Put the platter down here.

_____

19. Sit down.

_____

20. Pass those apples.

_____

21. Take my plate away.

_____

22. We need more milk.

_____

23. Have some dessert.

_____

24. Hand the vegetables to Mike.

_____

25. Get us some more ketchup.

_____

26. Sit here by me.

_____

27. Take the head of the table.

_____

28. Buy me a cigar.

_____

29. Go to Friendly's for some ice cream.

_____

30. Take Mary's mother home for dinner.

_____

31. Thank the chef for this excellent dinner.

_____

32. Come again.

_____

B. Write three invitations. Possible answers are given at the back.

Invite Ray to go to the movies with you and Nancy next Monday.

> Ray,
>   Would you like to go to the movies with Nancy and me next Monday?

1. Invite Mrs. Jones to come to your house with her son Michael at six on June 14th.

> Dear Mrs. Jones,

2. Ask Phil to take you out when you get back to town on January 25th. You would like to go for a drink at Crawdaddy's and then for dinner at Crustaceans.

3. Ask the Fidelsons (Bud and Poppy) to come to your house for the weekend and to bring their children. Ask them also to bring a porter crib for their baby and a bag of peaches from their peach tree so you can make a cobbler. They should arrive in time for supper Friday night.

Extra Exercise

This funny poem is from Lewis Carroll's **Alice's Adventures in Wonderland,** one of the most wonderful children's books in English. Here Carroll makes fun of polite expressions like those in this lesson.

The Lobster Quadrille

"Oh, **you** sing," said the Gryphon. "I've forgotten the words." So they began solemnly dancing round and round Alice, ...while the Mock Turtle sang this, very slowly and sadly: --

"Will you walk a little faster?" said a whiting to a snail.
"There's a porpoise close behind us, and he's treading on my tail
See how eagerly the lobsters and the turtles all advance!
They are waiting on the shingle - will you come and join the dance?
Will you, won't you, will you, won't you, will you join the dance?
Will you, won't you, will you, won't you, won't you join the dance?

"You can really have no notion how delightful it will be
When they take us up and throw us, with the lobsters, out to sea!"
But the snail replied, "Too far, too far!" and gave a look askance --
Said he thanked the whiting kindly, but he would not join the dance.
Would not, could not, would not, could not, would not join the dance.
Would not, could not, would not, could not, could not join the dance.

Can and **be able to** are used to express ability.

> *Fritz can lift 250 pounds.*
> *Fritz is able to lift 250 pounds.*

Notice the formation of questions, negative statements and contractions.

> ***Can** Fritz lift 250 pounds?*
> ***Is** Fritz **able to** lift 250 pounds?*

> *Fritz **cannot** lift 250 pounds.*
> *Fritz **is not able to** lift 250 pounds.*

> *Fritz **can't** lift 250 pounds.*
> *Fritz **isn't able to** lift 250 pounds.*

Notice the use of **can** and **be able to** with question words. (See Lesson 7.)

> *When **can** I see the doctor?*
> *Why **isn't** the doctor **able to** see me now?*

A. Fill in the blanks with **can** or **be able to**.

The maid *is able to* clean the top of the windows.

Mr. Martin _can_ sell insurance from his home.

1. Sally Sue _____ sing babies to sleep.
2. Our secretary _____ take dictation in shorthand.
3. That mechanic _____ fix anything.
4. I _____ translate this letter into Greek.
5. Sam _____ plant trees.
6. The hat check girl _____ get your coat for you.
7. That storyteller _____ make even Uncle Harry laugh.
8. This technical writer _____ make the directions perfectly clear.
9. These teachers _____ speak French very well.
10. That lifeguard _____ swim.
11. Our carpenters _____ build almost anything out of wood.
12. The plumber _____ come immediately to fix your toilet.

13. The singing waiter _____ pour coffee while he sings.

14. Pilots _____ see in the dark with their instruments.

15. Your priest _____ say mass in his sleep.

16. Those policemen _____ solve any crime.

17. Mary's kindergarten teacher _____ teach hundreds of songs.

18. Your house painters _____ work without spilling a drop.

19. Professor Hornbeam _____ lecture all day without notes.

20. The repairman _____ fix my TV.

B. Rewrite your sentences above using **can** for **is able to, is able to** for **can,** and changing affirmative statements into questions **(?)** or negative statements **(–)** as indicated.

(–) *The maid can't clean the top of the windows.*

(?) *Is Mr. Martin able to sell insurance from his home?*

1. (?) _____

2. (–) _____

3. (?) _____

4. (–) _____

5. (?) _____

6. (?) _____

7. (?) _____

8. (?) _____

9. (–) _____

10. (?) _____

11. (?) _____

12. (–) _____

13. (?) _____

14. (?) _____

15. (?) _____

16. (?) _____

17. (?) _____

18. (–) _____

19. (–) _____

20. (?) _____

(–) _____

C. These sentences are split into matched pairs. Put the two parts of the sentences together using **can** or **be able to.**

The dancing master		carry six cups of coffee.
The blacksmith		open anything from a car to a safe.
The waiter		bake fresh strawberry muffins.
The sailor	can	find any paper she has ever filed.
The locksmith		name all the kings of Hungary in order.
The cook	be able to	shoe a horse in ten minutes.
The secretary		play the Moonlight Sonata or the Tiger Rag.
The minister		handle boats of any size.
The scholar		waltz like a dream
The pianist		whistle Dixie while she kisses a baby.
The politician		preach so everyone feels sinful.

The dancing master is able to waltz like a dream.

_____

_____

_____

_____

_____

_____

_____

_____

_____

_____

_____

Modals of permission

35

Elementary school scenes

We use **may** and **can** to ask and give permission.

> **May** I speak to you?   Yes, you **may**.
> **Can** I speak to you?   Yes, you **can**.

We also use **could**, the past tense of can, but only in asking for permission.

> **Could** I speak to you?   Yes, you **can**.

For negative responses, we usually, use **can**.

> No, you **can't**.   No, you **cannot**!

Please is usually used with requests for permission.

> **May I please** speak to you?

Some people consider **may** and **could** to be more polite than **can**.

A. Write the requests for permission as indicated. Then give permission.

You want to go out and play.

(May) _May I go out and play?_   (No) _No, you can't._
(Could) _Could I go out and play?_   (OK) _OK, you can._

You and John want to have lunch now.

(Can) _Can we have lunch now?_ (Yes) _Yes, you can._

1. You want to speak to Bobby.

   (May) _____   (No) _____
   (Can) _____   (No) _____

2. You need to go to the bathroom.

   (Can) _____   (Yes) _____
   (May) _____   (Yes) _____

3. You want to help Molly.

   (May) _____   (No) _____
   (Could) _____   (No) _____

4. You want to take me to the dance.

   (May) _____   (Yes) _____
   (Could) _____   (No) _____

5.   You and I need to go back to the lunch room for a minute.
      (Can) _____

                                           (No)   _____

      (May, please,) _____

                                           (Yes)   _____

      (Could, please) _____

                                           (No)   _____

B.   Here are some requests of the kind you can hear in any grade school in the United
     States. Complete the sentences by adding **may** or **can.**

First Grade

Teacher: Class, _can_ I have your attention, please?

Freddy: Miss Lamb, _may_ I go to the bathroom?

Molly: _____ I please sharpen my pencil, Miss Lamb?

Principal: Miss Lamb, _____ I see you for a moment?

Teacher: Yes, Mr. Reed, but _____ I talk to you later?

Andy: _____ we go out to recess now? It's time!

Fourth Grade

Stu: Mr. Bell, _____ I get up and get another book?

Teacher: Yes, you _____

Dorothy: I don't understand this. _____ you help me please?

Teacher: _____ I ask you to wait while I help Stu, Dorothy?

Andy: _____ I go to the bathroom, Mr. Bell?

Teacher: _____ I ask you to wait until the bell rings in two minutes?

Principal: Mr. Bell, _____ I speak with you after class?

Sixth Grade

Willie: _____ I start my test now?

Gretchen: Mrs. Reynolds, _____ I do these problems on the board?

Sammy: _____ we do reading next, Mrs. Reynolds?

Paul: _____ Gretchen and I sit together, Mrs. Reynolds?

Andy: Mrs. Reynolds. Mrs. Reynolds! _____ I go to the bathroom?

Teacher: Andy, no. You _____

Andy: Oh, please, Mrs. Reynolds. I've really got to go.

Teacher: _____ I have quiet? Now! Please!!

Sammy: Please, _____ we do reading next, Mrs. Reynolds. Please.

Principal: Mrs. Reynolds, _____ I ask you to come to the hall?

The Teacher's Lounge

Mr Bell: Belle, _____ I fix you a cup of coffee? You look like you need it.

Miss Lamb: Sure, Bill, thanks. _____ I bum a cigarette at the same time?

The Principal's Office

Principal: Mrs. Reynolds, _____ I introduce you to Mr. and Mrs. Persons? Their son H.H. will be joining your class in two weeks.

Teacher: It's a pleasure. Mr. Persons, is it? _____ I have a seat, John? Thanks.

Mr. Persons: _____ I say that we are delighted to have H.H. going into a class with such an experienced teacher.

Principal: Mrs. Reynolds is one of our best in the whole school system.

Teacher: John, _____ I have a few minutes to talk to the Persons? I would like to get to know them a bit.

Principal: Certainly. _____ I leave you folks with Mrs. Reynolds for a few minutes? I'll just look in on her class. Sixth graders need to be watched, you know.

The Front Office

(The phone rings)

Secretary: Hello, Greeley School. _____ we help you?

Mrs. Berg: Yes, Miss Frank. _____ I speak to Mr. Reed, please?

Secretary: _____ I say who's calling?

Mrs. Berg: You _____. This is Sally Berg.

Secretary: Thank you. Hold the line please.
                  Mr. Reed, it's Sally Berg on line one. _____ I transfer her to you? She wants to talk about Andy again.

Principal: _____ I call her back, please? I've got to go upstairs for a few moments! What a day!

C. Ask for these permissions using either **may** or **can**.

Ask if you can be picked up at three this afternoon.

Can you pick me up at three this afternoon?

Ask if you can say something.

May I say something?

1. Ask if you can come to school late tomorrow.

_____

2. Ask if you can arrive at ten.

_____

3. Ask if you and Molly can leave.

_____

4. Ask if Jane can take the kids home early.

_____

5. Ask if you can show Gretchen your multiplication table.

_____

6. Ask if you both can sit with me in the lunch room.

_____

7. Ask if each of you can see Mr. Reed after school.

_____

8. Ask if either of you can take your class to the Field Museum.

_____

9. Ask if both of you can get a raise next year.

_____

10. Ask if you can help take Freddy to the school nurse.

_____

11. Ask if you and Bill Bell can leave early to go to the baseball game.

_____

12. Ask if you can give Andy a good spanking.

_____

D. Read this children's verse for fun.

Mother, may I go down to swim?
Yes, my darling daughter.
Hang your clothes on a hickory limb,
And don't go near the water.

HAVE and HAVE GOT 36

Medicine and illness

> Americans often use **have got** in place of **have** to express possession.
>
>   *I **have** poor eyesight.*   *I **have got** poor eyesight.*
>
> **Have got** is usually contracted in speech and informal writing.
>
>   *I**'ve got** poor eyesight.*
>
> Questions and negative statements are formed this way.
>
>   *Do you **have** glasses?*   ***Have** you **got** glasses?*
>   *No, I don't **have** any.*   *No, I **haven't got** any.*
>
> **Have got** is used only in the present.
>
>   *He **has** a problem.*   *He**'s got** a problem.*
>   *He **had** a problem last year.*
>   *He **will have** a problem next year.*
>
> (**Have to** and **have got to** are also used to express necessity. See *Grammar Exercises, Part II.* You **have (got) to** buy some glasses.)

A. Fill in the blanks with **have** or **have got**.

    I *have* a stuffed up nose.
    Do you *have* a nose spray?
    Ali *has got* a sore throat.
    Has he *got* a lozenge?

1.   Pam _____ a headache.

     _____ we _____ aspirins.

2.   You _____ a cold.

     _____ you _____ any Contac?

3.   Don _____ a hangover.

     _____ Bob _____ a couple of Alka-Seltzers?

4.   Dee _____ a little cut.

     She _____n't _____ a Band-Aid. Do you?

5.   Now she _____ a bigger cut,

     and she _____ six stitches.

6. Oh, I _____ a toothache!

    _____ you _____ the dentist's telephone number?

7. Bob _____ a stomach ache.

    _____ his mother _____ any Pepto-Bismol?

8. _____ Eli _____ a sinus headache?

    He _____ a strange expression on his face.

9. My girlfriend _____ bad breath

    but I _____ some Lavoris. Will it help?

10. Sue _____ her period.

    _____ you _____ a place where she can lie down?

B. Rewrite all of the above sentences changing **have** to **have got** and **have got** to **have**.

I have got a stuffed up nose.
Have you got a nose spray?
Eli has a sore throat.
Does he have a lozenge?

1. _____

2. _____

3. _____

4. _____

5. _____

6. _____

7. _____

8. _____

9. _____

10. _____

C. Fill in the blanks with the correct form of the verb indicated. Then rewrite the sentence as a question and then answer in the negative.

(have got) Rose *has got* the measles.
Has Rose got the measles? Rose hasn't got the measles.
(have) June *has* an earache.
Does June have an earache? June doesn't have an earache.

1. (have) Violet _____ something for my cough.

    _____

2. (have got) May _____ a bad cold.

    _____

3. (have) The little boy _____ a cut on his knee.

    _____

4. (have) May _____ a serious medical problem.

    _____

5. (have got) Daisy _____ enough polio vaccine for the kids.

    _____

6. (have) Poppy _____ cough medicine for sale at her store.

    _____

7. (have) Old April Tobias _____ a headache.

    _____

8. (have got) She _____ a broken hip.

    _____

9. (have) My daughter, Heather, _____ appendicitis.

    _____

10. (have got) She _____ a sharp pain in her side.

    _____

11. (have) She will _____ her appendix out in an hour.

    _____

12. (have got) We _____ good insurance.

    _____

37 Two-word verbs

Summer camp

Two-word verbs are idioms. We add a preposition to a verb and the meaning of the verb changes.

take	*I **take** the kids to camp each morning.*
take off	*Willie **takes off** his shoes before swimming.*

Some two-word verbs are separable. They can be used together or they can be used separated by their object.

*Willie **takes off** his shoes.*
*Willie **takes** his shoes **off**.*

When the object of a separable two-word verb is a pronoun, the two words must be separated.

*Willie **takes** them **off**.*

Other two-word verbs cannot be separated. They are always used together. For example, **take after** (resemble) must be used together: *"Willie **takes after** his grandmother"* or *"Willie **takes after** her."* We cannot say: *"Willie **takes** his grandmother **after**"* or *"Willie **takes** her **after**."*

A. The two-word verbs in these sentences are all separable. Underline them.

1. Mrs. Farrar wants to <u>use</u> Jimmy's energy <u>up</u>.
2. Before day camp started in June he broke her rocking chair up,
3. and then he broke Mr. Patterson's fence down.
4. Next he tried the lawn mower out in the garden,
5. and then he tried her best dress on riding his bike!
6. Mrs. Farrar signed Jimmy up for lots of sports.
7. She let him pick out his favorites.
8. First thing each morning he puts on his roller skates.
9. Then he takes off his clothes for swimming.
10. Then the coach passes out boxing gloves.
11. By the time Jimmy hangs up his baseball glove at 4 in the afternoon,
12. he's even too tired to beat up his baby sister.

B. Rewrite sentences 2 to 6 putting the two-word verbs together.

1. *Mrs. Farrar wants to use up Jimmy's energy.* _____
2. _____
3. _____
4. _____
5. _____
6. _____

C. Rewrite sentences 8 to 12 separating the two-word verbs.

7. *She let him pick his favorites out.* _____
8. _____
9. _____
10. _____
11. _____
12. _____

D. Rewrite these sentences changing the object of each two-word verb into a pronoun. Change the word order if necessary.

Most Americans enjoy bringing up their children,

Most Americans enjoy bringing them up,

1. but for a few weeks we like to send away the kids.

_____

2. We give up the pleasure of their company.

_____

3. We send our sons and daughters off to summer camp.

_____

4. We adults try out being alone again,

_____

5. and our children find out the pleasures of independence.

_____

6. Betty and I put off sending Brucie to camp until he was twelve,

_____

7. but this year we talked over his request to go sailing.

_____

8.   Finally we made up our minds.

_____

9.   We looked up the best sailing camp in Maine.

_____

10.   Then we filled out Camp Moosehead's application,

_____

11.   and packed up Brucie's bags.

_____

12.   Betty put on a brave face, but when Brucie left,

_____

13.   she turned on the tears.

_____

14.   I took out my handkerchief for her and said,

_____

15.   "Come on, darling. We don't want to throw away this chance.

_____

16.   Let's make up some travel plans, hit the road,

_____

17.   and look up some old friends."

_____

Vocabulary Summary

beat up (fight with)	put off (postpone)
break down (push down)	put on (dress)
break up (break into pieces)	put out (extinguish)
bring up (raise)	send off (send away)
comb out (straighten with a comb)	sign up (register)
find out (learn)	take off (remove)
give back (return)	take out (remove)
give up (abandon)	take over (become responsible for)
hang up (place on a hook)	talk over (discuss)
look over (examine)	throw away (discard)
look up (search for)	try on (test the fit)
make up (invent)	try out (test)
make up my mind (decide)	turn off (stop)
pack up (put in suitcases)	turn on (start)
pass out (distribute)	use up (finish)
pick out (choose)	wake up (arouse)
pick up (collect)	wash up (clean yourself)

Extra Exercise

Review the two-word verbs in the summary vocabulary. Read this story, replacing the words in bold type with the two-word verbs in this lesson.

Camp Tulares

Rick Robbins is a counselor at Camp Tulares, a sports camp for boys 12 to 16. The boys are very busy all day long. It is a long day. Rick **stops** ~~*turns off*~~ his alarm clock at five each morning, walks down to the lake, **cleans himself, straightens** his hair and beard **with a comb,** and smokes one pipe of tobacco. At six he goes back to his cabin to **arouse** his twelve sleeping boys. He **starts** the lights and makes a lot of noise. They get out of their beds, and **remove** their pajamas. "Take the plunge," Rick shouts, and they all run and jump in the lake.

After breakfast, Rick **becomes responsible for** the baseball team. Rick **examines** the list of boys who have **registered** for baseball and he **chooses** two teams. They play hard all morning. When he **sends** them **away** for lunch, he stays and **collects** the bats and balls the boys left on the field. "Why don't their parents **raise** them to **collect** their things when they are finished with them?" he complains to himself.

After lunch he helps the boys **learn** about Indian culture. They **search for** information about Indian crafts and clothes and dances in the camp library. Then they **return** the books and **invent** their own "Indian" culture.

After dinner around the campfire, Rick and his friend Frank **remove** their guitars and play folk songs. They **distribute** to the boys sheets of paper with the words. Everyone sings along.

At 9 o'clock Rick **extinguishes** the fire. Then in his cabin he **invents** a ghost story. By 10 pm he is really glad to go to sleep.

Post office

> **The** is called the definite article. We use **the** with specific or familiar objects, persons, or incidents. It is similar to the demonstratives **this, that, these** and **those** (see Lesson 41) because it indicates that **the one** thing or **the kind** of thing talked about is specific or definite. **The** is contrasted with **a**, the indefinite article (see Lesson 39), which is similar in meaning to **any** or **some** and is non-specific.
>
> | | |
> |---|---|
> | **The** *post office is on Main Street* | *(specific; singular)* |
> | *Alex is looking for **a** post office.* | *(non-specific; singular)* |
> | **The** *new airmail stamps are beautiful.* | *(specific; plural)* |
> | *You can buy stamps in post offices.* | *(non-specific; plural)* |
>
> Notice that **the** is used with singular and plural nouns; **a** is used with singular nouns only. Plural non-specific nouns do not require an article.
>
> These are examples of the use of **the** with specific objects or classes of objects.
>
> **The** *post office on Main Street . . .*
> **The** *oldest post office . . .*
> **The** *third post office . . .*
> **The** *Jerald Memorial Post Office . . .*
> *I went to **the** post office and **the** bank every day.*
> **The** *management of post offices . . .*
> **The** *administration of **the** post office over there . . .*
> **The** *running of **the** U.S. Post Office Department . . .*
> *Many of **the** post offices I have seen . . .*
> *Two of **the** post offices in Santa Fe . . .*
> *They built a court and **a** post office. **The** post office . . .*

A. Look at this picture. Fill in the blanks in these sentences with **the** or **a** or leave them blank.

The wind is blowing hard.

1. _____ Lincoln Post Office is closed.

2. It is Saturday so _____ post office is closed.

3. _____ post offices are usually closed on Saturdays.

4. _____ federal government has offices in _____ post office.

5. Even on Saturday, _____ mailmen have to deliver the mail.

6. _____ mailman in _____ picture is walking in _____ wind.

7. He is walking up _____ 12th St. to _____ two houses there.

8. Is there _____ dog at _____ Number Two 12th Street?

9. _____ dog is barking at _____ mailman.

10. _____ mailmen have _____ lot of trouble with _____ dogs.

11. _____ mailman here likes _____ dog at _____ Ball's house.

12. _____ dog always barks but it doesn't bite.

13. _____ family next door doesn't have _____ dog.

14. They have _____ cat.

15. _____ cat doesn't bother _____ mailman.

16. It sits in _____ sun in _____ window.

17. But _____ mailman doesn't like _____ cat.

18. He hates _____ cats.

19. _____ Balls have _____ Japanese girl living with them.

20. She is taking care of _____ children.

21. In January, she has to register with _____ federal government.

22. All of _____ foreigners in the U.S. must register.

23. Kioko should go to _____ post office in _____ Lincoln.

B. These are paired sentences. In one of them the definite article **the** should be used. In the other either **a** or no article is appropriate. Understand that it is possible to use **the** instead of **a** in most sentences, but it changes the meaning by suggesting that the speaker is referring to a specific object, person or incident. Fill in the blanks with **the** or **a** where they fit.

The mail clerk in the third window is pretty.

A mail clerk in another room began to laugh.

1. _____ bag of mail fell off the truck.

   _____ fattest bag of mail fell off the truck.

2. _____ new commemorative stamp has a beautiful picture on it.

   _____ commemorative stamps have beautiful pictures on them.

3. Six of _____ Tampa's post offices have been closed.

   Six of _____ post offices in Tampa have been closed.

4. _____ tall, thin mailman drives a truck.

   _____ mailmen drive trucks.

5. Lin likes _____ stamps.

   Lin likes _____ two-dollar stamp.

6. Mr. Simmons weighed _____ packages carefully.

   Mr. Simmons weighed _____ packages all afternoon.

7. _____ postmaster had a rough day yesterday.

   _____ postmasters have rough days sometimes.

8. Our little village has _____ postmistress.

   Sally has been _____ postmistress here for years.

9. It takes _____ letters six days to get to Hawaii.

   It took _____ letters I sent you six days to get to Hawaii.

10. Working for _____ U.S. Post Office pays well.

    Working for _____ post office pays well.

11. A letter and a package were lost, but later _____ letter was found.

    Two letters were lost, but _____ package was found.

12. Hank is _____ postmaster.

    Hank is _____ postmaster in Greenfield, Massachusetts.

13. What's _____ zip code for _____ University of Pennsylvania?

    _____ Yale University has _____ zip code of its own.

14. _____ air mail letter goes faster than _____ sea mail letter.

    _____ cost of surface mail is less than _____ cost of air mail.

15. There is _____ long line of people waiting to buy _____ stamps.

    There is _____ man whom I told you about waiting at _____ second window.

C. Read and enjoy these expressions and sayings.

The best part of a trip is **the** return home.

The first shall be last.

The more **the** merrier.

The meek shall inherit **the** earth.

Home is where **the** heart is.

The Man Upstairs (God) is always watching.

The Old Man (my father) wants me home early.

The morning after **the** night before...

The coward dies many times before his death.

She's on **the** level (honest).

You hit **the** nail on **the** head. (You are exactly right.)

The best things in life are free.

The proof of **the** pudding is in **the** eating.

The end justifies **the** means.

The customer is always right.

Who says I'm over **the** hill? (too old)

The bigger they come, **the** harder they fall.

The fool and his money are soon parted.

Don't let **the** cat out of **the** bag.

The wolf is at **the** door.

The pen is mightier than **the** sword.

This is **the** way **the** world ends

This is **the** way **the** world ends

This is **the** way **the** world ends

Not with **a** bang but **a** whimper.   T. S. Eliot

Machines

A (an) is called the indefinite article. It is used with unspecified or unfamiliar objects, persons, or incidents. It's meaning is similar to **one**; it is only used with singular nouns.

> **a** machine (one)   machines (more than one)

If the identity of the object, person or incident is known and we mean to stress that we are speaking of a specific object or group, we use the definite article **the** (See Lesson 38). If the specific identity is unknown or we do not mean to stress an object's specific identity, we use the noun with **a** in the singular or with no article in the plural.

> *Marvin bought **the** red typewriter.*
> *Which one?*
> ***The** red one. That one.*
>
> *Marvin bought **a** red typewriter.*
> *Which one?*
> *I don't know. Just **a** typewriter, **one of** the red ones.*

The indefinite article **a** is similar in meaning to the indefinite quantifying adjectives **some** and **any** (See Lesson 40).

> *Marvin needs **a** typewriter. **Any one** will do.*
> *Marvin needs **a** typist, **someone** who can type.*

Before a consonant sound we use **a** and before a vowel sound we use **an**.

> ***a** machine   **an** answering machine.*

Be careful of silent **h** and the letter **u**.

> **an** hour, **an** honor but **a** house, **a** helicopter
> **an** upper tooth, **an** unusual skill but **a** unit, **a** used car.

A. In these sentences, fill in the blanks with **a** or **an** or leave them blank. Then rewrite each one making the plurals singular and the singulars plural.

Can you fix _*a*_ lawnmower?

*Can you fix lawnmowers?*

1. Does Phil have _____ power drill?

   _____

2. Ed didn't buy _____ Apple computer.

   _____

3. Sylvia needs _____ chain saw.

   _____

4. Did Richard sell _____ hair driers?

   _____

5. _____ dishwasher helps prevent colds.

   _____

6. Today _____ farmer needs _____ good tractor.

   _____

7. Most farmers also have _____ reapers.

   _____

8. _____ fork lift would save your company _____ lot of time.

   _____

9. My lawyer needs _____ secretary who can use _____ word processor.

   _____

10. Does it take _____ hour to tune up _____ engine?

    _____

11. _____ pencil sharpeners are _____ simple devices.

    _____

12. _____ electric toothbrush is _____ unnecessary expense.

    _____

13. _____ internal combustion engines cause _____ pollution problems.

    _____

14. Is _____ broken gear _____ unusual problem or _____ expected one.

    _____

B. Add **a** or **an** to these riddles where necessary and then try to answer them.

   What has _____ keys and is used by _*a*_ typist?

   Answer: *A typewriter.* _____

1. What has _____ electric motor and can wash _____ shirt?

   Answer: _____

2. What has _____ hole in the front closed by _____ door and cleans _____ dirty dishes?

   Answer: _____

3. What has a _____ trunk but is not _____ elephant, _____ horn but is not ___ unicorn, starts with _____ "A" but is not _____ antelope, and has five wheels but is not _____ pentacycle?

     Answer: _____

4. What runs but doesn't have _____ feet and never moves, can add faster than _____ human but doesn't have _____ brain, and has _____ memory but not _____ eyes or _____ ears?

     Answer: _____

5. What has waves but not _____ drop of water, heats but does not get hot, and will melt _____ steel spoon but not burn _____ paper cup?

     Answer: _____

6. I have _____ face but not _____ head, two hands but no arms. I work by the hour, but never get paid _____ cent. The first sound in my name is "R". The first letter is "W". Who am I?

     Answer: _____

C. Fill in the blanks in these sentences with the most appropriate article **a (an)** or **the** or leave them blank. In many places either a definite or an indefinite article can be used, but the meaning of the sentence makes one a better choice.

     Paula had *an* important errand to do.

     She went to buy *a* car.

1. She wanted _____ brand new car, _____ Honda or _____ Nissan.
2. But Paula only had _____ couple of thousand dollars,
3. and she found out she couldn't get _____ loan.
4. _____ bank where she had _____ account wouldn't give her credit.
5. With _____ heavy heart, she shopped for _____ used car.
6. _____ first dealer she went to tried to sell her _____ wreck.
7. It needed _____ valve job and _____ crank shaft was bent.
8. _____ new dealer had just opened on Maple Street.
9. _____ owner was _____ old friend of Paula's mother.
10. So she took _____ chance, and went there next.
11. Mr. Blum, _____ owner, gave her _____ choice of three cars.
12. As soon as Paula saw _____ pink Dodge Dart, she was in love.
13. "It's not _____ new car, Honey, but it looks good," said Mr. Blum.
14. _____ few repairs, _____ good tune up, _____ new spark plugs!
15. "I'll have _____ paint touched up for you.
16. _____ engine will be as good as new."

17. Paula thought she had ____ good deal.

18. But in two weeks she got ____ leak in ____ radiator.

19. She didn't have ____ guarantee, so she fixed ____ leak.

20. Then ____ short burned out ____ speedometer.

21. She got ____ flat and had to buy ____ new wheel.

22. Next, ____ door on ____ passenger side fell off.

23. "This isn't ____ joke," she told her mother.

24. "I thought I had ____ plum, but I bought ____ lemon!"

25. When ____ cloud of smoke came from under ____ hood,

26. Paula took her car to ____ mechanic.

27. He said, "I bet she burns ____ quart of oil ____ week."

28. "That's ____ least of my problems," Paula replied.

29. "She needs ____ new rings, ____ seals, and ____ good tune up.

30. "It'll cost ____ pretty penny," he said cheerfully.

31. "I'll make ____ appointment for ____ day after tomorrow,"

32. Paula said ____ little crossly.

33. On ____ way home, ____ whole engine froze up,

34. and ____ block cracked.

35. She called ____ tow truck to tow ____ pink Dart away.

36. "I never want to see ____ thing again," she told ____ driver.

37. "And I'm not getting ____ new car, until I can get ____ new car!"

D. Extra Exercise. Correct this paragraph using indefinite article *an* wherever the indefinite article is appropriate. Correct copy is give at *an* back.

As we approach the 21st Century, average middle class American home has *the* the telephone with answering machine, the memory, a automatic redial button, and often portable handset. In the kitchen, there is microwave oven and programmable coffee maker; in the livingroom, not just TV with the cable connection, but also an VCR (often with minicam for home movies) and the tape deck, an compact disc (CD) player, and digital radio (DAB), all connected with fancy a amplifier and other a electronic wizardry.

Many of us also work with a gizmos like cellular phone and the computer system of a some sort, tied by the modem to telecommunications a network, and we have the fax machines and an photocopiers for a sending and making copies of an printed material. All of these wonders were unheard of only a few years ago.

Over the last hundred years, we have come to expect the change as constant in our lives. But in the new century, will each a year bring new wave of the change? It's an probable; however, each the year will also bring clutter of a unwanted, high-tech inventions as well. The past has brought us a many: an talking elevator, robot butler, video telephone, an home banking, flying car, and an hundred time-consuming gadgets for kitchen and a playroom.

Where to get advice

Some is used in affirmative statements but not in negative ones.

> *Juan needs some advice. He is looking for some advisors.*
> *He wants some now.*

Any is used in negative statements.

> *I can't give any advice. I don't know any advisors.*
> *There aren't any in the phone book.*

Any is also used in affirmative statements to stress the indefinite character of the noun.

> Ivan needs **some** help badly. **Any** help will do! **Any** will do!

Some and **any** are both used in questions.

> *Can you give Juan some advice?*
> *Can you give him any advice?*

Notice that **some** and **any** are used with non-count nouns — advice — and plural nouns — advisors. (See Lessons 11, 12, and 13.) They are also used with indefinite singular nouns to stress the indefinite quality of the nouns.

> *I'm sure **some** advisor can help Juan.*
> *I'm sure **any** advisor can help Juan!*

Note these compound words which follow the pattern described above for **some** and **any**:

someone	anyone
somebody	anybody
something	anything
somewhere	anywhere
someplace	anyplace
sometime	anytime
somehow	anyhow

> *Juan needs **someone** to advise him,*
> *but he can't find **anyone**.*
> *Do you know **anyone/someone**?*

A. Fill in the blanks with **some** or **any**.

Natasha has *some* problems,
and right now she doesn't have *any* solutions.

1. She needs to sell _____ of her paintings.
2. She has not sold _____ of them for a month.
3. Now she doesn't have _____ money.
4. Why does she need _____ money?
5. Natasha has _____ bills to pay.
6. She bought _____ expensive art supplies.
7. "It takes _____ money to make money," she complains.
8. Natasha needs _____ advice.
9. How can she get _____ money to pay her bills?
10. She asks her brother Pierre for _____ help.
11. He doesn't have _____ cash or _____ advice.
12. There are _____ priests at her church, and she asks one.
13. Father Ivan says _____ lawyers helped him once.
14. "I don't want _____ legal advice. It's too expensive."
15. "The Legal Aid Society might give you _____ free help."
16. Father Joe says, "Can't the Small Business Administration make _____ loans?
17. "No, they don't have _____ money, but _____ people go there for advice."
18. Father Gregor asked, "Do you have _____ money in the bank?"
19. "I've got _____ savings."
20. "Go to your banker for _____ guidance. He's in the business."
21. If only I could sell _____ paintings, I'd have enough."
22. "Why don't you call Mini's Art Gallery? Has she _____ of your work?
23. _____ people like Mini will give advice if you ask them
24. and then, if they like you, they will give _____ financial assistance."

B. Substitute or add **some** or **any** in these sentences.

             some
       There are ~~four~~ lawyers in that office.
               any
       Are there lawyers in this village?

1. I asked the police fifteen questions about safety.
2. Miguel paid a psychiatrist for counseling.
3. Does the welfare office offer help to poor people?
4. People with VD can call a VD Hotline for treatment.
5. That day care center is run by a lady with three kids of her own.
6. If you haven't got problems, you're not alive.
7. When Mrs. Blum was dying, a Hospice gave her care in her home.
8. Yesterday our minister visited lonely people at the Baptist Home.
9. Then the Rev. Lovejoy saw four sick people in the hospital.
10. The County Extension Service says we can't grow melons here.
11. Do you need work? Call your local Employment Office.
12. Alcoholics Anonymous won't let Miss Quinn drink one beer.

13. When his daughter ran away, Mr. Myers didn't ask anyone for help.
14. There wasn't a Parent's Anonymous Hotline in Clayton.
15. Neighbors finally called the Clayton Children's Aid Society.
16. They said the National Runaway Switchboard might be of help.
17. Molly Myers had taken drugs and was scared.
18. She heard two friends talk about the local Hotline.
19. The Hotline referred Molly to a rabbi for general counseling.
20. The rabbi got her a place to say and drug counseling.
21. After a time he got her to call her father.
22. "Trouble brings people closer to God," Mr. Myers said.
23. "And without a doubt, God brings some families closer, too," the rabbi replied.
24. Molly didn't get into more trouble after that.

25. Mrs. Lovejoy was given blood in the hospital.
26. Somehow without reason she decided she was HIV positive.
27. She called the Hotline to see if there was a way of being tested for AIDS without the Rev. Lovejoy finding out. In Clayton, news travels fast.

C. Add or substitute **some** or **any** in every place you can in this letter.
(The choice between **some** and **any** in questions is based on complicated rules of style which may vary from one part of the country to another or even from person to person. The answers given at the back are the answers which sound best to the author. See if you agree.)

November 4

Mr. Jake Wilkins
Principal
Thornberg School
Mallard Bay, IL

Dear Mr. Wilkins,

I am writing to tell you that I think you have *some* fine counselors at your school. Clarence was in *some* trouble earlier this year. He skipped classes. Several days he played hookey from school altogether. He didn't do work he didn't want to. In his old school, would one have noticed? Would one have cared? No. But of your teachers do care! They got together to talk about problem children - there aren't teachers without problem children - and then took questions to your counselors. I know. Miss Randolf told me things about it.

First Clarence's academic counselor had meetings with him. He couldn't find good explanations for my boy's behaviour, so he asked the school psychiatrist to spend time with him. First, Miss Blair learned Clarence has reading problems. They aren't terrible problems, but he has dyslexia and he also needs glasses for reading.

Then Clarence was caught one day smoking pot in the boy's room and then the next day buying angel dust behind the school garage. I couldn't take more. mother would feel the same way. But Miss Blair was there. She called my boy in and gave him advice. He agreed to get help and he has now joined other kids in a drug rehabilitation program given by policemen and Miss Blair at the school.

You probably know all this, but I don't think there is school which could have given us more support. When Clarence is back doing well in school, his academic counselors will be there to give him guidance. Should Clarence consider getting college education? Should he plan to get technical training? I know you will have counselors to help when the time comes. You and your school and your counselors are wonderful. God bless you!

Sincerely,

(MRS) I. Gomez
Irene Gomez

Beasts and birds

This and **that** (singular), **these** and **those** (plural) are demonstratives. They are used to indicate or "point to" specific objects, people, or events. They indicate the objects' distance from the speaker either in space or time.

1. **This** and **these** are used when the object is close to the speaker or when the time is the present.

   This dog in my lap has fleas!
   These mosquitoes are getting in my eyes!
   This year we are building a barn.

2. **That** and **those** are used when the object is far from the speaker or when the time is the past or the future.

   That cat over there caught my toad.
   Those sloths haven't moved in an hour.
   That week of our trip to Africa in 1982 was great fun.
   Those years will see us retired to a little farm.
   That mistake was the worst the cat ever made.

3. **This** is often used with **that**, and **these** with **those**, to show contrast.

   That pig is fat, but this one here is skinny.
   These mountains are dark green; those seem to be purple.

4. The demonstratives may be used before nouns as adjectives or alone as pronouns.

   These mountains are dark green; those seem to be purple.

A. Look at this picture. Complete these sentences with **this, that, these,** or **those.**

This animal looks like a horse, but
these stripes on it mean that it isn't a regular horse.

1. _____ kind of horse lives in the wild in Africa.
2. Wild horses with stripes like _____ are called zebras.
3. _____ end is called the head.
4. Notice _____ eyes and ears on the head, and
5. _____ wet spot here is the nose.

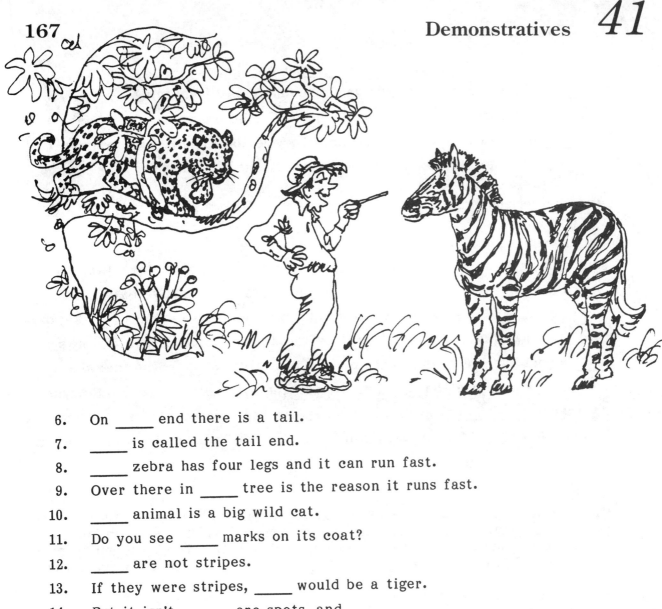

6. On _____ end there is a tail.

7. _____ is called the tail end.

8. _____ zebra has four legs and it can run fast.

9. Over there in _____ tree is the reason it runs fast.

10. _____ animal is a big wild cat.

11. Do you see _____ marks on its coat?

12. _____ are not stripes.

13. If they were stripes, _____ would be a tiger.

14. But it isn't. _____ are spots, and

15. _____ is a leopard.

16. Both of _____ animals live in Africa,

17. and both _____ zebra and I are going to leave now.

18. _____ is a dangerous place to be.

B. Use **this, that, these** or **those** in these sentences. In some places you may have a choice.

Those deer are eating apples over there.

1. Don't touch _____ raccoon I'm holding. It bites.

2. Did you see _____ whale surface?

3. _____ squirrels like to eat from my hand. See!

4. _____ wild cat is male. _____ one there is pregnant.

5. _____ possums are playing dead behind the barn.

6. Do you see ____ wolf stalking ____ sheep?

7. ____ skunks in Mrs. Percy's yard aren't afraid of anything.

8. Coyotes roam ____ hills so don't go out alone unarmed.

9. ____ coyotes here won't hurt me. They're too afraid.

10. Do you remember how many moose we saw in ____ days?

C. Add the demonstratives to this paragraph.

There are hundreds of common birds here in *these* New England forests. ____ song coming from ____ pines over there is the call of a chickadee. Last evening ____ birds we saw swooping for insects were swallows and bull bats. Then ____ morning we saw a chicken hawk over Blue Hill, and Elise swears ____ big dark bird you saw was a barn owl. ____ afternoon we'll look for wild turkeys in ____ woods over here, and tomorrow morning at dawn ____ geese that are flying overhead will be back on ____ lake over on the Sykes place. Look. Now here's my favorite. ____ little fellow is a common red breasted nuthatch. See how he hops down ____ tree upside down. They are all clowns and ____ one is almost tame.

D. Children in all lands and cultures enjoy games which use little nursery rhymes with ritual play. **These** rhymes use demonstratives as the grown up plays with the child's hands or feet or bounces her on his knee. Think of similar games from your language. In translating them do you use **this, that, these,** or **those**?

> This little pig went to market
> This little pig stayed home
> This little pig had roast beef
> And this little pig had none
> And this little pig ran wee wee wee
> All the way home.

> This is the way the ladies ride, trit trot, trit trot.
> This is the way the ladies ride
> All of a Sunday morning.

> This is the way the gentlemen ride, prancing prancing, prancing prancing.
> This is the way the gentlemen ride,
> All of a Sunday morning.

> This is the way the soldiers ride, gallopy gallopy, gallopy gallopy.
> This is the way the soldiers ride,
> All of a Sunday morning.

> This is the way the farmers ride, hobbledy gee, hobbledy gee.
> This is the way the farmers ride,
> All of a Sunday morning.

Magazines

We use Cardinal numbers

1. to count

>*1, 2, 3 .... 10, 11*
>*One, two, three .... ten, eleven*

2. to indicate quantities

>*14 magazines*
>*The Browns take **fourteen** magazines.*

3. to pronounce telephone numbers, and street addresses, and zip codes.

>*802-257-7779*
>*eight oh two   two five seven   seven seven seven nine*
>*164½ Maxwell Place*
>*One sixty-four and a half Maxwell Place*
>*East Palo Ato, California 94303*

We use Ordinal numbers

1. to indicate rank or position or order

>*1st: Boys Life*
>*Willy's **first** subscription was to **Boy's Life**.*

2. to express the number of a day in a date

>*9/14/1978 = Sept. 14th, 1978*
>*September **fourteenth**, nineteen seventy-eight*

See the vocabulary box at the end of this lesson.

A. Using the information from "The Best Selling U.S. Magazines" chart, write these sentences about circulation.

(5 – circulation) *National Geographic has a circulation of ten million, eight hundred and ninety thousand, six hundred and sixty.*

1. (The Star - circulation) _____

_____

_____

2. (13 - circulation) _____

_____

_____

3. (19 - circulation) _____

_____

_____

4. (**Woman's Day** - circulation) _____

_____

_____

5. (3 - circulation) _____

_____

_____

The Best Selling U.S. Magazines - 1990*

Rank	Title	Circulation
1.	Modern Maturity	21,430,990
2.	NRTA/AARP Bulletin	21,092,794
3.	Reader's Digest	16,343,599
4.	TV Guide	16,302,705
5.	National Geographic	10,890,660
6.	Better Homes & Gardens	8,005,311
7.	Family Circle	5,461,786
8.	Good Housekeeping	5,152,245
9.	McCall's	5,088,686
10.	Ladies' Home Journal	5,038,297
11.	Woman's Day	4,705,288
12.	Time	4,339,029
13.	Guideposts	4,203,934
14.	National Enquirer	4,100,740
15.	Star	3,588,753
16.	First for Women	3,509,688
17.	Sports Illustrated	3,424,393
18.	Playboy	3,421,203
19.	People	3,270,835
20.	Newsweek	3,180,011
21.	Prevention	3,134,914

* Source: The 1991 World Almanac.

B. Using the chart, write these sentences about rank.

(**Sports Illustrated** - rank) *Sports Illustrated is the seventeenth best selling U.S. magazine.*

1. (**Good Housekeeping** - rank)_____

_____

2. (**Better Homes and Gardens** - rank)_____

_____

3. (**Playboy** - rank)_____

_____

4. (**Woman's Day** - rank)_____

_____

5. (**The NRTA/AARP Bulletin** - rank)_____

_____

C. Using the chart, write the following sentences.

(20 - circulation) *The circulation of Newsweek is three million, one hundred and eighty thousand, and eleven.*

(**Family Circle** - rank) *Family Circle's sales rank seventh among U.S. magazines.*

1. (10 - rank)_____

_____

2. (**McCall's** - circulation)_____

_____

3. (14 - rank)_____

_____

4. (12 - circulation)_____

_____

5. (**The Star** - rank)_____

_____

6. (**TV Guide** - rank, circulation)_____

_____

_____

7.   (1 -   )_____

_____

_____

8.   (16 -   )_____

_____

_____

9.   (You choose)_____

_____

_____

10. (You choose)_____

_____

_____

D. Substitute words for numbers and numbers for words in the following sentences.

Sam bought thr̶e̶e̶ *3* copies of **Newsweek** last week.

The Village News Stand ordered 2̶0̶ *twenty* copies of the **New Yorker**.

1.   **Smithsonian** is my 1st choice for studying American culture.
2.   This magazine was addressed to four fifteen Maryland Court, not six oh nine!
3.   The ten leading advertizers in print media spend $1,927,478,640 last year.
4.   **Woman's Day** costs $1.25 per copy.
5.   It has a circulation of 4,705,288.
6.   Each issue of **Woman's Day** earns $5,881,610.
7.   **Woman's Day** is the sixth ranking women's magazine.
8.   The editorial address of **Newsweek** is 444 Madison Avenue,
9.   New York, New York 10022.
10. **Newsweek's** telephone number is 212-350-2000.
11. On June twenty-sixth, May Davis gave Chiang a present.
12. It was **Newsweek's** 50th Anniversary Issue.
13. **Newsweek** was founded in 1933 during The Depression.
14. Did you say **Hustler** is the 15th biggest U.S. magazine or the 50th?
15. The 50th, but **Playboy** is 17th.
16. The article starts on page 281 of this year's **National Geographic**.

Cardinal Numbers		Ordinal Numbers	
1	one	1st	first
2	two	2nd	second
3	three	3rd	third
4	four	4th	fourth
5	five	5th	fifth
6	six	6th	sixth
7	seven	7th	seventh
8	eight	8th	eighth
9	nine	9th	ninth
10	ten	10th	tenth
11	eleven	11th	eleventh
12	twelve	12th	twelfth
13	thirteen	13th	thirteenth
14	fourteen	14th	fourteenth
15	fifteen	15th	fifteenth
16	sixteen	16th	sixteenth
17	seventeen	17th	seventeenth
18	eighteen	18th	eighteenth
19	nineteen	19th	nineteenth
20	twenty	20th	twentieth
21	twenty-one	21st	twenty-first
30	thirty	30th	thirtieth
40	forty	40th	fortieth
50	fifty	50th	fiftieth
60	sixty	60th	sixtieth
70	seventy	70th	seventieth
80	eighty	80th	eightieth
90	ninety	90th	ninetieth
100	one/a hundred	100th	one/a hundredth
101	one/a hundred (and) one	101st	one/a hundred (and) first
1,000	one/a thousand	1,000th	one/a thousandth
2,000	two thousand	2,000th	two thousandth
10,000	ten thousand	10,000th	ten thousandth
100,000	one/a hundred thousand	100,000th	one/a hundred thousandth
1,000,000	one/a million	1,000,000th	one/a millionth
1,000,000,000	one/a billion	1,000,000,000th	one/a billionth

Extra Exercise

Ask two or three Americans to read these numbers and dates. Do they say them the same way? If not, make notes of the differences. Read them aloud to your teacher or some other American, explaining the differences you have discovered.

1. 409
2. Zip 60637
3. 446-0723
4. April 15, 1990
5. 10,627
6. 5/1/87
7. Zip 20052
8. 49%
9. 2002
10. 17.8
11. 9/16
12. 80.60
13. 868-4000
14. 3/4
15. 101,627,032
16. 1-800-527-4900
17. 432%
18. 8^2
19. 15^6
20. $\sqrt{64}$
21. 50÷5=
22. 32 x 6.8
23. 82,000 x 12.8%
24. (802) 257-2070

The usual, expected order of adjectives in a noun phrase is as follows.

1. **Partitives** (showing quantity): all (of), most (of), one-half (of), either (of)

2. **Determiners** — articles: a, the
   — demonstratives: that, these
   — possesives: George's, our
   — indefinite adjectives: some, many

3. **Numbers** — ordinals: third, first, fifty
   — cardinal: six, dozen

4. **Descriptive adjectives** (There are many kinds and their order is flexible; short adjectives often come before long ones. The usual order of some important kinds is as follows.)
   — general/opinion: beautiful, funny
   — size: huge, fat
   — shape: round, horizontal
   — condition: rusty, rainy, bright
   — age: young, brand-new
   — temperature: hot, freezing
   — color: blue, colorful, hot pink

5. **Proper adjectives/material**
   — nationality: French
   — religion: Catholic
   — style: Impressionist, oriental
   — material: clay,

6. **Adjuncts** (words which are almost part of the noun; they are rarely separated from the noun by other adjectives).

   — adjective: **modern** dance, **electronic** music
   — gerunds: **dancing** school, **opening** night
   — creator: **Ibsen** play **Beethoven** symphony
   — noun: **opera** singer, **paint** brush

We put a comma (,) or conjunction (and, but, or) between adjectives if they are the same kind, but we don't if they are not.

These red, white, and blue posters . . . Our six old, blue wooden bowls . . .

A. Build the noun phrases below using the adjectives given and then fit them into the paragraphs which follow.

noun: **artists**
(great) _great artists_
(these) _these great artists_
(U.S.) _these great U.S. artists_
(three) _these three great U.S. artists_
noun: **painters**
(famous) _famous painters_
(all) _all famous painters_
(very) _all very famous painters_

These three great U.S. artists are _all very famous_ painters.

1.   noun: **painting**
      (strange)_____
      (one)_____
      (oil)_____
      noun: **farmers**
      (very plain)_____
      (a pair of)_____
      (typical American)_____
      noun: **house**
      (white)_____
      (their)_____

(farm)_____

(old)_____

noun: **painting**

(this)_____

(modern)_____

(wonderful)_____

Grant Wood is well-known for _____ painting.

_____ farmers (a man and a woman) are

standing in front of _____ house.

_____ painting is called "American Gothic."

2.   noun: **canvases**

(large)_____

(complicated)_____

(Jackson Pollock's)_____

noun: **splashes**

(long)_____

(paint)_____

(hundreds of)_____

(multicolored)_____

noun: **public**

(today's)_____

(most of)_____

noun: **movement**

(international)_____

(the)_____

(abstract-expressionist)_____

noun: **art**

(strange)_____

(that)_____

(modern)_____

_____canvases covered

with _____ splashes are what

_____ public thinks of first when _____

movement or "_____ art" are mentioned.

3.   noun: **scenes**

(cheerful)_____

(sentimental)_____

(many)_____

noun: **life**

(everyday)_____

(our)_____

(American)_____

noun: **magazine**

(old)_____

(the)_____

(Saturday Evening Post)_____

(popular)_____

noun: **illustrations**

(delightful)_____

(a)_____

(many)_____

(great)_____

(Rockwell)_____

noun: **work**

(cover)_____

(front)_____

(art)_____

(its)_____

Norman Rockwell painted _____ scenes from

_____ life. _____ magazine

used _____ illustrations for

_____ work.

B. Here is a letter from the director of an amateur theater to his old drama school professor. Some of the adjectives in his letter are in the wrong order. Rewrite the letter unscrambling the adjectives. The adjectives which may be wrong are in bold type. One possible correct form of the letter is given at the back.

Play Our Neighborhood House

Professor dear Moran,

I need some of **professional good your** advice. We are putting on **American that classic** play, **funny but Tennessee Williams' painful** <u>Streetcar Named Desire</u>. So far **first our** preparations have been **well-organized fun and easy**. I have **hard-working and enthusiastic, happy a** organization. What I don't have is a Blanche Dubois, **but aging, glamorous, that Southern** belle who is **central play's the** character. I advertised in **local our weekly** newspaper: "Wanted: **middle-aged experienced an** actress to play Blanche Dubois." I got **amazing these four** characters.

Mercy Slidebeck, **ballet fourteen-year-old, nervous a** dancer. At the same time she looks **but young experienced too too also**.

Phillipa Block, **two-hundred-and-fifty-pound first sixty-five-year-old the** grandmother who ever thought of playing Blanche, I'm sure. She has **horse deep strange this** laugh, such statements as, "I've seen this play before. Har! Har! Har!!"

Willie May Jackson. She's got **warm, right Southern the** accent and **plump right slightly fortyish the** figure, and **hot and tired Blanche's** way of flirting with **sad young all the** men. She is also black. This is **Southern very a realistic** play, at least on the surface. What will **black a** Blanche do to it? It's **crazy and wonderful a rather** idea, isn't it? And then in walks:

Bobbie Coffin, **sexy, female, a thirtyish beautiful** impersonator in **pink hot skin-tight** pants and **blond white a** wig. "She" loves saying in **alto husky her** voice, "I can play anything-anything-anything you want to play, handsome. Believe me." Bobbie, too, would give <u>Streetcar</u> **new interesting an** twist.

Help, Professor! What do I do?

Our Neighborhood Play House

Dear Professor Moran,
   I need some of your good professional advice.

Latin America

Proper nouns and adjectives referring to nationalities always begin with a capital letter. There are many irregular forms.

Botswana *is a desert country.*
Fritz Stein is a **German.**
Sue is wearing a **Chilean** *dress.*
Can Wong speak **Korean** *and* **Japanese?**

A. First study this map of Latin American (not including Carribean countries) and fill out the following list from your memory naming all the countries you can. Check your work against the list given at the end of the lesson. Be sure to capitalize the proper nouns.

A. _Mexico_   I. _____   Q. _____
B. _____   J. _____   R. _____
C. _____   K. _____   S. _____
D. _____   L. _____   T. _____
E. _____   M. _____   U. _____
F. _____   N. _____
G. _____   O. _____
H. _____   P. _____

B. Using the map on the next page, fill out the following sentences using proper nouns and adjectives. If you are not sure of the proper forms, guess. Then check and correct your work using the answers at the back of the book.

José comes from (N) _Ecuador_ .

We met an (U) _Argentinian_ businessman named Max Schneider.

1. The (Q) _____ capitol is La Paz.
2. Can you take a trip to Rio for a (P) _____ vacation?
3. Juan Nakimoto is a native (R) _____.
4. The language of most (A) _____ is _____.
5. Montevideo is on the (T) _____ coast.
6. Many Mayans are (B) _____.
7. Simon Bolivar was not a native (Q) _____;
8. He was born a (J) _____.

9. The (J) _____, (I) _____, (N) _____,
    (Q) _____, and (H) _____ people all remember Bolivar
    as the Great Liberator.
10. To do business in Sao Paulo, one has to speak (P) _____.
11. Managua is the largest (F) _____ city.
12. (A) _____ are proud of their Spanish-Indian heritage.
13. Neither the (Q) _____ nor the (S) _____ have a coast.
14. The official (L) _____ language is Dutch.

C. First read the paragraph making any corrections in capitalization which are necessary and then add the nationality adjectives indicated to the sentences in D below. If you don't know the adjective, guess and then check your answer in the back.

              U.S.   *A*

    In the 1990 <u>u.s.</u> Census, 22,354,059 <u>a</u>mericans said they were of Spanish or hispanic origin, an increase of 53% from 14,605,883 in 1980. This was 9.1% of the U.s. population. For comparison, the 1990 population of Mexico city was 20,207,000. The next four largest portugese or spanish speaking cities were san Paulo (18,052,000), buenos aires (11,518,000), Rio de janeiro (11,428,000), and Lima (6,578,000). madrid had 4,451,000 people. The U.S. Hispanic population also compares to the populations of ecuador (10,560,000), Cuba (10,582,000), Portugal (10,528,000), chile (13,016,000), Venezuela (19,753,000), or peru (21,904,000). The south american countries, Bolivia, suriname, guyana, french guyana, Paraguay, and Uraguay are much smaller. argentina, Colombia, spain, the philippines, mexico, and brazil are much larger.

    All aliens living in the U.S. must register with the government. In 1980, 5,381,107 did. Fourteen countries had more than 100,000 Citizens registered in the u.s. The most came from mexico (1,058,596). Then came Canada, Cuba, great Britain, the philippines, Vietnam, Korea, italy, Germany, Portugal, the dominican republic, India, China, and japan. 84.2 percent of these aliens were immigrants, 3.2 percent were foreign students, 1.5 were foreign workers or visitors, and 4 percent were refugees.

D. First read C above. Then add the correct nationality adjectives to these sentences. If you don't know the adjective, guess, and then check your answers in the back. Can you add other interesting information below?

    Almost 21 million (U.S.) _Americans_ call themselves Hispanics. Many of these Hispanics are (Cuba) _Cubans_ .

1. There are more (Mexico) _____ in Mexico City
2. than there are (Venezuela) _____ .
3. The second largest group of U.S. aliens is (Canada) _____ .
4. The Philippines is a very large _____ speaking country.
5. The (Philippines) _____ are the fifth largest group of U.S. aliens.
6. The people in Rio de Janeiro speak _____ .
7. There are more (Brazil) _____ speakers in Sao Paulo
8. than there are _____ in all of Portugal.
9. There are 37,682,355 _____ in Spain and
10. 67,395,826 _____ in Mexico, the largest _____ speaking country.

11. The U.S. has many (Vietnam) _____ residents, but

12. there are more (Great Britain) _____ residents.

13. The (Chile) _____ population is greater than the (Bolivia) _____.

14. There are many (Europe) _____ living as aliens in the U.S.

15. particularly (Great Britain) _____, (Italy) _____,

16. (Germany) _____, and (Portugal) _____.

17. (Asia) _____ living here in large numbers are

18. (The Philippines) _____, (Vietnam) _____,

19. (Korea) _____, (India) _____, (China) _____, and (Japan) _____.

20. Most Hispanics are (believers in Christ) _____ at least formally.

21. The largest church is the (Catholicism of Rome) _____,

22. although there are many (Protestantism) _____ churches too.

_____

_____

_____

_____

_____

_____

_____

_____

Map Key

A.	Mexico	I.	Colombia	Q.	Bolivia
B.	Guatemala	J.	Venezuela	R.	Chile
C.	Belize	K.	Guyana	S.	Paraguay
D.	El Salvador	L.	Suriname	T.	Uruguay
E.	Honduras	M.	French Guiana	U.	Argentina
F.	Nicaragua	N.	Ecuador		
G.	Costa Rica	O.	Peru		
H.	Panama	P.	Brazil		

The American and his car

To form the comparative of adjectives:

1. We add **-er** to all one syllable adjectives

old	>	old**er**	*The Buick is older.*
hot	>	hott**er**	*My engine runs hotter.*
gray	>	gray**er**	*The dirt makes it look grayer.*
dry	>	dr**ier**	*The road is drier today.*

2. We must use **more** (or **less**) before all adjectives of 3 or more syllables.

expensive	>	**more** expensive	*This is **more** expensive.*

all adjectives derived from nouns or verbs which use these endings: **-ful, -ish, -less, -ous, -ing, -ed.**

beauty	>	beaut**iful**	>	more beaut**iful**
style	>	styl**ish**	>	less styl**ish**
price	>	price**less**	>	more price**less**
space	>	spac**ious**	>	less spac**ious**
interest	>	interest**ing**	>	more interest**ing**
polish	>	polish**ed**	>	less polish**ed**

3. We can use **-er** with all two syllable adjectives except those in 2 above, or we can use **more** for variation or greater emphasis.

   a. Two syllable adjectives ending in **-le** or **-y** almost always use **-er**

simple	>	simpl**er**	*Old cars have simpler motors.*
lucky	>	**luckier**	*I feel luckier in my VW.*

   b. With most other two syllable adjectives **-er** and **more** are both used often.

rugged	>	rugged**er**/**more** rugged
quiet	>	quiet**er**/**more** quiet
yellow	>	yellow**er**/**more** yellow
handsome	>	handsom**er**/**more** handsome
clever	>	cleverer**er**/**more** clever

Note that the two comparative forms are *never* used together, although this is a common mistake with children and non-native speakers.

*I never saw a ~~more~~ handsom**er** automobile!*

4. Adjectives with irregular comparative forms are never used with **-er** or **more**.

good	better	~~betterer~~/~~more better~~
bad	worse	~~worser~~/~~more worse~~
far	farther	~~fartherer~~/~~more farther~~

5. **Than** is used between the two parts of all complete comparisons.

*A V8 engine is more powerful **than** a V6 (is).*
*Your car is newer **than** mine (is).*

A. Fill in the blanks with comparative adjectives using the **–er** form.

(hot)   Jim's car is *hotter* than Mike's.

(pretty)   My VW is much *prettier* than Mike's.

1.   (fast)   Maria wants a _____ set of wheels.

2.   (costly)   Her dream car would be _____.

3.   (high)   My offer for the Honda was _____ than José's.

4.   (rough)   This engine runs _____ every day.

5.   (old, cheap)   Mrs. Conklin wants an _____, _____ car.

6.   (safe)   Sedans are _____ than sports cars.

7.   (tough)   Will's Chevy is _____ than his Renault.

8.   (good)   Subarus are _____ in rough country.

9.   (long, good)   "When I buy a car," he says, "The _____ the _____."

10.   (rusty)   Each year my Plymouth gets _____.

B. Combine these sentences using the comparative form **more**.

Working on my jalopy is fun. Working on Mom's Nissan.

Working on my jalopy is more fun than working on Mom's Nissan.

Cadillacs are expensive. Fords are expensive.

Cadillacs are more expensive than Fords.

1.   My Pontiac is stylish. Your VW is stylish.

_____

2.   This Toyota is quiet. That Saab is quiet.

_____

3.   The Mazda engine is interesting. The Datsun engine is interesting.

_____

4.   The dashboard of Suzie's Pinto is snazzy. Yours is snazzy.

_____

5.   This year's model is tinny. Last year's is tinny.

_____

6.   The flames painted on Nick's car are elaborate. Sally's are elaborate.

_____

7.   The new Continental is elegant. The old one is elegant.

_____

8.   A Jeep is trustworthy. A Landrover is trustworthy.

_____

9.   Frank's Porsche looks beaten up. An old stock car looks beaten up.

_____

10. Harvey thinks his MG is exciting. He thinks his wife is exciting.

_____

C. Rewrite your answers to B. 1-5 using the comparative form **less**.

Working on my jalopy is less fun than working on Mom's Nissan.
Cadillacs are less expensive than Fords.

1. _____
2. _____
3. _____
4. _____
5. _____

D. Rewrite these adjectives changing the **-er** comparatives to **more** and the **more** comparatives to **-er** if possible. If you cannot change a sentence, don't.

"OK, Molly's Chrysler LeBaron is ~~more flashy~~ *flashier* than my old Pontiac!"

1.   Her paint job is more fancy than mine.

2.   Her sheepskin seat covers are softer than mine.

3.   Even Molly's floor rugs are thicker than mine.

4.   But somehow my old car is still handsomer than Molly's new car.

5.   I think it's because of my more graceful racing stripes.

6.   Molly's are shinier,

7.   but mine are more classy.

8.   Furthermore, my mag wheels are more authentic than hers,

9.   and my radial tires have a thinner white wall stripe.

10. Her EPA mileage rating is higher than mine, of course;

11. it's a newer car and it's smaller.

12. But who cares! Mine's bigger.

13. She says the LeBaron is more comfortable than any Pontiac,

14. but my bucket seats are deeper and more luxurious.

15. My sound system is of much higher quality,

16. and the instruments in my dashboard are more useful

17. and more classic in their design.

18. Maybe Molly's is a more fashionable auto.

19. But my old jalopy seems more sexy to me,

20. more simple but more interesting.

21. Molly herself? She could be worse.

22. And her car's OK, too -- just more ordinary than mine.

To form the superlative:

1. We add **-est** to all one-syllable adjectives

> *Chicago has the tallest building in the World.*

2. We must use **most** or **least** before

all adjectives with three or more syllables.

> *The New York Stock Exchange is the **most** important in the U.S.*
> *Chester Arthur was the **least** memorable American President.*

All adjectives derived from nouns or verbs which use these endings: **-ful, -ive, -less, -ous, ing, -ed.**

> *The **most** expensive toy soldier in history cost $468.*
> *The **most** generous gift giver in history was John D. Rockefeller, who gave away $750 million.*

3. We can use **-est** with all two syllable adjectives except those in 2 above, or we can use **most** or **least** for variation or greater emphasis. (See Lesson 45.)

Two syllable adjectives ending in **-le** and **-y** almost always use **-est**.

> *The luck**iest** gambler won $5.5 million in a Lotto game.*

4. **The** is placed before all superlatives (except in the examples in 6 below).

> *Life Savers are **the** most popular candy. (29 billion rolls have been sold.)*

5. Adjectives with irregular superlatives are never used with **-est** or **most**.

good > best   bad > worst   far > farthest

6. The most common superlative construction is

> *Shakespeare is **the most** quoted author in America.*
> *The Mississippi is **the** longest river in North America.*

The following constructions are also common.

> *Shakespeare is America's **most** quoted author.*
> *The Mississippi is North America's longest river.*
> *Shakespeare is **the** author **most** quoted in America.*

A. In the blanks in these sentences, write in the superlatives of the adjectives given in the parentheses.

Texas was (large) *the largest* state in the U.S.A. before Alaska joined the union. Texans are proud of being (boastful) *the most boastful* people in the country.

Most Americans love superlatives. We joke about Texans who always say that Texas has (big) _____, (long) _____, (high) _____, (fat) _____, (sweet) _____, (fast) _____, (old) _____, (rich) _____ and (wonderful) _____, (famous) _____ and even (awful) _____ whatever you are talking about. We make fun of Texans, but we all love to boast and talk about records. I once heard a Texan boast, "Texas is so big that all Americans are Texans at heart." Maybe that is (good) _____, (perceptive) _____ boast a Texan ever made.

B. Rewrite these sentences using superlatives.

Smith is a common family name in the U.S.

Smith is the most common family name in the U.S.

Rhode Island is a small state in the United States.

Rhode Island is the smallest state in the United States.

1. Reader's Digest has a large U.S. magazine circulation.

_____

2. CBS News is a watched TV program.

_____

3. Proctor and Gamble has a fat advertising budget.

_____

4. The Toronto Star is a purchased Canadian daily paper.

_____

5. Chorus Line is a long running Broadway hit.

_____

6. The New York News is a widely read U.S. newspaper.

_____

7. Mount McKinley in Alaska is a high U.S. mountain.

_____

8. A towering mountain in the lower 48 states is California's Mt. Whitney.

_____

9. Admiral Robert Peary made a daring race to the North Pole in 1906.

_____

10.   A fast 100 meter race, 9.86 seconds, was run by Carl Lewis in 1991.

C. Correct this story using superlatives whenever they are appropriate.

the best   **The Tall Tale and the Last Laugh**

One of *funniest* ~~good~~ and ~~funny~~ stories about Texans is the story of the Texan who was sightseeing in the tiny State of Vermont. He saw an old Vermont farmer, and being a farmer himself, stopped to talk. Now Texans are known to be <u>good humored</u> and <u>boastful</u> Americans, while Vermoters have <u>less</u> to say and <u>dry</u> humor of any people in the whole U.S.A. (although they could boast of having <u>green</u> and <u>beautiful</u> mountains anywhere).

The Texan said, "Howdy, Partner. You sure have <u>a pretty</u> little farm in these parts. Yup, you sure do! <u>A quiet</u> and <u>peaceful</u> spread (farm) I've seen since Texas."

"Yup," said the Vermonter.

"Say, you know, I'm a farmer, too, my friend."

"Is that so?"

"Yes, sir! But my farm's larger. In fact it's <u>a big</u> farm in <u>a rich</u> county in <u>a lovely, fertile</u> part of the great State of Texas!"

"Oh," said the Vermonter.

"Yes, Ol' Buddy," said the Texan, "I don't mind telling you, my spread is <u>a spacious</u> and <u>lovely</u> ranch in all the Old Southwest. Why, it's so big I can drive my car all day from <u>an early</u> light of dawn until <u>a gorgeous</u> red Texas sun sets in the West without ever getting to <u>a far</u> corner of my property!"

The Vermonter sucked on his pipe. "Yup," he said quietly. "Had a car like that myself once, but I got rid of it."

(Footnote: Texas and Vermont are the only states which were independent nations before joining The Union. "The Lone Star State of Texas" makes <u>more</u> of its historical independence. Vermonters don't say too much about theirs. <u>They</u> don't have to.)

Extra Exercise

Americans are fascinated by records. Year after year <u>The Guinness Book of World Records</u> is <u>one of the best</u> selling reference books in the U.S. Here is some typical information from the book. If the superlatives are incorrect, correct them.

This year's Guinness Book is the ~~most big~~ *biggest* ever! Its full of ~~most late~~ *the latest* incredible facts! ** The most largest of all lizards are the Komono monitor of Indonesia. The giganticest one measured 10 ft. 2 in. and weighed 365 lb. ** The biggerest and littlest cathedrals in the world are St. John the Divine in N.Y.C. and St. Frances Cathedral Chapel in Laguna Beach, CA. ** The World's miniaturest ridable bicycle has 2 1/4 inch wheels and weighs 2 lbs. ** The all-time goodest selling authors are Earl Stanley Gardner (315 million in 37 languages) and Agatha Christie (300 million in 103 languages.). ** The most widely distributed book is The Bible (2.5 billion in 1,735 languages). ** An most ancientest living thing is a clone of the creosote plant in California which is about 11,700 years old. ** The popularest dog breed in America is the poodle. ** The most old athlete to win an Olympic title was Babe McDonald (U.S. - 42 years, 26 days old); the most young was Barbara Jones (U.S. - 15 years, 123 days). ** The expensivest TV Ad was $400,000 for 30 seconds during a Super Bowl. ** The farest Champagne cork flight was 105 ft. 9 in. in 1981. ** The most monsterous zucchini ever grown weighed 36 lbs. 3 oz. It was from Montreal, Canada. ** There is a tie for the record of the heavyest baby ever born: 22 lbs. 8 oz. ** The most great age a man ever lived to is 117 years for S. Izumi of Japan. ** Capt. Wilson Kettle of Canada had the morest living descendents. When he died at 102 he had 11 children, 65 grandchildren, 201 great grandchildren, and 305 great-great-grandchildren, a total of 582. ** The most largest number of children from one mother was 69 to one Russian woman. ** The longest-lived domestic bird on record was George, an English goose who died at the most advanced age of 49 years and 8 months. ** The least expensive automobile ever sold was the 1922 Red Bug Buckboard priced at $125.00 each.

47 Quantity words

American politics

1. We use **much, little,** and **less** with non-count nouns (see Lesson 13).

   Much is usually used with questions and negative statements.

   > *Does he have **much** hope of winning the election?*
   > *No, he doesn't have **much** hope.*

   Little and **a little** are usually used with questions and affirmative statements. **Little** is used to stress the negative lack of quantity; **a little** stresses the positive presence of quantity.

   > *Does he have a **little** hope of winning?*
   > *Yes, there is **a little** hope.*
   > *No, there is **little** hope.*

   Less and **least** are the comparative and superlative forms of **little**

2. We use **many** and **few,** with count nouns.

   Many is used with plural count nouns.

   > *Does the governor have **many** friends?*
   > *No, he doesn't have **many**;*
   > *he has **many** enemies.*

   Few and **a few** are usually used with questions and affirmative statements. As with **little** and **a little, few** stresses lack of quantity and **a few** stresses the presence of quantity.

   > *Doesn't the governor have **a few** friends?*
   > *He has always had **a few** political friends,*
   > *but he has **few** real friends now.*

   Fewer and **fewest** are the comparative and superlative forms of **few.**

3. **A lot of, lots of,** and **plenty of** are often used as quantity words with both count and non-count nouns. **Plenty** is not used in negative statements.

   > *A **lot of** people register to vote,*
   > *but **lots of** them don't vote.*
   > *Don't they have **a lot of** time to vote?*
   > *Sure, they have **plenty of** time.*

> **A great deal of** or **a good deal of** (like **much**) are used only with
> non-count nouns. **A great many** or **a good many** (like **many**) are used
> with count nouns.
>
> > *The governor is in **a good deal** of trouble*
> > *because he has made **a great many** enemies.*
>
> 4. **Of** is used after most quantity words when the noun is identified specifically
> with a demonstrative, a possessive or a modifying phrase, or when a
> pronoun is used.
>
> > *Many Democrats are loyal.*
> > *Many **of those** Democrats are loyal.*
> > *Many **of Roosevelt's** Democrats are loyal.*
> > *Many **of the** Democrats **from our town** are loyal.*
> > *Many **of them** are loyal.*

A. Fill in the blanks using **much** or **many**.

Many Americans are neither Republicans nor Democrats.

1. _____ of these people call themselves "independents."

2. The independents don't have _____ influence on public policy.

3. _____ politicians talk about winning the independent vote,

4. but they listen to the _____ party loyalists.

5. Independents don't give _____ money to support campaigns.

6. In general, they don't have _____ interest in political parties.

B. Fill in the blanks using **(a) few, (a) little, fewer,** or **lesser.**

7. _____ independents work hard for candidates they like,

8. and they give _____ money to them.

9. But today, although there are _____ real independents than 30 years
ago, there are also

10. _____ people registered as Republicans or Democrats.

11. The non-registered pay _____ attention to politics.

12. Party loyalists vote; too _____ "independents" do.

C. Fill in the blanks using **much, many, (a) few, (a) little, fewer** or **less.**

13. A true independent spends _____ hours judging:

14. "This man hasn't got _____ new ideas;

15.   that man wants to raise too _____ tax money.

16.   This man has too _____ experience,

17.   but that man has lived in Washington too _____ years

18.   and has too _____ contacts with the folks back home."

19.   Unfortunately not _____ voters take the time to be truly independent.

20.   It takes too _____ time.

21.   _____ lazy "independents" judge TV personalities

22.   and give _____ thought to a candidate's record

23.   and _____ to his and his party's philosophy.

24.   It should follow that we elect _____ philosophers today,

25.   but luckily there are still a great _____ in office.

D. Choose the best phrase in this politician's speech.

Good evening ladies and gentlemen. It's so good to see (a lot of/a good deal of) you here tonight. Now, of course, I am hoping (a great deal of/lots of) you will vote in this election. And I ask you to consider this: I don't have (plenty of/a great deal) of money. But I have (a lot of/a good many) enthusiasm for and dedication to my country. I hope (a great many of/a good deal of) you will vote for me. Now, I don't expect you to contribute (plenty of/a great deal of) money to my campaign. I don't want (a good many/lots of) money. But I do hope you can contribute (lots of/a great many of) time to my campaign by spreading the word. And the word is this: I believe people with (a lot of/a good many) money should not be in politics. What our country needs is (lots of/a good deal of) people like you and me in Washington D.C. -- people without (a great deal of/a good many) money. Our country needs congressmen like me -- men with (lots of/a great many) experience and dedication. When there are (a good deal of/a lot of) us in congress, this country will truly have a government of the people, by the people, and for the people. Thank you and God bless you.

Adverbs of manner 48

Cowboys and Indians

We <u>form</u> adverbs of manner by adding **-ly** to adjectives.

slow **+ ly** > slowly

We <u>use</u> adverbs of manner to tell how something is done.

Black Bart walked out of the saloon.
How did he walk?
He walked **slowly**.
He drew his gun, but his draw was too **slow**.

Slow is the adjective (*a* **slow** *draw*), **slowly** is the adverb (*he walked* **slowly**). Some Americans in some parts of our country use adjectives for adverbs. You will see signs saying "*go slow*" instead of "*go slowly*." This is not acceptable in formal speech or writing.

Spelling rules:
1. When an adjective ends in **-y**, change the **y** to **i** before adding **-ly**.

funny > funn**ily**   busy > bus**ily**

2. When an adjective ends in **-c**, add **-ally**.

basi**c** > basic**ally**   histori**c** > historic**ally**

3. When an adjective ends in **-ble, -ple -tle,** or **dle,** change the **-e** to **-y.**

gen**tle** > gen**tly**   proba**ble** > proba**bly**

A. Write the adverb form of one of these adjectives below each of these pictures.

cheap / expensive   **slow / quick**   **sad / happy**   **loud / soft**

a. *softly*

b. _____

c. _____

d. _____   e. _____   f. _____

g. _____   h. _____

B. Write a sentence for each picture using the adverb you wrote in exercise A. Possible answers are given at the back of the book.

a. *The Indian is speaking softly.*

b. _____

c. _____

d. _____

e. _____

f. _____

g. _____

h. _____

C. Write the adverbs into these sentences.

(colorful) In the movies, the cowboy hero dresses _colorfully_ .

(plain) He never dresses _plainly_ .

1. (expensive) His fancy clothes are _____ decorated

2. (real) because he is _____ only playing the hero.

3. (brave) Of course he faces danger _____,

4. (fierce) he fights bad guys _____,

5. (sudden) and then _____ he is either thrown out a window,

6. (unexpected) or he tumbles _____ off a racing stagecoach.

7. (shy) Is he hurt? As the dust clears, we find him smiling _____.

8. (neat) and _____ dressed with his hat still on.

9. (actual) In the 1870's, cowboys _____ lived a tough life.

10. (steady) They had to work hard and _____.

11. (heroic) They didn't have time to behave _____.

12. (unattractive) Real cowboys were often ugly and _____ unclean.

13. (poor) They were usually illiterate or at least _____ educated.

14. (separate) Usually the cowboys lived _____ from the Indians, and they left each other alone.

15. (fair) Sometimes like the movie heros they really did fight _____ with them,

16. (brutal) but too often they treated them _____.

17. (unexpected) _____ ambushing Indian camps, and

18. (cruel) _____ butchering defenseless men, women, and children.

19. (peaceful) Many cowboys, however, lived _____ near the Indians,

20. (eventual) trading, working, and _____ even living with them.

21. (free) Cowboys roamed _____ from job to job around the West.

22. (regular) Sometimes men worked _____, but too often

23. (anxious) they were _____ looking for any kind of work.

24. (actual) Come to think of it, maybe the old cowpokes who _____.

25. (slow) "built the West" by _____ building their ranches and towns,

26. (diligent) working _____ under great hardships and

27. (cooperative) living _____ with all their neighbors,

28. (real) _____ were heros.

D. Circle the right form
(careful/~~carefully~~)

The (~~Lone~~/Lonely) Ranger

One of the (~~exciting~~/excitingly) cowboy heros from the American movies was the Lone Ranger. He appeared (original/originally) on the radio. Every week, thousands of boys and girls waited (impatient/impatiently) and (expectant/expectantly) by their radios for the sound of the Lone Ranger's theme music, which until that time was (general/generally) known as Rossini's William Tell Overture. Today, (most/mostly) Americans hear the music and (immediate/immediately) think: "The Lone Ranger!"

Our hero was a (nice/nicely) man. He (usual/usually) dressed in white and wore the (usual/usually) white hat. He even rode a (large/largely) all-white horse called Silver. All of that was (common/commonly) for the "heros of the silver screen." What was (unusual/unusually) was that he wore a mask, traveled with an Indian named Tonto as his only friend and (faithful/faithfully) companion, and wasn't even (interested/interestedly) in girls. Furthermore, he couldn't sing! (Previous/previously) we thought of our heros as cowboys out on the range singing (romantic/romantically) either to their girlfriends or their cows.

The Lone Ranger was (real/really) a (different/differently) sort of hero. He was (mysterious/mysteriously), and he was always sneaking around (unexpected/unexpectedly) in disguise. There was something not quite (human/humanly) about him. He fought too (brave/bravely), he talked too (quiet/quietly), he seemed too (polite/politely), too (just/justly). (Real/really) people get angry (regular/regularly). The get (sad/sadly). They even fall (hopeless/hopelessly) in love or are driven by (passionate/passionately) hatreds. But not the Lone Ranger! He was above emotions. He was (quick/quickly) in drawing his gun, but he never fired his silver bullets to kill; (final/finally), all bad guys must go to court. The Lone Ranger was (basic/basically) an (ideal/ideally) superhero, and his action-packed adventures were (moral/morally) lessons. The Lone Ranger's world of good and evil was (simple/simply) to understand, and we Americans followed him (enthusiastic/enthusiastically) on radio, in many movies, and (ultimate/ultimately) on T.V.

Adverbs of frequency

49

Tourist information

1. The adverbs of frequency tell us approximately how often an action occurs.

Adverb	% of time	
always	100%	London's Big Ben **always** chimes the hour.
usually	75%–90%	Londoners **usually** drink beer.
often	60%–85%	Meg **often** has fish and chips for lunch,
sometimes	30%–60%	but **sometimes** she has steak and kidney pie.
rarely	10%–30%	She **rarely** takes dessert at lunch,
never	0%	and she **never** drinks coffee.

Other adverbs of frequency.

> **always** — constantly, continually, invariably
> **usually** — generally, ordinarily, habitually, regularly
> **often** — frequently, periodically
> **sometimes** — occasionally
> **rarely** — seldom, infrequently

2. Placement. These adverbs usually come after the verb **to be**.

> *Meg is **usually** thirsty at lunch time.*

They usually come before other main verbs.

> *She **often** drinks beer with her fish and chips.*

The adverbs grouped above with **usually**, **often**, and **sometimes** can also come at beginning or end of a sentence. **Never**, **seldom**, and **always** never come at the beginning or end. **Continually**, **constantly**, **invariably**, **rarely**, and **infrequently** do come at the end of sentences sometimes but very rarely at the beginning.

> *(Generally) Meg is thirsty at lunch (generally).*
> *(Never) Meg drinks coffee (never).*
> *(Constantly) She drinks beer (constantly).*

4. Some **Adverbial** phrases of **frequency**.

> All (of) the time, almost always, nearly always, most of the time
> much of the time, very often, fairly often
> some of the time, once in a while, every now and then, from time to time
> very rarely, hardly ever, scarcely ever
> at no time, almost never, nearly never

Some other adverbial phases of frequency.

once a(n)_____ (hour, day, week, year, century)
all_____ (day, night, week, etc)
every_____ (quarter hour, morning, day, etc.)
each_____ (hour, evening, month, etc.)
on_____ (Sundays, the tenth of each month, etc.)

*Meg goes out for lunch **every weekday**.*

A. Place the adverbs given in parentheses where they belong in the middle of these sentences.

(never) They *never* get a lot of snow in Mexico City.
(always) It is *always* warm in Yucatan.

1. (rarely) It rains in Chihuahua.
2. (often) Hurricanes hit Jalisco.
3. (usually) tourists enjoy the pyramids of Teotihuacan.
4. (generally) Mexican trains are late.
5. (constantly) Acapulco's beaches are crowded.
6. (nearly always) The sun shines in Cozumel.
7. (always) Lovers come to Cuernavaca.
8. (frequently) Mexicans eat tacos and drink Coke.
9. (ordinarily) The fishing off Mazatlan is wonderful.
10. (seldom) In Mexico City, workers take siestas nowadays.

B. Rewrite these sentences using the adverbs either in the beginning, in the middle or at the end of each sentence.

(seldom) Canadians are unfriendly.
Canadians are seldom unfriendly.
(frequently) It rains in Vancouver.
It rains in Vancouver frequently.

1. (regularly) Farmers come into Edmonton to shop.

2. (scarcely ever) I heard French spoken in Saskatchewan.

3. (sometimes) French Canadians don't speak any English.

_____

4. (almost always) Tourists love vacationing in Ontario.

_____

5. (constantly) New buildings are going up in Toronto.

_____

6. (seldom) In winter, Montreal shoppers have to go outdoors.

_____

7. (always) If I lived in the Yukon, I would go on vacation in the winter.

_____

8. (generally) Once a year Pierre takes the Candian Pacific west.

_____

9. (hardly ever) Tourists come to Newfoundland in January.

_____

10. (usually) Almost everyone enjoys visiting Old Quebec.

_____

11. (ordinarily) The Maritime Provinces are delightful.

_____

C. Where possible, rewrite the sentences in B changing the position of the adverbs.

X (not possible)
It frequently rains in Vancouver./Frequently it rains in Vancouver.

1. _____

2. _____

3. _____

4. _____

5. _____

6. _____

7. _____

8. _____

9. _____

10. _____

11. _____

Extra Exercise

I. Read the following paragraphs and add adverbs of frequency. There are many possible answers; one set of answers is given at the back of the book. Try to use all the adverbs at least once.

nearly never	always	frequently	occasionally
regularly	almost always	usually	scarcely ever
very often	commonly	nearly always	never
most of the time	often	very rarely	fairly often
sometimes	much of the time	ordinarily	

Travelers are ∧*often* amazed by the "strange" foods people from other countries eat. If you travel you will learn about new dishes even in areas of your own country. For example, in New England, people eat lobsters, the spiders of the sea. They also eat shellfish, clams and oysters, and they don't cook them; they eat them alive. This doesn't seem strange to New Englanders, but it seems horrible to many people from the Middle West.

French cooking is said to be excellent, but travelers are shocked to learn that they are eating horse meat. The French can cook marvelous dishes using calf's brains and thymus glands, which are called "sweet breads." If travelers don't know what they are eating, they love these dishes. However, you can eat frogs' legs or snails without knowing that you are eating "something very strange." Timid tourists try these delicacies.

In Germany, tourists who are lucky enough to be invited to a German house may be treated to blood sausage, cow's stomach (called "tripe"), or sandwiches made of ground raw meat. This raw meat, which is called "steak Tartar," is eaten in many parts of the world, but people eat good beef. They eat raw pork, as they do in Germany.

Another example of this cross-cultural "smorgasbord" or buffet is what the brave tourist finds himself eating in Japan: hunks of raw fish! This treat is served with bits of seaweed, and is very very fresh. Two kinds of raw fish which the Japanese enjoy but which tourists are enthusiastic about at first are sliced octopus and sea slug.

II. If you want more practice with these adverbs, on a separate sheet of paper rewrite some or all of the above essay replacing all of the adverbs with others which mean approximately the same thing. Use as many different adverbs as you can.

_____

_____

Prepositions of time 50

Schedules

These are some of the prepositions used with time.

1. **at, on, in** Notice the sequence from specific to general.

   at a specific time
   > at 10:37, at noon, at midnight, at dawn, at dusk,

   on a specific day
   > on Friday; on June 5th; on my birthday

   in a specific period of time, a part of a day or longer.
   > in a minute, in the morning, in the daytime, in June, in 1956

2. Explaining the limits of a period of time.

   from _____ **to/till/until** _____.
   > **from** 9 am. **to** 5 pm. **from** May **till** December
   > **from** 1968 **until** 1973.

   between _____ **and** _____.
   > **between** six **and** eight this evening
   > **between** now **and** then

3. Other prepositions of time

before	*Please come **before** six o'clock.*
after	*I'm going home **after** work.*
through	*Bob worked **through** his lunch hour.*
during	*I telephoned Bob **during** his lunch hour.*
for	*Donna works **for** eight hours (9-5).*
by	*Come **by** six o'clock, not after that.*
since	*It is now 5 pm. She has worked for 6 hours **since** 9 am.*

A. Put **in, on,** or **at** in these sentences.

I met Rudolph for coffee _at_ 9:30 this morning.

He told me a terrible story _in_ the ten minutes we sat there.

1. "It all started _____ Friday," he said.

2. "Everything was OK _____ the morning.

3. Then _____ noon I went to Captain Mack's for lunch.

4. I had oysters. You're not supposed to eat oysters _____ July.

5. Believe me, I never will again, not _____ a thousand years!

6. _____ 2:30 I started to feel kind of strange.

7. I got sicker and sicker _____ the afternoon and evening.

8. Phil found me on the floor of the bathroom _____ midnight.

9. In the hospital _____ Saturday, I didn't care if I lived or died.

10. I tried to watch the TV movie "Reds" _____ 8 o'clock _____ the evening,

11. but my head was spinning until dawn _____ Sunday morning.

12. Back _____ 1963, when I was a kid, I got food poisoning,

13. but it was nothing like my illness _____ the last three days.

14. I was supposed to go to church _____ 10 a.m. _____ Sunday.

15. Instead, Father Brown, the minister, came to me _____ noon.

16. I got out of the hospital two hours ago, _____ 7 this morning,

17. and here I am, weak but ready for work _____ 9:30.

18. Just don't suggest we have our luncheon meeting _____ three hours at Captain Mack's Pier 7."

B. Supply the prepostions needed in these questions, and then, using "Tonight's Television" listing at the end of this exercise, answer the questions using time prepositions.

At what time is CBN showing 700 Club?

It is showing 700 Club at 9 o'clock.

On what channel *at* 8 p.m. is the movie about submarines?

The movie is on Channel 56 at 8 p.m.

1. _____ what time is **McNeil/Lehrer Newshour** shown?

_____

2. _____ what time is **Evening at Pops** on Channel 57?

_____

3. _____ which year was the movie **Reds** released?

_____

4. _____ what time is **Business Report** shown on Channel 2?

_____

5. _____ 10 to 11, what music program is showing?

_____

Smalltown Daily

Tonight's television

8:00

② EVENING AT POPS "Steve Lawrence And Eydie Gorme" This husband-and-wife team sings with the Boston Pops Orchestra in a tribute to Irving Berlin.

(ESPNE) TENNIS U.S. Pro Championship final match (live from Boston).

③ ③ ⑥ ⑦ SCARECROW AND MRS. KING A chance encounter with Lee Stetson at a train station leads Amanda King into a web of espionage. (R)

④ ㉒ ㉛ ⑬ TV'S BLOOPERS AND PRACTICAL JOKES Featured: Danny DeVito and Kevin McCarthy are victims of practical jokes; animal bloopers; Canadian newscasters. (R)

⑤ ⑧ ⑨ ⑩ ㊵ BASEBALL At press time, scheduled games were St. Louis Cardinals at New York Mets or Chicago Cubs at Philadelphia Phillies.

(USA) MOVIE ★ ★ "The Triple Echo" (1973) Glenda Jackson, Oliver Reed. A soldier is drastically changed by his lover, the wife of a POW, until another soldier enters the picture.

⑪ SEEING THINGS

㉕ MOVIE ★ ★ ½ "The Steel Cowboy" (1978) James Brolin, Rip Torn. Hounded by bill collectors, an independent truck driver decides to pick up some extra money on the side by illegally transporting stolen cattle.

(LIFE) CABLE HEALTH WORLD REPORT

(CBN) CISCO KID

8:05

⑰ MOVIE ★ ★ ½ "The Tin Star" (1957) Henry Fonda, Anthony Perkins. A bounty hunter and a young sheriff team up to tame the town bully.

8:30

㊳ MOVIE ★ ★ ½ "The Sand Pebbles" (Part 1 of 2) (1966) Steve McQueen, Richard Crenna. An American expatriate is forced to take a stand when the gunboat he is on is held under siege.

9:00

② VICTORY GARDEN Bob Thomson tours Rogers Garden Center in Newport Beach, California, a retail garden establishment.

Tuneful Evening with
★ Steve & Eydie—'Pops' ᴱᵀᵛ

㊶ ⑤⑦ EVENING AT POPS "Steve Lawrence And Eydie Gorme" This husband-and-wife team sings with the Boston Pops Orchestra in a tribute to Irving Berlin. (R)

⑤⑥ MOVIE ★ ★ ★ "Run Silent, Run Deep" (1958) Clark Gable, Burt Lancaster. A submarine crew is divided between boys and men during a battle off the coast of Japan.

(LIFE) A WHOLE NEW YOU Featured: choosing wines; organizing your closet space; buying your first fur coat.

(HBO) MOVIE ★ ★ "Wavelength" (1983) Robert Carradine, Cherie Currie. Three creatures from outer space are captured and detained by the U.S. Air Force for medical experimentation. 'PG'

(NICK) NANNY

(CBN) PRIMENEWS

(TMC) MOVIE ★ ★ ★ "Reds" (1981) Warren Beatty, Diane Keaton. American journalist John Reed's involvement in the Russian Revolution of 1917 is depicted. 'PG'

8:05

⑨ SOLID GOLD

③ ③ ⑥ ⑦ CIRCUS OF THE STARS Beverly D'Angelo, Louis Gossett Jr., Ann Jillian, Robert Preston and Dottie West are the ringmasters for circus acts performed by celebrities including Tony Curtis, Lynn Redgrave, Brooke Shields, Phyllis Diller, Michele Lee and Pia Zadora. Taped at Caesars Palace in Las Vegas and Seaworld in San Diego. (R)

④ MOVIE ★ ★ ½ "The Golden Moment: An Olympic Love Story" (Part 2 of 2) (1980) Stephanie Zimbalist, David Keith. The love affair between an American and a Russian gymnast is complicated by pressures from Olympic competition and their countrymen.

㉒ ㉛ ⑬ MOVIE ★ ★ ½ "Child Bride Of Short Creek" (1981) Conrad Bain, Christopher Atkins. In a remote Arizona community, a Korean War veteran clashes with his polygamous father over the girl they both intend to marry. (R)

㊶ ⑤⑦ GREAT PERFORMANCES "Buddenbrooks" Christian sells his business, Tom is selected Senator in Lubeck, and Toni encourages Erica to marry a wealthy, older man. (Part 6 of 9) ▢

(CBN) 700 CLUB Featured: actress Kitty Moffat discusses Hollywood morality; a veterinarian reveals the criminal side of horse racing.

(CSPAN) VIEWER CALL-IN (LIVE)

⑨ GREATEST AMERICAN HERO

9:30

② GREAT CHEFS OF NEW ORLEANS

(HBO) NOT NECESSARILY THE NEWS

10:00

② ⑤⑥ (CNN) ⑨ NEWS

(ESPNE) POCKET BILLIARDS Luther Lassiter vs. U.J. Puckett

(USA) COVER STORY

⑪ GREAT PERFORMANCES "Buddenbrooks" Christian sells his business, Tom is selected Senator in Lubeck, and Toni encourages Erica to marry a wealthy, older man. (Part 6 of 9) ▢

㉕ 700 CLUB Featured: actress Kitty Moffat discusses Hollywood morality; a veterinarian reveals the criminal side of horse racing. (R)

㊳ GANGSTER GREATS AND OTHER MOVIE PARODIES A look at the gangster classics "Little Caesar" with Edward G. Robinson and "The Roaring Twenties" with James Cagney, and movie spoofs including "Young Frankenstein," "Airplane" and "Johnny Dangerously."

㊶ THE SANTA FE CHAMBER MUSIC FESTIVAL Highlights of the 1982 Santa Fe Music Festival feature the cultural heritage of the host city and interviews with Aaron Copland, Ned Rorem and William Schuman. (R)

⑤⑦ UNDER SAIL Robbie Doyle explains the guidelines by which sea persons conduct themselves and their vessels safely. ▢

(LIFE) NATURE OF THINGS

(HBO) MOVIE ★ ★ ½ "The Last American Virgin" (1982) Lawrence Monoson, Diane Franklin. A shy teen-ager in love is reluctant to join his buddies in their pursuit of sexual experiences. 'R'

(NICK) ONEDIN LINE

10:05

⑰ MOVIE ★ ★ ½ "Meatballs" (1979) Bill Murray, Chris Makepeace. A zany summer camp counselor leads his misfit charges into a no-holds-barred sports competition against a group from another camp with a much better reputation.

(CSPAN) BEST OF C-SPAN

10:30

② BUSINESS REPORT

(USA) SEEING STARS

㊳ ODD COUPLE

⑤⑥ ARCHIE BUNKER'S PLACE

⑤⑦ MACNEIL / LEHRER NEWSHOUR

(LIFE) HUMAN SEXUALITY Topic: issues concerning birth control.

(CBN) TOGETHER: WITH SHIRLEY AND PAT BOONE

11:00

② MACNEIL / LEHRER NEWSHOUR

(ESPNE) SPORTSCENTER

③ ③ ④ ⑤ ⑥ ⑦ ⑧ ⑨ ⑩ ㉒ ㉛ ㊵ ⑬ NEWS

(USA) ALFRED HITCHCOCK PRESENTS

⑪ NEW TECH TIMES Featured: a mystery novel written by a few thousand friends in Seattle; the use of personal computers in Kansas City. (R)

㉓ LEAVE IT TO BEAVER

㊳ ⑦ TWILIGHT ZONE

㊶ BUSINESS REPORT

⑤⑥ MARY TYLER MOORE

(LIFE) WORKING MOTHER Featured: special children; positive aspects for a child to have a working mother; family exercises; four meals from one roast.

(NICK) NOW IN PAPERBACK Guests: regional writers - Louise Shivers and Joan Chase.

(CNN) MONEYLINE

(CBN) ANOTHER LIFE

11:15

(ESPNE) RINGSIDE REVIEW (R)

11:30

③ ⑥ MAGNUM, P.I. A woman searching for her missing fiancé tries to persuade Magnum to enter a marathon swim-run-bike race. (R)

④ ㉒ ㉛ ⑬ TONIGHT Guest Host: Joan Rivers. Scheduled: comedian Gallagher, actress Susan Sullivan.

⑤ ⑧ ⑨ ⑩ ㊵ ABC NEWS NIGHTLINE

⑦ ENTERTAINMENT TONIGHT Featured: "Rocky" stars Sylvester Stallone and Talia Shire.

㊳ MISSION: IMPOSSIBLE

㊳ STARSKY AND HUTCH

⑤⑥ MARY TYLER MOORE

⑤⑦ NEWS

(LIFE) CABLE HEALTH WORLD REPORT

(NICK) INTERIOR DESIGN Guest Robert A.M. Stern.

6. _____ when _____ when is **The Sand Pebbles** showing on Channel 38?

_____

7. _____ how long is **Wavelength** showing on HBO?

_____

8. What is showing on Channel 2 _____ **Wavelength** _____ ten o'clock?

_____

9. _____ what year has **Run Silent, Run Deep** been popular?

_____

10. _____ eleven _____ midnight, how many channels show news?

_____

11. If Phil goes to sleep _____ 10, can he watch all of **Buddenbrooks**?

_____

12. _____ how many years has **The Steel Cowboy** been showing?

_____

13. _____ what hour does the baseball game start?

_____

14. _____ what time will it be over?

_____

15. How many movies start _____ the baseball game?

_____

16. If you like music, what programs will you watch and when?

_____

17. Using this TV schedule, tell what shows you want to watch. Use these prepositions: **by, at, in, before, after, for.** One possible answer is given at the back of the book.

_____

_____

_____

_____

_____

_____

_____

Extra Exercise

This was Rudolph's schedule last Friday before he got sick. Study it and then write a description of the day as it was planned using as many different prepostions of time as possible. One possible description is given at the back. In that description, underline all the prepositions of time.

FRIDAY **3** AUGUST

8:30   breakfast at Pussy's Breakfast Nook
        with Maion Hardcastle of Malamute Industries.
9:15-11:30 at our office in the big conference room
        present plans for Malamute's new ad campaign:
        Slim Styles for the Husky Guy.

9:15   Introductions of our staff to Malamute's people.
9:30   Present our basic concept.
10.00   Prentiss O'Malley interrupts to meet Malamute staff.
10:00-10:15 Coffee break; Prentiss stays.
10:15   I present rough sketches of the artwork: discussion.
10:45   Phil Monroe presents budget.
11:15   Present the schedule for the campaign.

12:00   Lunch at Captain Mack's with Hardcastle's staff,
        Phil, Betty and Prentiss, to discuss their overall reaction.
1-2   Buy necklace for H's birthday. Pick up suit at cleaners.
2:00   Get product safety reports on Husky Guy aftershave,
        shampoo/conditioner, and hair spray.
2:30-4:00 Write letters. Return phone calls.
4:00   Get market analysis on Husky Briefs. Write report.
5:00   Mail reports on product safety and market analysis
        to Malamute.

7:00   Pick up Heloise at her apartment.
7:30   Reservations at Ricci's for drinks.
8:15   Reservations at Casa Hermann for dinner.
10:00   Reservations at Club 2002 for dancing.
12:00   Pop the question!

These are some of the prepositions used to indicate place and position.

1. **at, on, in**   Notice the sequence from specific to general.

*Raoul's uncle's shop is **at** 46553 Palm Grove Ave. It is **at** the corner of Palm Grove and Dewey St., but **on** Palm Grove. It is right **on** the border of Shoreville and Crystal Cove, but **in** Crystal Cove. Uncle Juan likes it **in** Florida and in **the South**. "But maybe I'd like it anywhere **in** the United States," he says.*

2.
in	*Uncle Juan is **in** his jewelry shop.*
inside	*He always stays **inside** the store.*
outside	*"You sell vegetables **outside**, but not rubies."*
on	*He sits **on** a tall stool.*
on top of	*The watch he is fixing is **on top of** a pad **on** his desk.*
at	*He sits **at** his desk for hours,*
over	*bending **over** his work. He works alone,*
across	*but he feels safe. **Across** Palm Grove Avenue,*
opposite (from)	***opposite (from)** Juan's shop is the police station,*
next to	*and **next to** that is the fire station.*
near	*The bank is also **near** the shop.*
beside	*It is **beside** the Casa Grande department store.*
between	*There is a little hotel **between** the shop and Casa Grande.*
over	*The sign **over** the door says "Hotel de Luxe,"*
in front of	*but the men **in front of** the hotel*
by	*sitting **by** the front door or*
against	*leaning **against** the front window are poor.*
underneath	***Underneath** the pad on his desk, Juan has a button*
nearby	*he can push to call the police **nearby** his shop,*
beneath	*but he never uses it. Even the bum sleeping **beneath***
below	*the bench **below** the jewelry shop window is his friend.*
along	*All the men **along** the street are his friends. They are*
in back of	*all members of San Miguel's Church **in back of** the police*
behind	*station. Juan can see its spire **behind** the station.*

A. Use the prepositions **in, on,** or **at** in the following sentences.

The bank is not _on_ Dewey Street.

Dewey Street is _in_ Crystal Cove.

1.   What state is Shoreville _____?

2.   Is it _____ Georgia?

3.   Raoul and Uncle Juan live _____ Shore Drive.

4.   Shore Drive starts _____ the north end of Crystal Cove.

5.   Most of Shore Drive is _____ Crystal Cove,

6.   but _____ the corner of Dewey Street it bends,

7.   and from there south it is _____ Shoreville.

8.   Juan's apartment is _____ North Shore Drive

9.   _____ Crystal Cove.

10. His shop is _____ 46553 Palm Grove Ave.

11. Both his shop and his apartment are _____ Florida.

12. When he came to the U.S., he stayed _____ the South.

13. "It's too cold _____ New York," he says.

14.   "I came to live _____ America,

15.   not to die _____ the snow!"

16.   He adds, "I want Raoul to lie _____ the beach,

17.   to swim _____ the sea,

18.   and grow brown _____ the sun.

19.   _____ my youth _____ my island, I was strong and brown.

20.   _____ 65 years old I'm weak and white, but not my Raoul!"

The Critic . . .

Sempé.

B.   Look at the first picture of "The Critic" by Jean-Jacques Sempé.   Choose one of the prepostions in parentheses to complete these sentences.

(beside, in front of)   The artist is standing *in front of* his picture.

(in, on)   There are three trees *in* the painting.

1.   (behind, across)   There is a wall _____ the three trees.

2.   (in, between)   A river runs _____ the artist and the trees.

3.   (under, on top of)   His paints are _____ a paint box.

4.   (over, beneath)   The paint box is _____ the paints.

5.   (along, by)   The critic is walking _____ the painting.

6.   (between, across)   There is a bridge _____ the river.

7.   (through, in)   The artist has a pipe _____ his mouth.

8.   (by, on)   There are two street lights _____ the bridge.

9.   (above, on)   The critic has a black hat _____ his head.

10.   (against, in back of)   There are big buildings _____ the wall.

11.   (on top of, above)   We see smoke _____ the artist's pipe.

12.   (beside, opposite)   There is a tree _____ the stairs to the bridge.

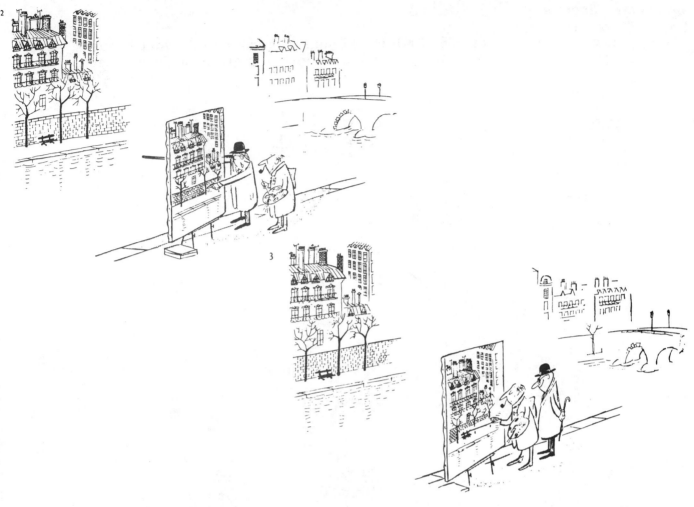

C. Look at the second and third pictures of "The Critic" and then complete the sentences below using prepositions.

In the second picture the critic has a walking stick *in* his hand.

He is pointing at a bench *beside* the river.

1.   The bench is _____ two of the trees,

2.   which are growing _____ the wall.

3.   which is _____ the bank of the river.

4.   The critic is standing _____ the painting.

5.   His left hand is pointing _____ the two trees.

6.   There is no bench there _____ the bank.

7.   The artist has a surprised expression _____ his face.

8.   He is holding his paints _____ his hands.

9.   In the third picture, the artist is working _____ his painting.

10. He is putting the bench _____ the wall for the critic.

11. The critic is holding his walking stick _____ his back.

12. He has a big "I'm-so-clever" smile _____ his face.

Extra Exercise

Look at the rest of "The Critic". In your own words, tell what happens. Use lots of prepositions. One possible description is given in the answers.

Circus!

The following prepositions show direction. They are often used with verbs of motion.

A. At	**E.** Away from	**I.** Around	**M.** Down
B. To	**F.** Into	**J.** Through	**N.** Up
C. From	**G.** Out of	**K.** Under	**O.** Along
D. Toward	**H.** By, past	**L.** Over	

52   Prepositions of direction   214

A. Fill in the missing prepositions of direction.

All the clowns are running *around* in the circus ring.

Like all clowns, they are getting *into* a lot of trouble.

1.   Clown A is staring _____ a mean gorilla.

2.   Clown B is giving his hat _____ Clown C.

3.   Clown D is running _____ the gorilla,

4.   while Clown E is running _____ it.

5.   F, the Human Cannon Ball, is climbing _____ one cannon.

6.   His brother, G, is being shot _____ of the other.

7.   Pretty Clown H is looking _____ Clown G,

8.   while she is walking _____ the cannons.

9.   Unicyclist I is riding _____ the tiger.

10. Miss J wants the tiger to jump _____ her hoop.

11. L, Ducky the Clown, is flying _____ the tiger.

12. While K, Foxy the Clown, is crawling _____ it.

13. Who is getting _____ the gorilla's way and _____ trouble? Clown _____.

14. Who wants to get _____ the gorilla's arms and _____ trouble? _____.

15. And who is making faces _____ the gorilla? _____.

16. Who is walking _____ the tight rope? Clown _____.

17. M and N are on the pole. N is climbing _____ it, but --

18. Watch out! M is coming _____ it!

19. Clown C may get more than a hat _____ Clown B. B has a big bat behind his back.

20. I love to go _____ the circus and laugh _____ the clowns.

B. The prepositions are missing from these sentences about the Tomasso Brothers Circus. Choose the best preposition from those given in parentheses.

Slim Jim's rope lasso is hanging *down*. (up, through, down)

The loop of the lasso is swinging *around* Jim's feet. (toward, around)

1.   Jim's left hand is twirling the lasso _____ his head. (over, up, along)

2.   Mr. Magic is pointing _____ the car with his sword. (past, from, at)

3.   He has a rabbit he can pull _____ his hat. (through, out of, down)

4.   Rikki is riding _____ on an elephant. (up, over, under)

5.   Rikki is sitting _____ an umbrella. (down, by, under)

6.   Zelda is riding _____ the ring. (by, into, out of)

7. She has stripes running _____ her body. (around, by, to)
8. Her horse is stepping _____ the elephant and Tommy. (over, between, from)
9. Hercules is holding a car _____ his head. (up, over, from)
10. He has a belt of stars _____ his waist. (along, around, by)
11. Little Lucy is looking _____ one car window, (through, by, out of)
12. while Ratso is climbing _____ the other. (over, to, out of)

C. Add prepostions _to_ these sentences. Possible answers are given.

Tomasso Brothers Circus is coming _into_ Clarksville.

Thursday evening they will have a parade _through_ town.

1. There will be three shows on Friday and Saturday _____ the tent.
2. In the circus they say. "_____ the Big Top."
3. Then Sunday the circus moves _____ to River Forest.
4. As they drive _____ from the fairgrounds, Joey will watch sadly.
5. Joey loves the circus. He wants to be a clown when he grows _____.
6. He would like to run _____ with Tomasso Brothers.
7. The circus people would understand if he came _____ with them,
8. but the boss, Tim Tomasso, cannot take children _____ home.
9. His circus moves _____ one town _____ another.
10. His people never settle _____ to a normal life.
11. The Tomasso's came _____ Italy in 1965; they own the circus.
12. When Tim walks _____ the spotlight, he is a magical Dr. Magic.
13. He pulls rabbits, snakes, and even a dog _____ his hat.
14. Then he closes Zelda _____ a big black box
15. and sticks six swords _____ it.
16. Somehow they go _____ her, because she isn't hurt.
17. After the show, Tim goes _____ the office and locks himself in.
18. He keeps his money _____ danger until he can pay his people.
19. Tom doesn't like business. He prefers to be high _____ the ring.
20. He is a singer and a trapeze artist. He climbs _____ his ropes,
21. sings a couple of love songs, and then swings _____ the air.

Extra Exercise

A lot of the prepositions in this story are incorrect. Cross them out and write in the correct ones. More than one preposition can be correct, but only the best ones are given in the answers.

Mary Lapointe has lived ~~at~~ *under* the Big Top almost all her life. At seventeen she wasn't able to get ~~on~~ *into* the circus, so she went **down** Europe. There aren't many circuses traveling **past** America, but in Europe there are circuses everywhere. Some are good, some bad. Mary didn't care. She wanted to learn, and she did. When she was twenty-two, she came **back at** America a star, Zelda the Zebra Lady. She went **up** a side show covered with interesting fake stripes. Children laughed and pointed **on** her, but men and women looked **on to** her large green eyes and took her very seriously. She is very beautiful, even with stripes running **up** and **by** her body.

When Zelda came **at** Tomasso Brothers', Tim took her **away through** the side show and made her his assistant. He threw knives **under** her, he laid her **in** a box and sawed her in half. He even locked her up **under** a magic cloth, and she got **of** the locks and **away to** the cloth while he tried to burn her up with a torch.

Zelda has a terrible problem hanging **to** her. Tim is in love with her. He wants to give an engagement ring **at** her. Tim is not her only boyfriend, however. Swinging and Singing Tommy is also mad for her. He is always following **after** her and singing songs **at** her. And then there is Mighty Hercules Jones. Herk wants to move **up** to Florida and go **through** the real estate business.

Zelda goes **by** Ratso the Clown for advice. Everyone wants advice **from** Ratso because he is old and wise and sweet. "Uncle Ratty," she calls him. "Uncle Ratty, how do I get **out by** this problem? The Tomasso's won't leave me alone. If I say no to Herk, he may kill someone."

Ratso turns **around** from her. "Who do you love, sweet Mary?" He looks **past** her at The Big Top. "Do you want any of them?"

"No, Ratty. None of them. **Around** the circus everything is always strange, right? Three good men turn **at** me for love, but I love another. There he is **up on** his elephant. 'Rikki the Rajah' beautiful little Rikki! But Ratty, he doesn't love me! What do I do?"

"I wish Old Ratty could help," he says with a sad smile, "Who knows? Maybe someday Rikki will climb **up off** his elephant. Who knows? He's young." He turns **away** again **over** the ring so Zelda can't see the tear drop **to** his eye and run **up** his cheek.

Summary Exercise on Prepositions

These idiomatic phrases use prepositions. Go over them with an English speaker and learn how to use them correctly.

Out of the blue

In the pink

Over the rainbow

Through rose colored glasses

Up and **at** 'em

In the nick of time

Down the primrose path

On hand

In the black

In the red

Over your head

Through the back door

Around and **about**

In and **out**

Beyond the Pale

In Dutch

Out of your mind

On the skids

In the money

On a dime

In your cups

Down hill, **up** hill

On ice

In a purple funk

Over the line

Against all odds

All in the same boat

Betwixt and **between**

Below the belt

Above it all

On the dot

On top of the situation

Beneath contempt

In the picture

On the map

Beyond the shadow of a doubt

Off of your duff

Into a fix

At the point of no return

Like falling **off** a log

Under the circumstances

Behind closed doors

On edge, edgy

In the bag

Under wraps

Out of a hat

Answers

Lesson 1

B.
1. is
2. teaches
3. starts
4. includes
5. follow
6. are
7. become
8. starts
9. come
10. include
11. studies
12. writes
13. are
14. checks
15. studies
16. corrects
17. are
18. need
19. ask
20. start

C.
4. each explanation
5. several exercises
6. the first exercise
7. the exercises
8. each exercise
9. examples
10. the examples
11. the student
12. he
13. the answers to each exercise
14. the student
15. he
16. he
17. these exercises
18. all students
19. good students
20. the answers

D.
4. examples
5. each explanation
6. easy
7. more difficult
8. with instructions
9. after the instructions
10. include the answers
11. the instructions and the examples
12. the exercises following the same pattern
13. at the back of the book
14. his answers carefully
15. his mistakes
16. all the mistakes he understands
17. for self study homework
18. help sometimes
19. for help
20. on page 219

E.
1. Only one answer will be correct for this sentence.
2. The appendix at the back of the book gives all the correct answers.
3. You should correct your exercises carefully.
4. All students make mistakes.
5. You can learn from your mistakes.
6. Each lesson in this book teaches one grammar point.
7. Each lesson also includes some vocabulary.
8. The vocabulary is listed in a box at the end of each lesson.
9. Some students study the vocabulary before starting the lesson.

F. Many of us learn best by speaking and listening.
Some of us learn quickly.
Adults can study the grammar of a language.
We need vocabulary.
Conversation practice is also very important.
Some of us need to write all of them.

Ex. enjoy   are
is   are
gives   are
is

Lesson 2

A.
1. The Atlantic and Pacific are not one big ocean.
2. The South Pole is not in the Arctic Ocean.
3. Hong Kong is not in Eastern Europe.
4. The Indian Ocean is not between the Americas.

B.
1. Australians do not come from Africa.
2. Saudi Arabians do not own Samoa.
3. Brazilians do not speak Spanish.
4. The American Indians do not live in South Asia.

C.
1. In 1492 Columbus was not a famous sea captain.
2. He was not a very rich man.
3. He did not want to go to America.
4. Columbus did not hope to find (the) Golden Gate.
5. His queen, Isabella, did not live in Rome.
6. She did not give Columbus twenty large ships.
7. He did not plan to sail west to find America.
8. Everyone did not believe the world was flat.
9. In 1492 the world did not change.
10. Columbus did not prove the world was round.
11. He did not sail around the world.
12. He did not discover the United States!
13. He did not call the people "Americans."
14. Columbus was not a popular hero back in Spain.
15. He did not return with lots of gold and silver.
16. Queen Isabella did not want to call it "Columbia."
17. "Columbus was not the first European here," say the Scandinavians today. The Scandinavians do not say, "Columbus . . ."
18. The Irish do not believe the Vikings discovered the new world.
19. This argument is not very important.
20. After 1492, the Spanish did not civilize the Americans.
21. Everyone was not rich and happy.
22. The Indians of the new world did not love Columbus.

D. The sun and the stars do not go around the earth.
It does not go around the Earth.
The Moon is not a planet.
We cannot see Uranus, Neptune, and Pluto.
The Sun is not a planet.
All the other stars do not go around the Sun.
It is not the center of the Universe.
Now we know this is not true.
The universe is not made for us, but we forget.

Answers

E.
1. In 1778 Captain Cook did not colonize Hawaii.
   About 700 AD Polynesians colonized Hawaii.
2. In 1909 Robert Peary did not reach the South Pole.
   In 1911 Roald Amundsen reached the South Pole.
3. Charles Lindburg was not the first to fly the Pacific alone.
   Charles Lindburg was the first to fly the Atlantic alone.
4. The first man to climb Mt. Everest was not Lord Everest.
   The first man to climb Mt. Everest was Sir Edmund Hillary.
5. Captain Magellan did not sail alone around the world.
   Capt. Joshua Slocum sailed alone around the world.
6. Laika, a Russian cat, was not the first animal in space.
   Laika, a Russian dog, was the first animal in space.
7. John Glenn was not the first man on the Moon.
   Neil Armstrong was the first man on the Moon.
8. Sally Ride was not the first woman in space.
   Valentina Tereshkova was the first woman in space.
9. The U.S.A. did not reach the Sun, Moon, Venus, and Mars first.
   The U.S.S.R. reached the Sun, Moon, Venus, and Mars first.
10. Lunik 10 was not the first space ship to leave our solar system.
    Pioneer 10 was the first space ship to leave our solar system.
11. Apollo 11 did not return to Earth with a little green Moon man.
    Apollo 11 returned to Earth with Moon rocks.
12. The first reusable space shuttle was not Sputnik 1.
    The first reusable space shuttle was Columbia.
13. The first U.S.S.R.-U.S.A joint space flight was not in 1983.
    The first U.S.S.R.-U.S.A joint space flight was in 1975.
14. The world's favorite spaceman is not R2D2.
    The world's favorite spaceman is ET.
15. The space shuttle Columbia is not named for a Viking sea captain.
    The space shuttle Columbia is named for a Italian sea captain.
16. The best use for space is not war.
    The best use for space is (peace, science, industry, tourism?)

Lesson 3

A.
1. Is French 520 at 7:30 am?
2. Is physics fun?
3. Is economics easy?
4. Is philosophy difficult?
5. Are biology, chemistry, and physics called the natural sciences?
6. Does our Language Department give a course in Chinese?
7. Does Mary take French twice a week?
8. Do you take German from Mrs. Doppfeldorf?
9. Does June want to study Chinese?
10. Did we sign up for algebra in room 609?

B.
1. Can a freshman take Bookkeeping?
2. Will my advisor let me take typing?
3. Should John study physics?
4. Is geometry a prerequisite for modern art?
5. Can anyone get credit for physical education?
6. Are philosophy and history called social sciences?
7. Did Political Science 421 meet in Keller Hall today?
8. Did Maria fail the geography exam?

C. Is algebra difficult? Was she the best student? Must all students take physical education? Does everyone pass English?

D.
1. Did I pass music history this term?
2. Should I sign up for American History 345 next term?
3. Will my physics course meet at ten o'clock?
4. Do we have trigonometry on Tuesday?
5. Can I get to my computer science class on time?
6. Will I like this English history course?

Lesson 4

A.
1. No.
2. No.
3. Yes.
4. No.
5. Yes. Thank you. - No, thank you.
6. Yes, please. - No, thank you.
7. No, thanks. - Yes, thanks.
8. No. - Yes.
9. No. - Yes.
10. Yes. - No.
11. No. - Yes.
12. Yes. - No.

B.
1. Yes, they are. No, they are not. No, they aren't.
2. Yes, they do. No, they do not. No, they don't.
3. Yes, they do. No, they do not. No, they don't.
4. Yes, they can. No, they cannot. No, they can't.
5. Yes, you may. No, you may not. No, you can't.
6. Yes, I do. No, I do not. No, I don't.
7. Yes, you can. No, you cannot. No, you can't.
8. Yes, it is. No, it is not. No, it isn't. No, it's not.
9. Yes, it is. No, it is not. No, it isn't. No, it's not.
10. Yes, you can. No, you cannot. No, you can't.
11. Yes, I will. No, I will not. No, I won't.
12. Yes, it is. No, it is not. No, it isn't. No, it's not.

C.
1. Yes, we can.
2. Yes, it will.
3. No, it doesn't.
4. Yes, it does.
5. Yes, it does.
6. Yes, it is.
7. Yes, we can.
8. Yes, it is.
9. No, it isn't.
10. Yes, it will.
11. Yes, we will.
12. Yes, we can.
13. No, we can't.
14. No, they aren't.
15. No, you don't.
16. Yes, you do.
17. Yes, you do, probably.
18. The best way to travel is to go by (car) because it is (cheapest). If you want to save time, the best way to make this trip is to fly.

Lesson 5

A.
1. Who
2. Who
3. What
4. Who
5. What
6. Who
7. Who
8. Who
9. Who
10. Who
11. What
12. Who

B.
1. Who
2. Which
3. Who
4. What, which
5. What, which
6. Whose, which
7. Whose, which
8. Which, whose
9. What, which
10. Who
11. Which
12. Who, which
13. What
14. Who
15. Who
16. Which

C. 1. What is new?
2. Who sells computer software?
3. Whose new customer needs to see her immediately?
   Which customer needs to see her immediately?
   Who needs to see her immediately?
4. What must be typed for Manning and Company?
5. What is not part of Janet Johnson's job?
6. Who doesn't have the necessary time?
7. Which contract must be ready by tomorrow?
   Whose contract must be ready by tomorrow?
   What must be ready by tomorrow?
8. What should be perfectly typed?

Ex. 2. who
3. which
4. who
5. which
6. whose
   which
7. which
   what
8. whose
   what
9. which
   what

10. which
11. who
12. who
13. what
   which
   whose
14. which
15. which
16. who

Lesson 6

A. 1. Whose breakfast herring is he very fond of?
   What is he very fond of?
2. What does Sam like for lunch?
3. What does he adore?
4. Who does Jim give shrimp to for Sunday dinner?
   To whom does Jim give shrimp?
5. Whose lobster does he share with Sam?
   What does he share with Sam?
6. What does Sam like for dessert?
7. When given a choice, what does Sam always prefer?
8. Whose house does Sam eat well at?
9. Whose house does he love to come to?
10. Whose goldfish is his very favorite food?
   What is his very favorite food?
11. What does he like to eat fresh?
   Who does he like to eat fresh?
12. What does Sam sit patiently next to?
13. Whose fish does he close his eyes and dream about?
   What does he dream about?
   Who does he dream about?
14. Who am I not fond of?
   Who are you not fond of?

B. 1. Who did I get together with . . . ?
   With whom did I get together . . . ?
2. Who did I see on Christmas Day?
   Whom did I see . . . ?
3. Who did she show her new Pekinese puppy to?
   To whom did she show . . . ?
4. Who did Aunt Flossie give the name Poopsie?
   To whom did Aunt Flossie give the name Poopsie?
5. Who did she go to the Doggie Beauty Salon with . . . ?
   With whom did she go . . . ?
6. Who did she have tinted pink?
   Whom did she have tinted pink?
7. Who did they put gold nail polish on?
   On whom did they put Puppy Perfume?
8. Who did Flossie buy a new rhinestone collar for?
   For whom did Flossie buy . . . ?
9. Who should you see?
   Whom should you see?
10. Who do all the ladies love?
   Whom do all the ladies love?
11. Who do they feed candy all day long?
   To whom do they feed candy all day long?
12. When they cuddle him, who does Poopsie love?
   . . . whom does Poopsie love?
13. To whom does Flossie say, "Poopsie, darling, you're a new dog!"?
   Who does Flossie say, "Poopsie, darling, you're a new dog!" to?
14. Who is brave little Poopsie afraid of?
   Of whom is brave little Poopsie afraid?

C. Whose dog did she want a bone for. Hers.
What did she find in the cupboard. Nothing.
To whom did she go for tripe? The butcher.
What did she find when she got home? Her dog smoking her pipe.
What did she buy at the grocer's shop? Some fat.
Who was he feeding? What was he feeding? The cat.
What did she do at the barber's. She bought a wig.
What kind of dance was he dancing? A jig.
To which shop did she go for bread? The Baker's.
Whose dog was dead? Her dog.

D. 1. Who do we give human names to?
2. In whose homes do our pets live?
3. What kinds of pets to most of us have?
4. Which kinds of fancy dogs to people prefer?
5. What kind of cats do most people have?
6. Which kind of fish do children enjoy growing?
7. What exotic animals do some Americans have?
8. What animals do children on farms raise?
9. Which animals do a lot of boys and girls keep?
10. Whose pets don't American eat?

Answers

Lesson 7

A.
1. Where will you be waiting?
2. Why do you want to go out so early?
3. When is the movie?
4. When will the movie be over?
5. How will you be dressed?
6. Where do you want to eat supper?
7. Why do you want to go dancing?
8. Where is the dance?
9. How can we get to the dance on time?
10. Why is the dance so important?
11. How should I dress for the dance?
12. Why is this party so expensive?
13. How do you want to go home?
14. When can we go out again?

B.
1. Why was she unhappy in Portland?
   Where was she unhappy?
2. When did her brother take her to a party at Tommy's house?
   Where did her brother take her?
3. Where did she meet Mike and Tommy?
   When did she meet Mike and Tommy?
4. Why did Tommy joke a lot?
   How much did Tommy joke?
5. How did Mike seem at the beginning of the party?
   When did Mike seem very serious?
6. How did Molly feel because Mike talked to her seriously?
   Why did Molly feel pleased?
7. When did Molly and Mike become good friends?
   Where did Molly and Mike become good friends?
8. When did Molly begin to date Mike?
   Why did Molly begin to date Mike?
9. When did Mike and Molly fall in love and marry?
   How did Mike and Molly live ever after?

Ex. Where is the man kneeling in picture 1?
Why is the man offering the woman a ring?
How does the woman react to the fur coat in picture 6?
When does the man bring the woman a necklace?
Where is the woman sitting in picture 4?
How does the man try to interest the woman?
Why does the man look happy in picture 7?
How does the woman feel in picture 8?

Lesson 8

A.
1. Bob's
2. I'll
3. It's/isn't it
4. They're
5. They've
6. Jack'll
7. rehearsal's
8. They'll
9. don't
10. We'll
11. bells're
12. doesn't
13. They're/aren't they?
14. They've
15. you've/wouldn't
16. wouldn't/ We're (aren't)/they're
17. can't/it's
18. I've
19. couldn't
20. you're (aren't)/you're
21. X
22. I'll (won't)/I'm

B. Now they're saying they're going to get married . . . Isn't that great news. She doesn't know when her father'll be back from Spain. He'll probably be back in May, so they're planning. . . . We're not (We aren't) going to be here in August, so I'm hoping it won't be postponed. You'll be able to go in August, but I don't want to miss Mary's wedding.
They're not (They aren't) having a big wedding. Mary'll have a maid . . . Joe's having a best man and that's all. It's possible that they'll change their plans, but I'm sure, if they're going to get married, they'll end up . . . , if it doesn't rain as it's raining today! And don't worry, Joe's mother's going to bake the wedding cake . . . so you'll be there, I'm sure.

Don't forget to write!

Ex. They'll, we'll, wouldn't, They'd, weren't, wasn't, couldn't, we'll, he'd, we'll, didn't, We're not (We aren't), she'd, weren't, mustn't, can't you?, I'm, didn't, He'd, wasn't, must've, didn't, she'd, can't, weren't, couldn't, didn't, we'd, You'll not (You won't), They're

Lesson 9

A.
1. The Tigers come from Michigan, don't they? Yes, they do.
2. Seattle is the home of the Mariners, isn't it? Yes it is.
3. Ray saw the Astros in Chicago, didn't he? Yes, he did.
4. Jon is a Red Sox fan, isn't he? Yes, he is.
5. The Cleveland Indians play good baseball, don't they? Yes, they do.
6. The St. Louis Cards are a great team, too, aren't they? Yes, they are.
7. So is Baltimore, isn't it? Yes it is.
8. The Angels play home games in Los Angeles, don't they? Yes, they do.
9. Luis wants to be a Met someday, doesn't he? Yes, he does.
10. Molly can get tickets for the Expos' game, can't she? Yes, she can.
11. The Phillies are from Philly, aren't they? Yes, they are.
12. The Red Sox are the world's best team, aren't they? You bet they are! (Yes, they are.)

B.
1. The Royals don't come from Kansas City, do they?
2. The Boston team doesn't wear white socks, does it?
3. You don't remember the Brooklyn Dodgers, do you?
4. An American team won't always win the World Series, will it?
5. The Milwaukee Brewers don't sell beer, do they?
6. Yoshi isn't a Ranger fan, is he?
7. Pierre isn't nuts about the Expos, is he?
8. Your grandfather doesn't think the Braves are from Boston, does he?
9. The Cubs didn't beat the Pirates yesterday, did they?
10. The A's aren't going to lose in the tenth inning, are they?

C.
1. Both leagues have the same number of teams, don't they? No, they don't.
2. Chicago doesn't have more teams than any other city, does it? No, it doesn't.
3. Fourteen states in the U.S. have teams, don't they? Yes, they do.
4. The Atlanta Braves were the American League champions in 1983, weren't they? No, they weren't.
5. The Pirates aren't in the National League, are they? Yes, they are.
6. Four teams have names of birds, don't they? No, they don't.
7. Three teams are named for animals, aren't they. Yes, they are.
8. The Mets are from Pennsylvania, aren't they? No, they aren't.
9. There are two teams from Texas, aren't there? Yes, there are.
10. No, there aren't three teams from Missouri, are there? Yes, there are.
11. There is a good team from Arizona, isn't there? No, there isn't.
12. Canada doesn't have two teams in the American League, does it? No, it doesn't.
13. California doesn't have more teams than Canada, does it? Yes, it does.
14. The Yankees are the most famous team in the world, aren't they. Yes, they are.

Lesson 10

A.
1. wine, and Dad had a beer.
2. salad, and Dad had some soup.
3. potato, and Mom ordered spaghetti.
4. dinner, and they had coffee with dessert.
5. strawberries, and Dad . . . .with nuts.
6. dollars, and they left a six dollar tip.
7. time, and they almost missed the movie.
8. tickets, and Mom bought popcorn.
9. movie, and Dad was mad.
10. film, and Mom loved it.
11. cried, and Dad fell asleep.
12. before, and he had eaten too much dinner.

B.
1. Sally is sixteen, and Suzie is nineteen.
2. Sally wants to go roller skating, and her. . . .
3. Sally wants a ride from Suzie, but Suzie. . . .
4. She likes roller skating, but tonight. . . .
5. Bob called her, and he has. . . .
6. Riverside is an amusement park, and Suzie. . . .
7. She likes Bob a lot, and she. . . .
8. Sally likes Riverside too, but Suzie. . . .
9. . . . your kid sister, but this. . . .
10. Suzie likes the Haunted House, and Bob. . . .
11. . . . ride the parachute, but Suzie. . . .
12. . . . the Ferris Wheel, but she. . . .
13. . . . dogs for dinner, and later. . . .

Ex.
. . . at noon, or I. . . .
. . . love Pop's, but I. . . .
. . . Grill now, but he. . . .
. . . from Pop's, or he. . . .
. . . lounge, or. . . .
. . . Fine Dining, but I. . . .
. . . man's bar, or I. . . .
. . . this town, but I. . . .
. . . pizza, or I. . . .
. . . good food, but I. . . .
. . . it's cheap, or I. . . .
. . . live music, or he. . . .
. . . to you, but don't. . . .
. . . music, but I. . . .
. . . opera, or folk. . . .
. . . Western, but Alfredo. . . .
. . . to dance, but Alfredo's. . . .
. . . teenagers, but he. . . .

Lesson 11

A.
1. bedrooms
2. beds
3. bureaus
   dressers
   chests of drawers
4. floor lamps
5. light switches
6. rugs
   carpets
7. mirrors
8. pictures
9. doorways
10. bathrooms
11. toilets
12. basins
   sinks
13. bathtubs
14. showers
15. medicine cabinets
16. dining rooms
17. tables
18. chairs
19. side boards
20. table lamps
21. vases of flowers
22. living rooms
23. couches
   sofas

24. easy chairs
   arm chairs
25. televisions
   TV's
26. stereos
   speakers
27. floor lamps
28. rugs
29. coffee tables
30. kitchens
31. stoves
32. vents
   hoods
33. refrigerators
   ice boxes
34. kitchen sinks
35. counters
36. cabinets
   cupboards
37. radios
38. front porches
   front stoops
39. front steps
40. chimneys
41. porches
42. windows
43. bushes
44. laundry
   clothes lines

B.

attics	brushes
cabinets	thinners
basins	soaps
sinks	detergents
pantries	cleaners
porches	removers
utilities	cleaners
switches	kitchens
windows	toilets
doors	cleaners
cellars	lots
chimneys	lubricants
workshops	oils
boxes	cans
trunks	tomatoes
paints	peaches.
stains	

Answers

Lesson 12

A. **I**

geese B
feet B
women C
calves A
indexes/indices H
teeth B
loaves A
species D
deer D
media, mediums H
children C

II

half A
shorts F
sheep B
stimulus H
wolf A
crisis H
Chinese E
pajamas F
series D
mouse B
scissors F

B.

wives	teeth
children	thieves
women	wildman
people	bags
animals	houses
cats	knives
cats	clubs
mice	people
cats	fools
women	ourselves
oxen	thieves
cows	cats
calves	animals
sheep	scissors
ducks	eye glasses
geese	pots
chickens	tongs
eggs	shelves
pools	tins
trout	pipes
bass	nuts
salmon	leaves
fish	loaves
students	halves
mountains	mice
days	squirrels
beasts	cats
people	signs
trousers	thieves
shirts	footprints
shoes	paws
feet	marks
men	hills
pajamas	echoes
shorts	wolves
coats	dogs
clothes	farm animals
Swiss	thieves

C. **Across**

1. paw/paws
4. time/time
7. ox/oxen
8. knife/knives
10. sheep/sheep
12. hill/hills
13. people/people
15. mouse/mice
16. shelf/shelves
17. shoe/shoes

Down

1. pot/pots
2. woman/women
3. thesis/theses
5. cow/cows
6. goose/geese
9. trousers/trousers
11. pipe/pipes
12. hoof/hooves
14. life/lives
15. man/men

Lesson 13

A.

Countable Nouns	**Non-countable nouns**
egg	milk
cookie	butter
strawberry	bacon
tissue	coffee
paper towel	sugar
mop	cream
battery	wine
match	soap
toothbrush	silver polish
potato	charcoal
paper plate	toothpaste
flower	fish
cornflake	steak
	steak sauce
	corn
	pie
	ice cream
	salt
	scotch tape
	parsley
	fruit
	grass seed
	coke
	ginger ale

B.
a carton of eggs/milk/cream/ice cream
a dozen eggs
a quart of strawberries/milk/ice cream
a gallon of milk/wine/ice cream
a pound of cookies/potatoes/butter/coffee/bacon/sugar/
  fish/steak/salt/grass seed
a package of cookies/batteries/matches/paper towels/
  paper plates/soap/corn/toothbrush
a pint of cream
a box of cookies/strawberries/tissues/
  matches/corn flakes/silver polish/salt/grass seed
a bar of soap
a bottle of milk/wine/steak sauce/coke/ginger ale
a bag of sugar/charcoal/grass seed
a tube of toothpaste/silver polish
a piece of soap/pie/parsley
a bouquet of flowers
a roll of paper towels/scotch tape

C. **Count Nouns**

joke	computer
dollar	calendar
baseball (ball)	date
chair	automobile
book	laugh
garden	map
leaf	

Non-count Nouns

geology	fun
groceries	economics
industry	propaganda
rage	garbage
baseball (game)	youth
fear	cooking
luggage	space
stationery	hope
emotion	art
vocabulary	history
physics	wealth
money	joy
pavement	paper
hunting	traffic
dancing	glory
furniture	Mohammedism
happiness	poverty
truth	knowledge
philosophy	laughter
literature	education
law	French
slang	

Lesson 14

B.
2. the policeman's
3. Susan's
4. Bill's
5. James'
6. the mailman's
7. Joan's
8. the nurse's
9. Ellen's
10. the Balls'
11. Lou's
12. Thomas'
13. Joy's
14. the monkeys'

C. the length of this sleeve
the soles of his shoes
the handle of my umbrella
the buckle of that old belt
my favorite designer's fashions
the style of his new outfit
my brother Frank's taste
the pockets of my new pants
the buttons of these fancy shirts
the clothes of today's teenagers
the trends of the 1980's
the stripes of that red shirt

Ex. 1. *The legs of these pants are too short.
These pants' legs are too short.
2. The handle of my umbrella is leather.
My umbrella's handle is leather.
3. *What's the size of her skirt?
What's her skirt's size?
4. There's a hole in the sole of his shoe.
There's a hole in his shoe's sole.
5. I don't like the color of your umbrella.
I don't like your umbrella's color.
6. *The laces of old Mrs. Wilson's shoes are always untied.
Old Mrs. Wilson's shoes' laces are always untied.
7. The boots of an urban cowboy are his pride and joy.
*An urban cowboy's boots are his pride and joy.
8. *The stitching on the pocket of his designer jeans is in gold.
The stitching on his designer jeans' pocket is in gold.
9. The outfits of Frank are always stylish. (awkward)
*Frank's outfits are always stylish.
10. *The stripes of his shirt match his tie and socks.
His shirt's stripes match his tie and socks.
11. There's a stain on the sleeve of my shirt.
There's a stain on my shirt's sleeve.
12. Can you mend the right leg of my pants?
Can you mend my pants' right leg?

Lesson 15

A.
1. They
2. he
3. she
4. it
5. you
6. it
7. we
8. it
9. they
10. they/we
11. she
12. they
13. they
14. it
15. it
16. we

B.
1. TV Guide is published once a week.
2. Adult listeners often prefer FM radio.
3. The turntable on my stereo.
4. The instructions come with the set.
5. May and I listen to FM radio all the time.
6. VHF channels are numberd 14 and higher.
7. Joe lives with his AM rock station on.
8. The knob marked "on/off" is also marked "volume."
9. The Japanese made both my FM receiver and amplifier.

C.
They don't answer. . . .
If you do. . . .
She will. . . .
We have. . . .
They are both. . . .
They are at the right. . . .
It comes. . . .
You must pull. . . .
It is marked. . . .
If you turn. . . .
it makes. . . .

it comes off. . . .
it has two. . . .
you can choose. . . .
it is too the left. . . .
they are difficult. . . .
they need fixing.
they can both. . . .
he's a nice guy. . . .
he said.
he would. . . .
we are good. . . .

Lesson 16

A.
1. him
2. us
3. her
4. it
5. me
6. her
7. us
8. them
9. them
10. them . . . them
11. it
12. her

B.
1. them O
2. it O
3. her O
4. they S
5. her O
6. she S
7. them O
8. they S
9. it O
10. it S
11. they S
12. you S
13. us O
14. them O
15. them for you O
16. them O
17. him O
18. her O
19. them O
20. they S
21. him O
22. it O
23. her O
24. he S
25. me O
26. we S
27. you S
28. us O

C.
1. Could *Miss Clair* give the razor blades to Miss Curry, please.
2. Please take the mirror to the Thompson's house.
3. Mrs. Taylor needs the hair dye now.
4. Mrs. Taylor gave three combs to *Miss Clair*.
5. Buy *Max* some pills, please.
6. Bruce will need scissors tonight.
7. *Miss Clair* found the lipstick for us.
8. Ernie met Sally in the drugstore.
9. Ernie wants a new toothbrush.
10. Ernie wants the toothbrush to be a good one.
11. *Max* saw an ad for the cold medicine.
12. Grace takes vitamins every day.
13. Please use some facial tissues.
14. Molly buys razor blades every week.
15. Mr. Perkins used a Band-Aid last time.
16. Take the cough medicine after supper.
17. Bruce bought the cough medicine for Sally.
18. Can Mrs. Taylor afford to buy the hair brush, the mascara, and the pregnancy test kit tonight?
19. Mr. Perkins and Molly told us that the store was out of after shave lotion and deodorant.
20. *Miss Clair* and *Max* put the shampoo, comb, and scissors in front of Joe, the Barber.

D.
A boy I know named William met his girlfriend Linda yesterday at Perkins' Drugstore. William had planned to meet her at six o'clock, but he was late. He wanted to buy her a birthday present. When he got to the store, they looked for a good hair dryer, but they couldn't find one. William asked Mr. Perkins, the druggist. He found a good hair dryer right away, and William bought it for Linda. Then they sat down at the counter of the snack bar, and William bought them a soda.

When William and Linda left the drugstore, he took her to the movies. A Tarzan picture was showing. Linda had seen it before, but she didn't care. They saw it anyway. I was at the movie too, and we sat together. I didn't like the film but they did. They loved it! They were just happy being together. Love is wonderful, isn't it?

Lesson 17

A.
1. Return this package to Rayco for Henrietta, please.
2. Send the Model R211 to Radio Shack.
3. Ask Henry to fix that disk drive for James.
4. Mr. Phillips will give the message to Yolanda.
5. Pass on the instruction manual to Mr. Phillips.
6. Wayne tells everything he hears to Yolanda.
7. The repair manual was written for Radio Shack.
8. Today Henrietta sold the complete product line to Mr. Phillips.
9. Pay $2,575 to Rayco for this shipment.
10. Mr. Phillips buys Rayco products for Radio Shack every Tuesday.
11. Wayne needs to borrow a company car for Henrietta.
12. Rayco offers a special discount to Henry.

B.
1. The salesman delivered the calculator to her.
2. The salesman delivered them to her.
3. The salesman delivered them to Mr. Phillips.
4. The salesman delivered a package to Mr. Phillips.
5. The salesman delivered a package for Henry.
6. The salesman got a package for Henry.
7. The salesman got a receipt for Henry.
8. The salesman got it for Henry.
9. The salesman got it for me.
10. The salesman loaned it to James.
11. The salesman loaned the manual to James.
12. The salesman loaned the manual to him.
13. The salesman loaned it to him.
14. The salesman sold it to him.
15. The salesman sold her the typewriter.
16. The salesman sold us the typewriter.
17. The salesman sold the typewriter to you.
18. The salesman gave the typewriter to you.
19. The salesman gave him the typewriter.
20. The salesman gave it to her.

C.
1. My broker sold some stock for me.
   ("sold me stock" means "sold stock to me")
   X
2. IBM pays big dividends to its stockholders.
   IBM pays its stockholders big dividends.
3. Will you please cash this check for me?
   Will you please cash me the check?
4. Your company owes more money to us.
   Your company owes us more money.
5. Get a receipt for the bookkeeper.
   Get the bookkeeper a receipt.
6. Did the manager say anything to her?
   X
7. The salesman delivered the new model to them.
   The salesman delivered them the new model.
8. His secretary buys office supplies for us.
   His secretary buys us office supplies.
9. I sent the shipment to them on April 15.
   I sent them the shipment on April 15.
10. Mary offered the calculator to the new owner.
    Mary offered the new owner the calculator.
    The new owner offered the calculator to Mary.
    The new owner offered Mary the calculator.
11. Please take this receipt to her.
    Please take her this receipt.
12. Get the Wilcox file to the president right now!
    Get the president the Wilcox file right now!
13. The bank will loan the cash to you.
    The bank will loan you the cash.
14. Her accountant wrote three checks for us.
    Her accountant wrote us three checks.
15. Can Sharp fix this calculator for Elise?
    Can Elise fix this calculator for Sharp?
    X
16. Pat buys all the office supplies for them.
    Pat buys them all the office supplies.

Lesson 18

A.
1. Theirs are football and baseball too.
2. Yours and mine is soccer too.
   Ours is soccer too.
3. Tennis is his too.
4. Mohammed Ali watches mine on TV too.
5. You need clubs to play hers too.
6. Rodeo clowns risk theirs in rodeos too.
7. Theirs is in Chicago too.
8. We have lost ours too.
9. Hers is in the water too.
10. Mark Spitz worked out in ours too.
11. I'd like to play nine holes with his too.
12. Bob has his too.
13. Theirs are strong too.
14. His were remarkable too.
15. His was cut short too.
16. I shot mine and missed by a mile too.
17. Mine is missing too.

B.
Theirs is a good life
Hers is with a medical laboratory
his is with the administration
hers is swimming
Mine is swimming
than mine
Yours is not the best
ours doesn't have to be
If ours is volleyball
yours is a lot better
then hers
ours are better

Lesson 19

A.
1. her nose	13. your hand
2. his stomach	14. their ears
3. his feet	15. her hair
4. her fingers	16. her legs
5. his eyes	17. his son's head
6. his hips	18. his hands/her waist
7. his knee	19. his thumb
8. her neck	20. her face
9. his nose	21. our faces
10. their eyes	22. our heads
11. his foot in his mouth	23. his butt
12. his chin	24. face of the tiger
	its face

B.
1. His	13. Her
2. Her	14. Your
3. Your	15. His
4. Our	16. Their
5. Her	17. Her
6. Its	18. Our
7. My	19. Her
8. Their	20. My
9. His	21. Our
10. Your	22. His
11. His	23. My
12. Our	24. His

Lesson 20

B.
2. It is cold out here.
3. It is dark,
4. and it is stormy.
5. It's very early.
6. What time is it?
7. It was 3:34.
8. It's just before 4.
9. It's early.
10. It is icy.
11. It is too far.
12. It is 3 miles.
13. It is 10° outside.
14. It will be an hour.
15. It's so nice and warm.
16. It isn't every night.

C.
1. What date was it? It was February 14, 1923.
2. What day is it? It is Thursday.
3. What year will it be? It will be 2014.
4. What temperature is it? It is minus 14 degrees.
5. Was it raining yesterday? No, it was sunny.
6. What time of day is it? It is late afternoon.
7. Is it time to go swimming? Yes, it is.
8. How far is it to Chicago? It is 290 miles.
9. How far is it by car? It is 5½ hours.
10. What time is it in Chicago. It is 12:25 am.
11. Is it time for breakfast? No, it's time for lunch.
12. How far is it to San Diego? It is 1600 miles.
13. How far is it by plane? It is 4 hours.
14. What time of day is it in San Diego? It is morning.
15. Is it 8:25 am. on February 14, 1996 in San Diego?
    Yes, it is.
16. What temperature is it in Chicago? It is 5 degrees.
17. Is it hot in Chicago? No, it is bitterly cold.
18. Is it a sunny day there? No, it is cloudy and very windy.
19. Is it nice in San Diego? Yes, it's hot.
20. Is it clear? No, it is still and smoggy.
21. What time is it in your country? It is 8 pm.
22. Is it cold and cloudy? It is hot and clear at home.
23. How far is it to your home? It is 7000 miles.
24. How long is it by plane? It is 16½ hours.

Answers

Lesson 21

A.
1. There are steps in front of the house.
2. There is an elevated train, the L, above the house.
3. There is a subway below the house.
4. There are two restaurants next door to 56 3rd Avenue.
5. First there is a Chinese restaurant.
6. There is a Jewish delicatessen next to that.
7. There is a taxi stopped on front of Fong's Fast Food.
8. In the taxi there is a fat woman.
9. Through Fong's window, there is a Chinese man watching.
10. There is a woman in Gottlieb's doorway.
11. There isn't a pleased expression on her face.
12. There are lots of noises on 3rd Avenue today.
13. There appears to be something wrong on 3rd Avenue.
14. There goes "peace and quiet!"

B.
1. There are trains rumbling by.
2. There is a fat woman paying her taxi driver.
3. Between Mrs. Gottlieb and Mr. Fong, there is tension growing.
4. There is a fight brewing on 3rd Avenue.
5. There is a dog barking at Mrs. Gottlieb's cat; it is Fong's.
6. In front of number 56, there is a boy sitting on the steps.
7. There is a boy watching the excitement build.
8. There is nothing unusual happening here.
9. There is always a battle coming between the Fongs and the Gottliebs.
10. Now there remains only one hope for peace.

C.
1. There aren't steps in front of the house.
Oh, but there are.
2. There isn't an elevated train above the house.
Oh, but there is.
3. There isn't a subway below the house.
Oh, but there is.
4. There aren't two restaurants next door to 56 3rd Avenue. Oh, but there are.
5. There isn't a Chinese restaurant first.
Oh, but there is!

D.
6. Is there a Jewish delicatessen next to that?
You bet there is!
7. Is there a taxi stopping in front of Fong's Fast Food?
You bet there is!
8. Is there a fat woman in the taxi?
You bet there is!
9. Through Fong's window, is there a Chinese man watching? You bet there is!
10. Is there a woman in Gottlieb's doorway?
You bet there is!

E.
1. There is a bigger Asian population than Black or White in Honolulu.
Are there more Blackes, Whites, or Asians in Honolulu?
2. There are more Hispanics in New York than people in San Antonio.
Are there more Hispanics in New York or San Antonio?
3. In Detroit there are more Blacks than Whites.
Are there more Blacks or Whites in Detroit?
4. There is a large Asian population in Honolulu.
In what American city are there lots of Asians?
5. In Atlanta there are only 5,750 Hispanics.
In the cities of the South, there are a lot of Hispanics, aren't there?
6. In Detroit there is an Asian population of only 7,614.
There are a lot of Asians in Chicago. How about in Detroit?
7. There are almost as many Blacks in Chicago as _____.
What can you compare The Black population in Chicago to?
8. There are about the same number of _____ in San Antonio as in _____.
Are there more or less _____ in San Antonio than in _____?

Ex.
1. is
2. is
3. be
4. is
5. is
6. are
7. is
8. is
9. are
10. is
11. is/is
12. is
13. is
14. is
15. is/is
16. are
17. be
18. to be
19. is
20. are
21. be
22. is
23. is
24. are
25. is

Lesson 22

A.
1. is
2. are
3. is/am
4. are
5. am/are
6. are
7. am
8. is
9. am/are
10. is
11. are
12. are/is
13. is
14. is
15. is/is
16. are/is
17. he's
18. are
19. Mom's
20. are/is/you're
21. you're
22. It's/we are

B.
1. Mr. Bowers is very shy.
2. Mr. Bowers isn't very shy.
3. Mr. Bowers isn't very ugly.
4. Mr. Bowers is very ugly.
5. Mr. Bowers is too ugly.
(Mr. Bowers is very ugly too.)
6. Mr. Bowers is too industrious.
7. We are too industrious.
8. I am too industrious.
9. I am too friendly.
10. Texans are too friendly.
11. Texans are too complacent.
12. Texans are too conceited.
13. You three are too conceited.
14. You three are too greedy.
15. You three are too crazy about Patty.
16. We are too crazy about Patty.
17. We are too up-tight.
(We are too up-tight about Patty.)
18. Susan is too up-tight.
(We are too up-tight about Susan.)
19. Susan is too studious.
20. Susan is too stuck up.

Ex.

are crooks	is for O'Brien
is the same	is young
is good	are the ideas
are both	is a bit
are Bob	is honest
are loyal	am for him
are the best	is no stuck up
is the party	is sad
are not	am more
we're very	are right
are in office	is honest
is more	is a tried

Lesson 23

A.
1. were	12. was
2. was	13. were/was
3. was	14. were/was
4. was	15. was
5. were	16. was
6. was	17. was
7. was/was	18. were
8. were	19. was
9. was	20. were
10. were/was	21. were
11. was/was	22. were

B.
1. were	16. was
2. was	17. was
3. was	18. were
4. was	19. was
5. X	20. were
6. were	21. was
7. X	22. was
8. was	23. was
9. X	24. was
10. was	25. were
11. were	26. were
12. was	27. X
13. X	28. was
14. were	29. X
15. were	30. were

C.
1. Lyndon Johnson and Jimmy Carter were both Democrats.
2. The Republican Party was in power from 1969 to 1977.
3. Three of these Presidents were Vice President first.
4. Carter and Reagan were governors.
5. Carter was a physicist and a peanut farmer.
6. Nixon and Ford were both lawyers.
7. Both Democrat Presidents were from the South.
8. Four of these five Presidents were born between 1908 and 1913.
9. There were three Presidents during the 1970's.
10. Nixon was a native Californian.

Lesson 24

A.
1. use	6. know
2. sells	7. stop
3. steals	8. starts
4. commit	9. happens
5. watches	10. die

B.
1. belong	10. sentences
2. steals	11. need
3. stop	12. find
4. commit	13. collects
5. use	14. happen
6. helps	15. needs
7. hides	16. becomes
8. kill	17. turns
9. sell	

C.
1. catch	8. rushes
2. blackmail	9. radios
3. rushes	10. tries
4. tries/happens	11. kills
5. steal	12. radios
6. catches	13. tries
7. blackmails	

Ex.
misses news	
likes strange	tries to trap
becomes interested	understand the crime
bring difficult	collect lots
asks his friend	is right
listen while	laughs at Holmes
seems to be	works like
overlooks	stays on the trail
watches the victim	want to talk
tries not	catches the villian
forgets nothing	seems very simple
develops several	says, "Elementary,"
goes to the scene	plays his violin
finds lots	

Lesson 25

A.
1. likes	11. hesitates
2. wants	12. promises
3. considers	13. trusts
4. asks	14. hates
5. values	15. fears
6. need	16. knows
7. enjoy	17. holds
8. realizes	18. like
9. imagines	19. feels
10. believes	20. equals

B.
2. loves	7. prefers
3. hates	8. realizes
4. considers	9. laughs
5. wishes	10. believes
6. hesitates	

C.
wants	write
believes	like
like	give
shows	has
values	writes
seems	thinks
tells	makes
is	underline
uses	leave
ask	want

D.
live	expect
prefer	consider
like	regard
shop	tends
prefers	remembers
enjoys	feel
enjoy	weigh
go	measures
intend	agree

Lesson 26

A.
1. are flying	11. are they trying
2. are talking	12. is she going
am riding	13. are not staying
3. are you sailing	14. are traveling
4. are not riding	15. am renting
is raining	16. is eating out
5. is leaving	17. are you sightseeing
6. is her ship arriving	18. is she touring
7. are walking	19. is taking
8. is taking off	20. are being
9. is always running	are spending
10. are taking	

B. 1. When is your train leaving?
2. Aren't you traveling by car?
3. Ali's hitch-hiking all the way to Reno!
4. She is sleeping in that hotel again tonight.
5. Gwen is taking Interstate Highway 95 into Jacksonville.
6. Where are you, Jack, and I sleeping tonight?
7. Is Mickey leaving for the Coast Wednesday?
8. We are going for a skiing vacation in Vail.
9. Is our train departing at six?
10. Is he waiting in line for customs or immigration?

C. 1. Are they staying
2. is buying/is picking up
3. are running
4. are flying
5. is not riding
6. are you renting
   are you picking up
7. is racing
8. is ticking
9. is sailing
10. are we walking
    are we window
    shopping
11. am checking in

Lesson 27

A. 1. accepted
2. cashed
3. loaned
4. borrowed
5. insured
6. deposited
7. endorsed
8. debited
9. opened
10. saved
11. signed
12. unlocked
13. explained
14. deposited
15. checked
16. charged
17. closed out
18. cashed
19. bounced
20. stopped
21. borrowed

B. 1. Bill canceled his credit cards last May.
Did Bill cancel his. . .?
Bill didn't cancel. . . .
2. Miss Pickering endorsed all the checks.
Did Miss Pickering endorse all. . .?
Miss Pickering didn't endorse all. . . .
3. The bank accepted traveler's checks last week.
Did the bank accept traveler's. . .?
The bank didn't accept traveler's. . . .
4. Felinda received a receipt for her payment.
Did Felinda receive a receipt. . .?
Felinda didn't receive a receipt. . . .
5. Ralph always charged everything he wanted last year.
Did Ralph always charge . . . he wanted. . .?
Ralph didn't always charge . . . he wanted. . . .
6. My children tried to pay with half of a dollar bill.
Did my children try to pay. . .?
My children didn't try to pay. . . .
7. Our bank closed promptly at three this afternoon.
Did our bank close promptly. . .?
Our bank didn't close promptly. . . .
8. That damned bank charged a service charge for everything!
Did that bank charge. . .?
That bank did not charge. . . .
9. The 1st National Bank canceled a check for us on May 6th.
Did the bank cancel a check. . .?
The bank didn't cancel a check. . . .
10. I denied that this was my signature on this check.
Did I deny that. . .?
I didn't deny that. . . .
11. Humphrey used the drive-in teller last Friday.
Did Humphrey use the drive-in. . .?
Humphrey didn't use the drive-in. . . .
12. You applied for a car loan from the Merchant's Bank.
Did you apply for a car loan. . .?
You did not apply for a car loan. . . .
13. Butch canceled his appointment at the bank.
Did Butch cancel his. . .?
Butch didn't cancel his. . . .

Ex. looked around
spotted one
picked it up
filled it out
carried it up
called her Frankie
smiled sweetly
asked if she could
answered that
needed to take
pushed me
shoved a note
grabbed the note
turned white
he whispered
she replied
whipped out
waved it
he hissed
tried to walk
stopped me
I stayed
laughed at me
felt sick

looked sick
smiled weakly
straigtened his dark
tapped his fake
pointed the gun
I fainted
alarm sounded
shouted angrily
fired his gun
all ducked
he ran
and escaped
pulled myself
asked politely
waited for
dropped my
picked it up
checked my savings
handed me
she laughed
stepped back
wondered if
was dreaming

Lesson 28

A. 1. held
2. did it cut
3. sold
4. came
5. cut
6. kept
7. had
8. paid/was
9. lost
10. threw/broke
11. sang/played
12. built
13. left
14. put

B. 1. fell/The painter didn't fall . . . .
2. fed/Farmer Cobb didn't feed . . . .
3. paid/Did you pay . . . .?
4. got/Did the secretary get . . . .?
5. had/The cashiers didn't have . . . .
6. rode/Did the police officer ride . . .?
7. read/The meter reader didn't read. . . .
8. took/Did the priest take. . .?
9. taught/Did the teachers teach. . .?
10. went/Did the night watchman go. . .?
11. cost/Lawyers didn't cost. . . .
12. gave/Did Mary give. . .?
13. swept/Did the janitor sweep. . .?
14. grew/The farmer didn't grow. . . .
15. read/Did the librarians read a lot?
16. blew/The hotel doorman didn't blow. . . .

Ex. got all wet
caught a cold
fell in sheets
blew in gusts
tore my umbrella
stole the hat
took the bus
did it do?
broke down
we stopped
hit us
got blocked
took a minute
I said
I put
threw myself
I pushed
and fought
I escaped
ran two blocks
flew four blocks
got to
made my train
rode along
bought a table
lit a cigarette
read a bit
noticed the Devil
was sitting
was noticing
felt ashamed
found me
lost power
heard this sigh
conditioner quit
train groaned

and shuddered
and stood still
I swore
and wept
I sat
and smiled
eyes met
lost no time
he smiled
he found
he spoke
stood up
took my hand
led me
head swam
I thought
I was
sang in my ears
I forgot
got off
found a cafe
bought me
left me
we sat
and drank
made small talk
told stories
came with
we got to
lept out
held the door
he said
I said
We shook
left me

Lesson 29

A.
1. is going to boil
2. are they going to roast
3. is going to mince
4. is going to squeeze
5. is going to melt
6. are going to mix
7. are going to stir
8. are going to spoon
9. are going to turn
10. are they going to cook
11. am going to grind
12. is going to measure
13. is going to need
14. is going to add

B.
1. Andy is going to spread. . . .
   Andy is not going to spread. . . .
   Is Andy going to spread. . .?
2. Sue is going to slice the bread.
   Sue isn't going to slice the bread.
   Is Sue going to slice the bread?
3. The old cook is going to mash. . . .
   The old cook isn't going to mash. . . .
   Is the old cook going to mash. . .?
4. Ingrid is going to lick the mixing bowl.
   Ingrid isn't going to lick. . . .
   Is Ingrid going to lick. . .?
5. Harold is going to barbecue. . . .
   Harold isn't going to barbecue. . . .
   Is Harold going to barbecue. . . ?
6. Kitty is going to spoon out. . . .
   Kitty isn't going to spoon out. . . .
   Is Kitty going to spoon out. . . ?
7. Paula is going to beat. . . .
   Paula isn't going to beat. . . .
   Is Paula going to beat. . .?
8. Ralph is going to chill. . . .
   Ralph is not going to chill. . . .
   Is Ralph going to chill. . .?
9. Elise is going to fry her eggs. . . .
   Elise isn't going to fry her eggs. . . .
   Is Elise going to fry her eggs. . .?
10. You are going to whip. . . .
    You aren't going to whip. . . .
    Are you going to whip. . .?

C. You are going to divide the ground meat.
You are going to make round balls.
You are going to flatten the meat balls.
You are going to fry the meat patties.
You are going to put the cooked hamburger on a hamburger bun.
You are going to add ketchup, mustard, and a slice of onion.

Ex. First, I am going to mince 1 small onion. Next, I am going to saute it in butter . . . ., etc.

Lesson 30

A. Larry will be a fireman.
Kenneth will make millions. . . .
Daisy will be a painter.
Gloria will study to be a lawyer.
Stu will play as a football star. . . .
Wally will star as a ballet dancer.
Ginny will be the mayor.
Ted will become famous. . . .
Joy will be President.
Walt will box Mohammed Ali.
Anita will be a mother.
Mandy will drive a big truck.
Clark will be an accountant.
Mr. Moran will be a tennis star. . . .

Answers

B. 1. Bruce will play baseball. . . .
Bruce'll play baseball. . . .
Will Bruce play baseball. . .?
Bruce won't play baseball. . . .
2. She will finish *War and Peace*. . . .
She'll finish. . . .
Will she finish. . .?
She won't finish. . . .
3. The job will be done soon.
The job'll be done soon.
Will the job be done soon?
The job won't be done soon.
4. Victoria will study. . . .
Victoria'll study. . . .
Will Victoria study. . . .?
Victoria won't study. . . .
5. It will rain forever.
It'll rain forever.
Will it rain forever?
It won't rain forever.
6. They will both be doctors.
They'll both be doctors.
Will they both be doctors?
They won't both be doctors.
7. I will always remember you.
I'll always remember you.
Will I always remember you?
I won't always remember you.
8. Bob and I will be lawyers.
Bob and I'll be lawyers.
Will Bob and I be lawyers?
Bob and I won't be lawyers.

Ex. we will keep
receivers will be called
we will listen
we will use
we will slip
we will have
will come through
we will still be able
Compacs will also be
they will help prevent
Compacs will be that
They will allow
we will have to do
code will put us
code will then tell
system will put us

compac will keep
2002 will be
people will still have
They will use them
They will run on
will be invented
he will now be called
he will own all
Megacorp will have
drivers will enjoy
which will provide
Piggies will have made
people will work at home
work will use the Piggies
we will usually leave
will be so terrific
will be better
will make modernization

Lesson 31

A. 1. Please take one free.
Don't take one free
2. Buy two for the price of one, please.
Don't buy one two for the price of one.
3. Please try it.
Don't try it.
4. Put your money on Mike's, please.
Do not put your money on Mike's.
5. Ride the rails, please.
Don't ride the rails.
6. Please see the World at Woolsey's Opticians.
Do not see the World at Woolsey's Opticians.
7. Please buy American.
Do not buy American.
8. Get a dozen while they last, please.
Don't get a dozen while they last.
9. Take her home, please, you Macho, you.
Don't take her home, you Macho, you.
10. Please eat at Joe's.
Don't eat at Joe's.
11. Fly me to Tahiti, please.
Don't fly me to Tahiti.
12. Please think small
Do not think small.
13. Come up and see me sometime, please.
Don't come up and see me sometime.
14. Please send it Speedexpress to get. . . .
Don't send it Speedexpress. . . .
15. Please be a man. Please smoke a mule.
Don't be a man. Do not smoke a mule.
16. Please taste one.
Do not taste one.

B. There are 22 imperatives.

Lesson 32

A. 1. Let's swim
2. Let's go skiing
3. let us leave
4. let's all go
5. let us drive
6. let's go
7. let's go
8. let us

B. let's do
let's go
let's go
let's not
let's do it
she'll let us
she may let us
let's do
let's catch
let's get
let's cut it out.
let's have
let's quiet
let's get out
let's go

let's go running
let's go swimming
let's go over
let's go fishing
let's take
let's go over
let's go fishing
let us borrow
let us have
let's not
let's go do it
let's go get it
let us go
let's go
let's all three get

C. 1. Let't go hunting. No. Thanks anyway.
2. Let us borrow your car. OK. Sure. When?
3. Please, let us go swimming. No, sorry. Not today.
Please, let's go swimming. No thanks. Another time.
4. Please, let us have $30 for dinner. No.
5. Let's go jogging together. OK, that sounds great.
6. Please let us go. Nope. Sorry.
7. Let's go on a hike. I'd really love to, but I just can't.
Let us go on a hike. No, not today.
8. Let's go hiking. Sure, great.
Let us go hiking. Impossible. You can't.
9. Let's go (let us go) for a bike ride. Sure.
10. Ginny, let's go (let us go) fishing. Why not? When?
11. Let us go bowling, Mrs. Smith. No.
12. It's starting to snow! Let's go skiing. OK.

Lesson 33

A.
1. Will you go to Maxim's with us?
2. Could you please buy me a drink?
3. Would you please hand Mary the gravy.
4. Will you ask the waitress for our check, please?
5. Would you mind getting me some ice water?
6. I want some apple pie with ice cream, please.
7. Would you like to dance with me?
   May I have this dance?
8. Please follow me to your table.
9. Would you mind finding us another fork?
10. Could you bring us some more rice, please?
11. Would you like to take me out to dinner tomorrow?
12. Won't you please catch the waiter's eye?
13. Excuse me, please. We are out of salt.
14. Can you pick me up at six thirty-five, please?
15. Please, won't you fix me another cocktail?
16. Take the meat, please.
17. Wouldn't you like to pour the wine, please?
18. Would you mind putting the platter down here?
19. Please, sit down.
20. Will you please pass those apples.
21. You may take my plate away now, please.
22. We need some more milk, please.
23. Won't you please have some dessert?
24. Could you please hand the vegetables to Mike?
25. Would you mind getting us some ketchup?
26. Sit here by me, won't you?
27. Can you please take the head of the table?
28. May I please have a cigar?
   Could you please buy a cigar for me?
29. Would you like to go to Friendly's for some ice cream?
30. Would you mind taking Mary's mother home for dinner?
31. Will you thank the chef for this excellent dinner, please?
32. Please come again.

B.
1. Dear Mrs. Jones,
   Would you and your son Michael come to my house on June 14th at six?

2. Dear Phil,
   Would you mind taking me out for dinner when I get back to town on the 25th? I'd love to go to Crawdaddy's for a drink first, and then maybe we could have dinner at Crustaceans. It would be such fun.

3. Dear Bud and Poppy,
   You've got to come to our house for the weekend. Please do! Bring a porter crib for the baby. If you don't mind, also bring a bag of peaches from your wonderful peach tree so I can make a cobbler. Please arrive in time for supper on Friday night. We are looking forward to seeing you!

Lesson 34

A.
1. Sally Sue can sing babies to sleep.
   (Sally Sue is able to sing babies to sleep)

2. can	12. can
3. is able to	13. is able to
4. am able to	14. can
5. can	15. can
6. can	16. are able to
7. can	17. can
8. is able to	18. are able to
9. can	19. can
10. is able to	20. is able to
11. are able to	

B.
1. Is Sally Sue able to sing babies to sleep?
2. Our secretary isn't able to take dictation in shorthand.
3. Can that mechanic fix anything?
4. I cannot translate this letter into Greek.
5. Is Sam able to plant trees?
6. Is the hat check girl able to get your coat for you?
7. Is the story teller able to make even Uncle Harry laugh?
8. Can this technical writer make the directions perfectly clear?
9. These teachers aren't able to speak French very well.
10. Can that lifeguard swim?
11. Can our carpenter build almost anything out of wood?
12. The plumber isn't able to come immediately to fix your toilet.
13. Can the singing waiter pour coffee while he sings.
14. Are pilots able to see in the dark with their instruments?
15. Is your priest able to say mass in his sleep?
16. Can those policemen solve any crime?
17. Is Mary's kindergarten teacher able to teach hundreds of songs?
18. Your house painters cannot work without spilling a drop.
19. Professor Hornbeam isn't able to lecture all day without notes.
20. Can the repairmen fix my TV?
   The repairmen can't fix my TV.
   Can't the repairmen fix my TV?

C.
The blacksmith is able to shoe a horse. . . .
The waiter can carry six cups of coffee.
The sailor is able to handle boats. . . .
The locksmith can open anything. . . .
The cook is able to bake fresh. . . .
The secretary can find any paper. . . .
The minister is able to preach so. . . .
The scholar can name all the kings. . . .
The pianist is able to play the Moonlight. . . .
The politician can whistle Dixie. . . .

Answers

Lesson 35

A.
1. May I speak to Bobby?
   No, you can't.
   Can I speak to Bobby?
   No, you can't.
2. Can I go to the bathroom?
   Yes, you can.
   May I go to the bathroom?
   Yes, you may.
3. May I help Molly?
   No, you cannot.
   Could I help Molly?
   No, you can't.
4. May I take you to the dance?
   You certainly may!
   Could I take you to the dance?
   No, I'm sorry, you can't.
5. Can we go back to the lunch room for a minute?
   No, you can't.
   May we please go back to . . . .?
   Yes, sure. Go ahead.
   Could we please go back to . . . .?
   No, you cannot. Not now.

B.

1st Grade	Lounge
can	can
may	can
may	
may	**Principal's Office**
can	may
can	may
	may
4th Grade	can
can	may
can	
can	**Front Office**
may	may
can	may
can	may
may	may
	can
6th Grade	can
can	
can	
can	
may	
can	
can't	
can	
can	
may	

C.
1. Can I come to school late tomorrow?
2. Can I arrive at ten?
3. May we leave?
4. Can Jane take the kids home early?
5. May I show Gretchen my multiplication table?
6. Can we please sit with you at lunch?
7. May we see Mr. Reed after school?
8. Can either of us take our class to the Field Museum?
9. Can we get a raise next year?
10. May I help take Freddy to the school nurse?
11. Can Bill and I leave early to go to the baseball game?
12. May I give Andy a good spanking, please?

Lesson 36

A.
1. has
   Do we have
2. You've got
   Have you got
3. Don's got
   Does Bob have
4. has
   hasn't got
5. She's got
   she has
6. I've got
   Have you got
7. has
   Does his mother have
8. Has Eli got
   has
9. has
   I've got
10. has
    Do you have

B.
1. Pam has got a headache.
   Have we got aspirins?
2. You have a cold.
   Do you have any Contac?

C.
1. has/Does Violet have something for my cough?
   No, she doesn't have anything for it.
2. has got/Has May got a bad cold?
   No, she hasn't got a bad cold.
3. has/Does the little boy have a cut . . . ?
   No, he doesn't have a cut on his knee.
4. has/Does May have a serious . . . ?
   No, she doesn't have one.
5. has got/Has Daisy got enough . . . ?
   No, she hasn't got enough.
6. has/Does Poppy have cough medicine . . . ?
   No, she doesn't have any.
7. has/Does old April Tobias have a headache?
   No, she doesn't have one.
8. has got/Has she got a broken hip?
   No, April hasn't got a broken hip.
9. has/Does Heather have appendicitis?
   No, she doesn't have appendicitis.
10. has got/Has she got a sharp pain. . . ?
    No, she hasn't got one.
11. has/Will she have her appendix out. . . ?
    No, she won't have it out in an hour.
12. have got/Have we got good insurance?
    No, we haven't got good insurance.

Lesson 37

A.
1. use up
2. broke up
3. broke down
4. tried out
5. tried on
6. signed up
7. pick out
8. puts on
9. takes off
10. passes out
11. hangs up
12. beat up

B.
2. . . . he broke up her rocking chair.
3. . . . he broke down Mrs. Patterson's fence.
4. . . . he tried out the lawnmower. . . .
5. . . . he tried on her best dress. . . .
6. Mrs. Farrar signed up Jimmy for. . . .

C.
8. . . . he puts his roller skates on.
9. . . . he takes his clothes off for. . . .
10. . . . coach passing boxing gloves out.
11. . . . Jimmy hangs his baseball glove up at. . . .
12. He's even too tired to beat his baby sister up.

D.
1. . . . to send them away.
2. We give it up.
3. We send them off to. . . .
4. We adults try it out again,
5. . . . children find it out.
6. Betty and I put it off until. . . .
7. . . . we talked it over.
8. . . . we made them up.
9. We looked it up.
10. Then we filled it out,
11. and packed them up.
12. Betty put one (it) on, but. . . .
13. She turned them on.
14. I took it out for. . . .
15. . . . to throw it away.
16. Let's make some (them) up, . . .
17. and look some (them) up.

Ex.
washes up
combs out his hair
wakes up his boys
turns on the lights
take off their pajamas
takes over
looks over
signed up
picks out
sends them off for lunch
picks up the bats

bring them up
pick up their things
find out
look up
give the books back
make up their own
take out their guitars
pass out
puts out
makes up

Lesson 38

A.
1. the
2. the
3. X
4. the/the
5. X
6. the/the/the
7. X/the
8. a/X
9. the/the
10. X/a/X
11. the/the/the
12. the
13. the/a
14. a
15. the/the
16. the/a
17. the/the
18. X
19. the/a
20. the
21. the
22. the
23. the/X

B.
1. a
the
2. the
X
3. X
the
4. the
X
5. X
the
6. the
X
7. the
X
8. a
the
9. X
the
10. the
a
11. the
a
12. a
the
13. the/the
X/a
14. an/a
the/the
15. a/X
the/the

Lesson 39

A.
1. a/Does Phil have power drills?
2. an/Ed didn't buy Apple computers.
3. a/Sylvia needs chain saws.
4. X/Did Richard sell a hair drier?
5. a/Dishwashers help prevent colds.
6. a/a/Today farmers need good tractors.
7. X/Most farmers also have a reaper.
8. a/a/Fork lifts would save . . . .lots of time.
9. a/a/needs secretaries . . . use word processors.
10. an/an/take hours . . . .up engines?
11. X/X/A pencil sharpener is a simple device.
12. an/an/Electric toothbrushes are unnecessary expenses.
13. X/X/An internal combustion engine causes a pollution problem.
14. a/an/an/Are broken gears unusual problems or unexpected ones.

B.
1. an/a - a washing machine.
2. a/a/X - a dishwasher.
3. a/an/a/a/an/an/a - an automobile.
4. X/a/a/a/X/X - a computer.
5. a/a/a - a microwave oven.
6. a/a/a - I am a wristwatch.

C.
1. a/a/a
2. a
3. a
4. the/an
5. a/a
6. the/a
7. a/the
8. a
9. the/an
10. a
11. the/a
12. the
13. a
14. a/a/X
15. the
16. the
17. a
18. a/the
19. a/the
20. a/the
21. a/a
22. the/the
23. a
24. a/a
25. a/the
26. a
27. a/a
28. the
29. X/X/a
30. a
31. an/the
32. a
33. the/the
34. the
35. a/the
36. the/the
37. a/a

D. As we approach the 21st Century, **an** average middle class American home has a telephone with **an** answering machine, **a** memory, **an** automatic redial button, and often **a** portable handset. In the kitchen, there is **a** microwave oven and **a** programmable coffee machine; in the livingroom, not just **a** TV with **a** cable connection, but also **a** VCR (often with **a** minicam for home movies) and **a** tape deck, **a** compact disk (CD) player, and **a** digital radio (DAB), all connected with **a** fancy amplifier and other electronic wizardry.

    Many of us also work with gizmos like **a** cellular phone and **a** computer system of some sort, tied by **a** modem to **a** telecommunications network, and we have Fax machines and photocopiers for sending and making copies of printed material. All of these wonders were unheard of only **a** few years ago.

    Over the last hundred years, we have come to expect change as **a** constant in our lives. But in the new century, will each year bring **a** new wave of change? It's probable; however, each year will also bring **a** clutter of unwanted, high-tech inventions as well. The past has brought us many: **a** talking elevator, **a** robot butler, **a** video telephone, home banking, **a** flying car, and **a** hundred time-consuming gadgets for kitchen and playroom.

Answers

Lesson 40

A.
1. some	13. some
2. any	14. any
3. any	15. some
4. any	16. any
5. some	17. any/some
6. some	18. any
7. some	19. some
8. some	20. some
9. some	21. some
10. some	22. some
11. any/any	23. some
12. some	24. some

B.
1. police some questions	15. some neighbors
2. for some counseling	16. of some help
3. offer any help	17. take some hard drugs
4. for some treatment	18. heard some friends
5. with some kids	19. for some general
6. got any problems	20. and some drug
7. her some care	21. After some time
8. visited some lonely	22. brings some people
9. saw some sick	23. without any doubt
10. grow any melons	24. into any more
11. need some work	25. given some blood
12. drink any beer	26. without any reason
13. for any help	27. was any/some way
14. wasn't any parents'	Clayton, some/any news

C.
some classes	some glasses
any work	some pot
anyone	some angel
anyone	any more
some of	Any mother
some problem	some advice
any teachers	some help
some problem	some other
some questions	some policemen
some things	any school
some meetings	some guidance
any good	some college
some time	some technical
some reading	some counselors

Lesson 41

A.
1. this	10. that
2. these	11. those
3. this	12. those
4. these	13. that
5. this	14. those
6. that	15. that
7. that	16. these
8. this	17. this
9. that	18. this

B.
1. this	6. that/those
2. that	7. those
3. these	8. these
4. this/that	9. those
5. those	10. those

C.
these	these
that	those
those	that
those	this
this	this
that	this
this	

Lesson 42

A.
1. The Star has a circulation of three million, five hundred and eighty-eight thousand, seven hundred and fifty-three.
2. Guidepost has a circulation of four million, two hundred and three thousand, nine hundred and thirty-four.
3. People has a circulation of three million, two hundred and seventy thousand, eight hundred and thirty-five.
4. Women's Day has a circulation of four million, seven hundred and five thousand, two hundred and eighty-eight.
5. Reader's Digest has a circulation of sixteen million, three hundred and forty-three thousand, five hundred and ninety-nine

B.
1. Good Housekeeping is the eighth best selling U.S. magazine.
2. Better Homes and Gardens is the sixth best selling. . . .
3. Playboy is the eighteenth best selling. . . .
4. Women's Day is the eleventh best selling. . . .
5. The NRTA/AARP Bulletin is the second best selling. . . .

C.
1. Ladies' Home Journal's sales rank tenth among U.S. magazines.
2. The circulation of McCall's is five million, eighty-eight thousand, six hundred and eighty-six.
3. The National Enquirer's sales rank fourteenth. . . .
4. The circulation of Time's magazine is four million three hundred thirty-nine thousand, twenty-nine.
5. The Star's sales rank fifteenth. . . .
6. T.V. Guide's sales which rank fourth in the U.S. are sixteen million, three hundred and two thousand, seven hundred and five.

D.
1. first
2. 415 Maryland Court, not 609
3. 10/one billion, nine hundred twenty-seven million, four hundred seventy-eight thousand, six hundred and forty dollars.
4. one dollar and twenty-five cents
5. four million, seven hundred and five thousand, two hundred eighty-eight.
6. five million, eight hundred eighty-one thousand, six hundred and sixty-one
7. 6th
8. four forty-four (four hundred forty-four/four four four)
9. one oh oh two two
10. two one two, three five oh, two thousand.
11. 26th
12. fiftieth
13. nineteen (hundred and) thirty-three
14. fifteenth/fiftieth
15. fiftieth/seventeenth
16. two hundred (and) eighty-one

Lesson 43

A.
1. Grant Wood is well-known for one strange oil painting. A pair of very plain typical American farmers are standing in front of their old, white farmhouse. This wonderful modern painting is called "American Gothic."

2. Jackson Pollock's large, complicated canvases covered with hundreds of long, multicolored paint splashes are what most of today's public thinks of first when the international abstract-expressionist movement or "that strange modern art" are mentioned.

3. Norman Rockwell painted many cheerful, sentimental scenes from our everyday American (American everyday) life. The popular old Saturday Evening Post magazine used a great many delightful Rockwell illustrations for its front cover art work.

B. - your good professional advice
- that classic American play
- Tennessee Williams' painful but funny *Streetcar*
- our first preparations
- fun, easy, and well organized
- a hard-working, enthusiastic, and happy organization
- that aging but glamorous Southern bell
- the play's central character
- our local weekly newspaper
- an experienced, middle-aged actress
- these four amazing characters
- a nervous, fourteen-year-old ballet dancer
- too young but also too experienced
- the first sixty-five-year-old, two hundred-and-fifty-pound grandmother
- this strange, deep horse laugh
- the right warm Southern accent
- the right slightly plump, fortyish figure
- Blanche's hot and tired way
- all the sad young men
- a very realistic Southern play
- a black Blanche
- a rather crazy and wonderful idea
- a thirtyish, beautiful, sexy female impersonator
- skin-tight, hot pink pants
- a white blonde wig
- her husky alto voice
- an interesting new twist

Lesson 44

B.
1. Bolivian	10. Portuguese
2. Brazilian	11. Nicaraguan
3. Chilean	12. Mexicans
4. Mexicans	13. Bolivians
Spanish	Paraguayans
5. Uruguayan	14. Surinamese
6. Guatamalan - adj.	
(Guatamalans -n.)	
7. Bolivian	
8. Venezuelan	
9. Venezuelan	
Colombian	
Ecuadorean	
Bolivian	
Panamanian	

C.
U.S.	Suriname
Americans	Guyana
Hispanic	French Guiana
U.S.	Argentina
Mexico City	Spain
Portuguese	Philipines
Spanish	Mexico
Sao Paulo	Brazil
Buenos Aires	U.S.
Rio de Janeiro	Mexico
Madrid	Great Britain
Ecuador	Philipines
Chile	Italy
Peru	Dominican Republic
South America	Japan

D.
1. Mexicans	14. Europeans		
2. Venezuelans	15. Britains		
3. Canadian	Italians		
4. Spanish	16. Germans		
5. Filipinos	Portuguese		
6. Portuguese	17. Asians		
7. Portuguese	18. Filipinos		
8. Portuguese	Vietnamese		
9. Spanish	19. Koreans		
10. Mexicans	Indians		
Spanish	Chinese		
11. Vietnamese	Japanese		
12. British	20. Christians		
(English)	21. Roman Catholic		
13. Chilean	22. Protestant		
Bolivian			

Lesson 45

A.
1. faster	6. safer
2. costlier	7. tougher
3. higher	8. better
4. rougher	9. longer/better
5. older/cheaper	10. rustier

B.
1. is more stylish than your VW.
2. is more quiet than that Saab.
3. is more interesting thatn the Datsun.
4. is more snazzy than yours.
5. is more tinny than last year's.
6. are more elaborate than Sally's.
7. is more elegant than the old one.
8. is more thrustworthy that a Landrover.
9. looks more beaten up than an old stock car.
10. Harvey thinks his MG is more exciting than his wife.

C.
1. is less stylish than your VW.
2. is less quiet than that Saab.
3. is less interesting than the Datsun.
4. is less snazzy than yours.
5. is less tinny than last year's.

D.
1. fancier	12. X
2. X	13. X
3. X	14. X
4. more handsome	15. X
5. X	16. X
6. more shiny	17. X
7. classier	18. X
8. X	19. sexier
9. X	20. simpler/X
10. X	21. X
11. X	22. X

Lesson 46

A.
biggest	richest
longest	most wonderful
highest	most famous
fattest	most awful
sweetest	best
fastest	most perceptive
oldest	

B.
1. the largest	6. the most widely read
2. the most watched	7. the highest
3. the fattest	8. the most towering
4. the most purchased	9. the most daring
5. the longest running	10. the fastest

Answers

C. The best humored
most boastful
the least
the driest
the greenest
most beautiful
the prettiest
the quietest
most peaceful
the biggest

the richest
the most lovely,
most fertile
the most spacious
most lovely
the earliest
the most gorgeous
the farthest
the most

Ex. the largest
the most gigantic
the biggest
most miniature
best
the most ancient
the most popular
the oldest

the youngest
the most expensive
the farthest
the heaviest
the greatest
the most
the largest

Lesson 47

A.
1. many
2. much
3. many

4. many
5. much
6. much

B.
7. a few
8. a little
9. fewer

10. fewer
11. little
12. few

C.
13. many
14. many
15. much
16. little
17. many
18. few
19. many

20. much
21. many
22. little
23. less
24. fewer
25. many

D. a lot of
lots of
a great deal
a lot of
a great many of
a great deal
lots of

lots of
a lot of
lots of
a great deal of
lots of
a lot of

Lesson 48

A.
a. softly
b. loudly
c. happily
d. quickly

e. slowly
f. sadly
g. cheaply
h. expensively

B.
a. The Indian is speaking softly.
b. The Indian is speaking loudly.
c. The cowboy is singing happily.
d. The cowboy is riding quickly.
e. The cowboy is riding slowly.
f. The cowgirl is singing sadly.
g. This person lives cheaply.
h. These people live expensively.

C.
1. expensively
2. really
3. bravely
4. fiercely
5. suddenly
6. unexpectedly
7. shyly
8. neatly
9. actually
10. steadily
11. heroically
12. unattractively
13. poorly
14. separately

15. fairly
16. brutally
17. unexpectedly
18. cruelly
19. peacefully
20. eventually
21. freely
22. regularly
23. anxiously
24. actually
25. slowly
26. diligently
27. cooperatively
28. really

D. exciting
originally
impatiently
expectantly
generally
most
immediately
nice
usually
usual
large
common
unusual
faithful
interested
previously
romantically
really
different
mysterious

unexpectedly
human
bravely
quietly
polite
just
real
regularly
sad
hopelessly
passionate
quick
finally
basically
ideal
moral
simple
enthusiastically
ultimately

Lesson 49

A. 1. It rarely rains. . . .
2. Hurricanes often hit. . . .
3. tourist usually enjoy. . . .
4. trains are generally late.
5. beaches are usually crowded.
6. sun nearly always shines. . . .
7. Lovers always come. . . .
8. Mexicans frequently eat. . . .
9. Mazatlan is ordinarily wonderful.
10. workers seldom take

B. 1. Regularly farmers. . . .
Farmers regularly come. . . .
to shop regularly.
2. I scarcely ever.
3. Sometimes French. . . .
Canadians sometimes don't. . . .
any English sometimes.
4. Almost always tourists. . . .
Tourists almost always love. . . .
in Ontariao almost always.
5. New buildings are constantly. . . .
In Toronto constantly.
6. shoppers seldom have to go. . . .
7. I would always go. . . .
8. Generally, once a year, Pierre. . . .
Once a year, generally, Pierre. . . .
9. Tourists hardly ever come. . . .
10. Usually almost. . . .
everyone usually. . . .
Quebec usually.
11. Ordinarily the Maritime. . . .
Provinces are ordinarily. . . .
delightful ordinarily. . . .

C. See B. above.

Ex. eat sometimes.
travel regularly, you
will very often learn
people frequently eat
also commonly eat
don't always cook
but fairly often it seems
to be almost always excellent
are sometimes shocked
can ordinarily cook
are commonly called
they usually love
can never eat frogs'
tourists nearly never try
are occasionally lucky
sandwiches much of the time made
is ordinarily called
people ususally eat
they scarcely ever eat
eating much of the time in Japan
is very often served
is nearly always very very
are very rarely enthusiastic

Lesson 50

A.
1. on	10. at/in
2. in	11. on
3. at	12. in
4. in	13. in
5. in	14. at/on
6. at	15. at
7. in	16. at
8. at	17. at
9. on	18. in

B. 1. at/It is shown at 10:30 and 11 o'clock.
2. at/It is on Channel 57 at 8 o'clock.
3. in/It was released in 1981.
4. at/It is shown at 10:30 on Channel 2.
5. from/The Santa Fe Chamber Music Festival is showing from 10 to 11.
6. from/till (to, until)/ It's on from 8 till 10.
7. for/It's showing for two hours.
8. after/at/The news is on Channel 2 at 10 after Wavelength.
9. since/It has been popular since 1958.
10. between/and/Fifteen channels show news between 11 and midnight.
11. at/Yes. It's over by ten.
12. for/It's been showing for years.
13. at/It starts at 8 o'clock.
14. by/It will be over by 11.
15. during/Eleven movies start during the game.
16. I'll watch Evening at Pops at 8 and the Santa Fe Festival at 10.
17. Before the Golden Moment, I want to watch TV's Bloopers at 8 o'clock. The movie runs for 2 hours and ends by 11. After it's over in the last hour before I go to bed, I want to watch the news and ABC Nightline on Channel 9.

Ex. On Friday, August 3rd, Rudolph was going to have breakfast at 8:30 at Pussy's before going to the office. During breakfast he planned to meet with Marion Hardcastle. Between 9:15 and 11:30 in the big conference room, he was going to present plans for Malamute's new ad campaign. By 10 o'clock, he planned to introduce our staff and present the basic concept. At 10, Prentiss O'Malley planned to interrupt to meet the Malamute staff. He planned to stay for a 15 minute coffee break. After that, Rudolph was going to present and discuss rough sketches of the art work. At 11:15 after Phil Monroe was going to present the budget, Rudolph planned to present the schedule for the campaign.

Through lunch at Captain Mack's, Rudolph, Phil, Betty, Prentiss, and Hardcastle's staff were going to discuss their reaction. Between 1 and 2, Rudolph planned to buy a necklace for H's birthday and to pick up his suit at the cleaners. At 2 he was going to get product safety reports, and from then until 4 he planned to write letters and return phone calls. At 5 he planned to mail the product safety reports and his report on the market analysis on Husky Briefs to Malamute.

Rudolph planned to pick up Heloise at 7, and from 7:30 to 8:15 they were to have drinks at Ricci's. After dinner at Casa Hermann, between 10 and 12 they were going dancing at Club 2002, and then at midnight he planned to pop the question!

Answers

Lesson 51

A.

1. in	11. in
2. in	12. in
3. on	13. in
4. at	14. in
5. in	15. in
6. at	16. on
7. in	17. in
8. on	18. in
9. in	19. in/on
10. at	20. at

B.

1. behind	7. in
2. between	8. on
3. on top of	9. on
4. beneath	10. in back of
5. by	11. above
6. across	12. beside

C.

1. between	8. in
2. beside (along)	9. on (at)
3. along	10. in front of (beside, next to)
4. next to (beside)	
5. at	11. behind
6. on	12. on (across)
7. on	

Ex. In the fourth picture, the critic is pointing at a chimney on top of one of the buildings across the river. The chimney is not shown in the picture. The expression on the critic's face is very happy. The artist doesn't look very happy.

In the fifth picture, he is adding the missing chimney at the edge of the roof. A wind comes up in back of the critic and blows his black hat off his head and up in the air.

In the sixth picture, the hat lands in the middle of the river. There are great circles around it in the water. The artist carefully paints the hat into the picture. The artist has no smile on his face. The critic is not pleased.

Lesson 52

A.

1. at	11. over
2. to	12. under
3. toward	13. out of/out of/E
4. away from	14. into/in (into)/D
5. into	15. at/A
6. out of	16. along/O
7. at	17. up
8. by (past)	18. down
9. around	19. from
10. through	20. to/at

B.

1. over	7. around
2. at	8. between
3. out of	9. over
4. up	10. around
5. under	11. out of
6. into	12. out of

C.

1. in	12. into
2. under	13. out of
3. on	14. into
4. away	15. through
5. up	16. past
6. away	17. to (out to)
7. along	18. away from
8. from	19. above
9. from/to	20. up
10. in	21. through
11. from	

Ex.

to Europe	ring to her
around America	songs to her
back to America	down to Florida
into a side show	into the . . . .business
at her	to Ratso
into her . . . .eyes	out of this problem
up and down her body	away from her
to Tomasso	to me for love
away from the . . . .show	down from his elephant
at her	towards the ring
out of the locks	from his eye
away from under the cloth	down his cheek
over her	

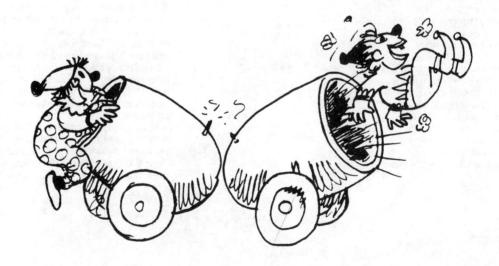

Numbers refer to lessons and not to pages.

Cultural topic index

Numbers refer to lessons and not to pages.

Clair, Nancy. **The Grammar Handbook: Part One.** Brattleboro, Vt.: Pro Lingua Associates, 1990.

Clair, Nancy. **The Grammar Handbook: Part Two.** Brattleboro, Vt.: Pro Lingua Associates, 1986.

Clark, Raymond C., Patrick R. Moran, and Arthur A. Burrows. **The ESL Miscellany, A treasury of cultural and linguistic information — 2nd edition**. Brattleboro, Vt.: Pro Lingua Associates, 1991.

Clark, Raymond C., ed. **Index Card Games for ESL.** Brattleboro, Vt.: Pro Lingua Associates/Experiment Press, 1982.

Clark Raymond C. **Language Teaching Techniques**. Brattleboro, Vt.: Pro Lingua Associates, 1987.

Celce-Murcia, Marianne, and Diane Larsen-Freeman. **The Grammar Book: An ESL/EFL Teacher's Course**. Rowley, Mass.: Newbury House Publishers, 1983.

Danielson, Dorothy, and Rebecca Hayden. **Using English: Your Second Language**. Englewood Cliffs, N.J.: Prentice-Hall, 1973.

Frank, Marcella. **Modern English: Exercises for Non-Native Speakers: Parts I and II**. Englewood Cliffs, N.J.: Prentice-Hall, 1972.

Frank, Marcella. **Modern English: A Practical Reference Guide.** Englewood Cliffs, N.J.: Prentice-Hall, 1972.

Hayden, Rebecca E., Dorothy W. Pilgrim, and Aurora Quiros Haggard. **Mastering American English: A Handbook-Workbook of Essentials.** Englewood Cliffs, N.J.: Prentice-Hall, 1956.

Krohn, Robert. **English Sentence Structure**. Ann Arbor, Mich.: The University of Michigan Press, 1971.

Praninskas, Jean. **Rapid Review of English Grammar: A Text for Students of ESL: 2nd edition**. Englewood Cliffs, N.J.: Prentice-Hall, 1957, 1975.

Rein, David P. **Grammar Exercises: Part Two**. Brattleboro, Vt.: Pro Lingua Associates, 1986.

Yorkey, Richard. **The English Notebook: Exercises for Mastering Essential Structures**. New York City, N.Y.: Minerva Books, Ltd., 1981.

Word order	*It is brown.* page 1 *It isn't brown.* p. 5 *Is it brown?* p. 10 *Yes, it is.* p. 13 *It is, isn't it?* p. 33
Question words	*Who? What? Where? Why?* pp. 16, 20, 25
Conjunctions	*and, or, but* p. 37
Nouns — regular plural irregular plural non-count possessive	*book, books* page 40 *child, children* p. 44 *bread* p. 48 *Sam's* p. 51
Pronouns — subject object indirect object possessive	*I, we, you, he, she, it, they* p. 56 *me, us, you, him, her, it, them* p. 60 *to me, for me* p. 65 *mine, ours, yours, his, hers, its, theirs* p. 70
Possessive adjectives	*my, our, your, his, her, its, their* p. 73
Expletives	*it is* p. 77 *there is* p. 81
Verbs — to be present present progressive past — regular past — irregular future imperative polite expressions modals of ability modals of permission two-word verbs	*I am* page 88 *I was* p. 91 *I walk* p. 95 *I am walking* p. 105 *I walked* p. 108 *I gave* p. 113 *I am going to walk* p. 119 *I will walk* p. 123 *I am walking tomorrow* p. 119 *Walk!* p. 128 *Let's walk* p. 131 *Walk, please* p. 135 *can, be able to* p. 140 *may, can* p. 143 *take out, take off* p. 150
Adjectives — articles demonstratives numbers comparative superlative quantity	*the, a, an* pages 154, 158 *some/any* p. 162 *this/that, these/those* p. 166 *one, first, 1, 1st* p. 169 *bigger* p. 184 *biggest* p. 188 *much, many, a lot of* p. 192
Adverbs of manner of frequency	*slowly* p. 195 *always, sometimes* p. 199
Prepositions of time of place of direction	*at 6 o'clock* p. 203 *at my place* p. 208 *throw the pie at me* p. 213